HOUSE OF PAGE'S

HOUSE OF PAGE'S

—also—ENG 10-1

in

COUNTY OF SUFFOLK, ENGLAND

Viking Influence in

Denmark—France—England—Virginia

ROBERT E. PAGE

Author of Carolina Page's

authorHOUSE®

AuthorHouse™
1663 Liberty Drive
Bloomington, IN 47403
www.authorhouse.com
Phone: 1-800-839-8640

For information contact the below address.
87465 Old Hwy, Islamorada, Florida, 33036

Published by AuthorHouse   05/02/2013

ISBN: 978-1-4817-4736-3 (sc)
ISBN: 978-1-4817-4780-6 (e)

Library of Congress Control Number: 2013907767

CONTENTS

- Robert Page III

PREFACE

In the year 1659 when Thomas Page and Mrs Alice (Garrett) Page first arrived in Perquimans District, North Carolina and settled in Isle of Wight, Virginia (which was the N.C. border area) and began a large family that later spread out to many southern states. (560-181) Who was Thomas Page and where did he come from was always a question by descendants? Finally about 35 years ago, Jesse M. Page Jr, (1914-1991)(560-181B) author of "Page Family in North Carolina" began his 10 year Page research which was published in 1987. He finally released a Family History Chart which revealed he was from the Thomas Page/Alis line—through his son John Page, b.1685 married to Hanner ? (see chart T 3-1 in CAROLINA PAGE's) for his line from Thomas Page married to Alis from County Suffork, England down to him. (560-181A)

Robert E. Page then spent the next three years trying to connect all the many Page families reported by Jesse Page, and developed many family history charts (by North Carolina counties) showing the "possible" blood and marriage connections—supported by additional documents—like land transactions, wills recorded in court records, birth, marriage and death records. Many Page families were finally "clearly connected" but when DNA finally entered the genealogy world—it then confirmed the connections—that the "paper trail" had produced. Much of the DNA confirmations pointed back to the early family history charts provided to Robert E. Page by Jesse Page—just before his death in 1991. In 1990 Robert E. Page published "Carolina Page's" after several years of studying the "official documents" that Jesse Page found all over North Carolina, plus many other research documents by other family historians. I was just the gatherer and consolidator of this effort. The Page families had grown so much—since 1700 A.D. and appear to be prosperous—and were spreading all over the southern states. These old "family charts" have provided many "new" genealogist—a foundation in where to search for their particular family and then with Y-DNA—it has made the connections "proof positive" and replaced the "guessing" game—that many family historians had been using for hundreds of years.

Now further research has "finally" revealed that the "long sought after answer" that focused on finding out—who was Thomas Page (arrived Isle of Wight, Virginia area—just before 1659—see (560-181)) and the efforts to trace his family from his birth place backward—as far back—as written documents will reveal took place. This research began before Y-DNA was available—which later—supported the paper trail—that Jesse Page Jr—spent 10 years gathering—before he published his research and provided me additional information that was NOT in his book. It was amazingly accurate—for its time—but missing many connections, which were later discovered—to make it a more accurate picture of PAGE family "C", which he later claimed his line. He was working on his 2nd book, when he died, in 1991 and his additional research documents have disappeared.

CHAPTER 1

HISTORY AND BACKGROUND

So the focus of my genealogical research has been—back to the country of origin (England) and little comment is reported on the expanded Page Family in Virginia—as they started to migrate down to North Carolina and further south and westward. There are other books and ways to track the movement of Pages in the 1700 and 1800's.

What was an "amazing discovery" by my daughter Robin Page—who found out about this English publication "Who Lived in Your House"—"People at Homes in Early Walsham le Willows, County of Suffolk, England" by Audrey McLaughlin. Our research team had already focused on this small village town in England—but this local publication—which focused on many families—many of which—was the Page family—loaded with photographs of the houses of the "expanding middle class" English families lived in and passed on to other Page relatives. The value of this book—is—it goes into great depth about the Page family— as they grew and prospered—and passed on important residences and land ownership—from father to usually the oldest son—as each generation—died out—before their emigration to the Colonies began to take place, which by the end of 1600's—most of the PAGE family "C" line had left England for Virginia.

Several serious Page researchers have tried to focus—just on FTDNA Page Family line "C", out of about 15 different PAGE lines, all with the surname PAGE—which are NOT blood related—during the past many years. Bobby W. Page (Okla), Chris Page (Ark) (his son and computer whiz), Harry L. Page (SC) and Robert Page (Fla) are among the many that have contributed to this narrative along with George W. Page, (MD) Administrator of the Page family DNA project, which has grown to identify over 15 "different" families of Pages. Our Y-DNA—Page line "C" **haplogroup is I1a3. Haplogroup I** is the most common haplogroup in the British Isles.

Not sure how many have contributed their Y-DNA to make this Page DNA Project happen, but I am sure it is over 150 individuals by now. Our Line "C" has a few markers that indicates Viking bloodline like DYS 449 (10) and DYS 460 (10) and Anglo-Saxon is DYS 390 (22) and DYS 455 (8). The Vikings have a reputation as "great warriors", but were also merchants, artists, kings, seafarers, explorers, shipbuilders and creators of remarkable mythology and brilliant literary sagas.

Focusing on Page line "C" has been Christopher Page (Ark), who continues to amaze me with his computer skills, and his father Bobby W. Page (Okla), who almost lives in libraries, as he travels around the states, and with Harry L. Page, the "local" historian in Marion, S.C—where the ABRAHAM PAGE line seems centered in the 1700's and the local library has the genealogical archives for our PAGE Line "C". There are so many others that have assisted in this research and some will be mentioned at the end of this document. My task has been to take all the "bits and pieces" since my effort began in the 1980's and "try" to connect all the dots, to tell the genealogical story. This has not been an easy genealogical effort and Chris Page and I—often disagree—with the conclusions offered in this document. I do intend to go back later and review this very complicated English family history charts that I have prepared on page 28 to 32, and invite everyone to help me verify the connections. Most of the information came from important documents like Parish Records, Wills and Land Transfer documents—BUT—accurately showing the parents of the person being discussed—is sometimes very difficult.

PAGE LINE "C" DEVELOPMENT

The following document is a "joint" attempt to give a little history of the beginning of the PAGE family "C", with some genealogical charts, to make it easy to see the family connections. For a long time, we all wanted to know . . . where did Thomas Page, (I believe b. 1640, Hunston (County Suffolk), England) (560-43, -84 & -181) is the apparent English immigrant. I believe this Thomas Page comes from Hunston—and NOW we know. He appears in Isle of Wight, Va, area just before 1659, that family history says he married Alis (Alice) Garrett on a ship in Mid-Atlantic traveling with her Garrett family on the same ship—meeting some members of the Garrett (Yarrett) family already established in Isle of Wight, Va,. Our small research group searched most of England, looking for something to connect the Thomas Page (arriving in Isle of Wight, Va. circa 1680) back to England, and this appears to be the answer.

Chris (Ark) Page disagrees with me and alleges that the Thomas Page—that arrived in Perquimans District, N.C.—in 1659—(that was already married to Alis ?) and Chris "claims" it is—Thomas Page, b.18Apr1653 in Chevington, (Co. Suffolk), England. (see 560-43, -84, -181) I see nothing to support a family history chart to support that claim, and Chris offers nothing to support this "Guess". LDS IGI N.C. records (560-181) clearly reveal that Thomas and his wife "Alis" are recorded in Perquimans Dist, N.C. in 1659. (560-181) Chris Page "also" believes Thomas Page married Alice Hollowell (Holloway) in Isle of Wight, Va—but my source documents (173 & 173A) fail to support this unsupported marriage. Chris Page has turned this serious research into a "guessing" game. (see 560-182)

I am of the opinion that the (Isle of Wight) THOMAS PAGE, was born 1640 in Hunston, (Co. Suffolk), England. (see 560-183) I have prepared a very detailed family history chart of this PAGE family—as it "popped up" in early 1300—in County Suffolk, England—as last names—were being forced for tax purposes. This is footnoted—in many documents—noted by the designation (see 560—??)—which the index can be found at the very end of this document. As you read through this very long and complicated document—that has taken years to put together—is probably NOT—free of errors. As the bits and pieces were developed—trying to piece them together—many often went without conflict—but—there are several connections—that I kept getting conflicting connections—from one generation to the next generation—and that can only be resolved by further research—by those that are still young—and have the time. I am slowly turning over much of my research material to the Archives in Marion County Library, South Carolina—so at least—this research will not be lost—when I am gone and others can continue.

For those interested in Y-DNA and would like to see the breakdown of the many Page Y-DNA families and see which lines go back to which oldest ancestor. You can access this information by hitting—www.pagey-dna.org. There you can see the results of well over 150 male Page individuals and many non-Page names and where they fall into the big picture. For those only interested in my family "C" line and who the individuals are, you can request a list from me and ask for the SAXON list. This very large list contains both PAGE and non-PAGE names, with a brief family background—all connected by Y-DNA.

Walsham le Willows is a small town in County Suffolk, England, ten miles from Bury St. Edmunds, which is about 60 miles north of London, that this genealogical information is being focused. It's name was given to the village by the Anglo-Saxons. Waaels or Wals being, perhaps, the name of the person holding this settlement or enclosure of land known as a ham. A Saxon church is recorded in the Domesday Book (1086) of Norman times. What more natural, than that the Saxon cultivators, who settled along the south facing slopes of a fertile valley, fixing tracks and field boundaries which, in many ways, are the same today, yet leaving little evidence of their presence here, except for a few sherds of pottery. Elsewhere of course, in the heathlands to the east of our county, at Sutton Hoo, near Woodbridge, field systems, settlements and most elaborate burials have been excavated, recorded and most recently interpreted in Martin Carfverae's book. "Burial Ground of Kings". But for Walsham, we can only manage a computer reconstruction of a domestic pot from the discovered sherd. Other sherds of pottery carry the story of settlement on Joly Cote Hill forwards.

The Domesday Book predates the PAGE surname. The Domesday book is divided. Book One is devoted to the counties of Essex, Norfolk and Suffolk and Book Two, to the rest of England. (560-1, p.656) There is mention of Pagenham/Pagham (a form of Page Home, or a home where Pages were schooled to serve the various Kings and courts.) There were two schools in England and one was near Bury St. Edmunds and Walsham le Willows.

Charles Nash Page in his (238) History and Genealogy of the Page Family (1257-1911) provides us a look, at what he presents as the beginning of the surname PAGE, on his chart #1. The following is NOT saying, (little evidence points to it) that we "might" be descended from this John de Pagham, but does seem to provide the foundation for the many Page lines, we are all chasing. So with that warning about the "conclusions" of Charles Nash Page—let's take a look at his findings.

1151-1157 John de Pagham, d. 1158, Rome, Italy, was the 4th Bishop of Worcester, England. (399, p. 28)(see my chart ENG 15)

1257   John lived at Ebor, Co. Yorkshire, England and was the son of a feudal Baron. (name not known)

The name de Pagen was not a family name, but descriptive of a place or occupation. Which means, he was in charge of a school to train "Pages". Hugo de Pageham, bc.1220, England (see my charts—ENG 1-1 & CONN 3) the senior son of a Baron or Knight was sent on an important mission (1256-1257) to Spain by Henry III, King of England. Charles Nash Page claims he was knighted in 1260, as Sir Hugo Page, by King Henry III but evidence of this is missing. In 1257, he was living in Ebor, Co. Yorkshire, England. It appears that Hugo and others were ordered to be captured and detained in the king's prison, at de Pageham, for the death of Roger de Belsham in Sussex in 1267. Hugo disappears after this event. (399, p. 29)

Hugo's brother, William de Pageham, knight, was sent by King Henry III (1207-1272), to Palestine to be Commander of the Crusaders in 1270. He returned to Sussex in the southern part of England, after four unsuccessful years of holy wars with Prince Edward, who becomes King Edward I. Edmund Page, of Pageham, Yorkshire was probably son or grandson of William de Pageham (399, p.30) (472-1, page 3) and 281-1, p. 2) In 1240 William le Page appeared as a witness in the Court of Fines for Essex. Research by **Rick Bentley Page** reveals he found a burial monument of William de Pageham, at Titchfield Church, in County Hampshire, England, who "may" also have been a son, but his line "appears" to have daughtered out.

Pakenham, or **De Pirou**, from the **Castle of Pirou**, in Coutances region, Normandy, France. To see a picture of the Castle Pirou—go to Google and type Castle Pirou, Normandy, France and the picture and history of the castle will appear. The **Baron of Pirou** came to England in 1066, and is mentioned at Battle of Hastings. **William de Pakenham**, his son, was Dapifer to Henry I, (more on Henry I later) He was last with Prince William in 1120.

His son William held the office of Dapifer. (Dapifer is the chief officer arranging the journeys of a king or emperor and by 1701 was the chief officer and head of the Army and administrator of the royal family). His son William held a barony of eleven fees in Normandy 1165. **William Pirou** also held five fees from Earl Bigot in Norfolk, and one from Montfichet, and William Fitz-Humphry held a fee of the honour of Eye.

In 1198 William, son of William Pirou, complained that the Earl Bigot had seized his lands as feudal superior and the Earl was obliged to restore his fief, which was Pakeham or Pakenham. This name now was adopted as the **family surname**, and William de Pakenham and Simon de Pakenham occur 1199. Hence the Pakenhams of Suffolk, and the Earls of Longforde. (560-13, p. 350)

Our PAGE family "C" Y-DNA **Haplogroup** is :l1a3 (M253+) and this lineage "likely" has its roots in northern France. Today it is found most frequently within Viking/Scandinavian populations in northwest Europe. According to Family Tree DNA our line "C" began its journey in what is today Kuwait, traveled north thru Turkey, then through old Yugoslavia, then turns west into lower France, into Normandy, then north to Scandinavia, probably by sea or land, that permitted the Scandinavian countries to develop and then some returned to Normandy, France.

Family Trees
EMMA AND HER NORMAN FAMILY

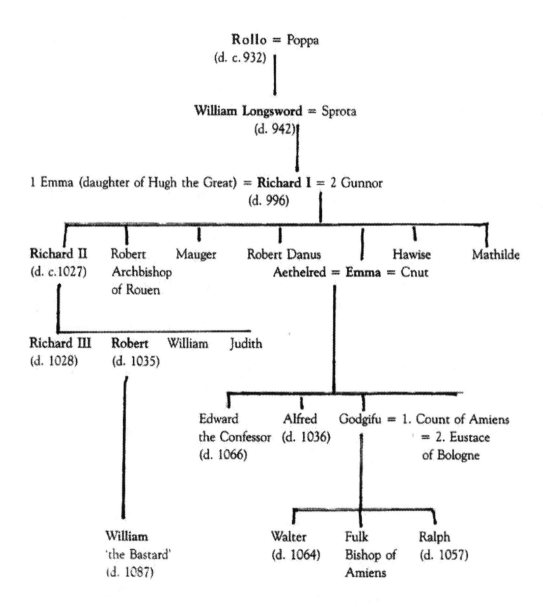

ROLLO, (bc.846, Denmark—dc. 931, Normandy, France), (551F, p.183) "the Viking" and baptized as **Robert I**—that left Fakse, Denmark in the 870s and plundered England and Holland landed in northern France.

By 911, the French King Charles "the Simple" ceded land to him—as a means of keeping him under control. The territory of the North men was subsequently known as Normandy. As ROLLO, and his fellow Vikings put down roots in Normandy, they inevitably loosened their ties with their Scandinavian homeland,. The old Norse language was quick to go. The first wave of invaders had come with few, if any women; when they settled down, they took French wives and concubines. The children grew up speaking their mothers tongue. (551 I, p. 72)

William "the bastard" (b.1027-d.1087) who conquered England in 1066, and became King of England Christmas 1066—was a descendant of Rollo. (551D) I have visited Caen, France and the abbey church of St. Stephen where William "the bastard" is buried.

Tomb of William "the bastard" in the choir of St. Stephen's church, Caen, France.

It was recently announced that bones of two of Rollo's relatives, Richard I and Richard II are being dug up to determine the Y-DNA. (see 551D, p. IX) It "appears" that his haplogroup "might" be I1—which is Page Family "C" haplogroup. We are awaiting the DNA results. For more information on Rollo, go to: http://en.wikipedia.org/wiki/Rollo. And www.explicofund. org/index-3.html

Another discovery is a "possible" connection to Robert de Bruce (b.11Jul1274-d.7June1329) whose fathers family came from House of Brus (now Brix), in Normandy, France—very near (15 miles) to Coutances, where Castle Pirou was located on the coast. The first was Robert de Brus (1030-1080) then—Robert de Bruce—the First, d. 1094 was a Norman Knight—that took part in the Norman invasion of England in 1066, with William the Conqueror (1027-1087) who won the battle at Hastings and became King of England. (519C, p.28)

Robert de Bruce VIII, b.11Jul1274-d.7Jun1329 (later King of Scotland) was born in Writtle, (some debate about this) a village just outside Chelmsford, Co. Essex, England, where the Abraham Page line lived. Robert de Bruce seized the Scottish throne in early 1306, just as the Knights Templars were arrested or fleeing out of France.

The Page Y-DNA Project administrator George W. Page has provided us with better research. He has searched the "Close Rolls" beginning in the year 1231 and found **Walter Page** and **Johnnes le Page** (from the vicinity of Northhamptonshire) and in 1234 the name Serlonem (Serlonis) Page appears in the "Rolls" that were started by King Henry III (1207-1272) (399, p. 28) These two **Bold Print** names are later found in Co. Suffolk Subsidy Returns on Burials. (560-12C), (page 11 & 18)

From the Dictionary of the Ancestral Heads of the New England Families (1620-1700) by Frank R. Holmes, we learn that "Page" was an "occupational" name given to youths of the gentry class between seven and fourteen years of age, while receiving their education to become a squire and then a knight. The origin of the word "Page" is supposed to be Italian for "Paggie" or from the Latin "Pagius", meaning a boy or youth attending the king. Boys of noble parentage, who were at the royal court were called "Pages". It was quite an honor much sought after, as the surroundings and the acquaintances made at court were valuable to personal advancement. A course of training in courtesy, etiquette, and diplomacy was given these boys, and the place where they lived and trained was called a "Page Home", shortened to "Pageham", also sometimes written "Pagham" or "Pagenham". (399, p.27)

The origins of the Knights of Saint Edmund or Milites de Sancti Edmundi. Shortly after the Norman Conquest, William the Conqueror, ordered that all major nobles, bishops and Abbeys had to provide a certain number of Knights to the crown. This service was normally for 3 months every year. The Abbey of St. Edmund had the unique privilege of holding the eight and half hundreds of west Suffolk, known as the Liberty of St. Edmund, and consequently 40 knights were demanded by the King. When not on campaign these knights had to perform garrison duty at Norwich castle on a three month rota. The original Knights were granted land in return for undertaking this military service on behalf of the Abbey. Many of the leading Anglo-Norman families in Suffolk became Knights of St. Edmund including the de Clare, de

Vere, de Valognes, Blundus and Bigod families. Even old Anglo-Saxon families held Knights fees from the Abbey, most notably the de Cockfield family. The Knights therefore formed a club of local families holding land in Suffolk.

Apart from guarding Norwich castle, the Knights of St. Edmund also had to act as advisors, jurors and feudal tenants of the Abbot of Bury St. Edmund who was also the Baron of St. Edmund. Like other Barons the knights swore allegiance to the Abbot of St. Edmunds as their feudal overlord. This was important as if they died, without issue, or before their children were old enough to inherit the Abbot could take their estates into his hands until either an heir matured or until the Abbot could marry-off the heiress.

The zenith of the Knights career occurred in 1173 when they led the royalist army into battle, defeating and routing the largely Flemish mercenary rebel army led by Robert Beaumont, the Earl of Leicester, at the battle of Fornham, St. Genevieve. The Knights were led into battle by the banner of St. Edmund—which was carried by **ROGER BIGOD, t**he Norman founder of a house that dominated East Anglia (560-1, p.625) and Earl of Norfolk de Monfort (560-163, p.152) that forced King John to sign the Magna Carta, in 1215 (560-163, p.26), that abolished the absolute monarchy Anglo-Norman state. (560-163, p.153). It is interesting that in 1263 the Queen had pawned her jewels to the **Templars**, but a trick by King Henry (son of King John) permitted him to regain the jewels. (560-163, p.156) The property around **Somerleyton** eventually wound up in the Jernegan family, which is closely tied to the Page family name in Co. Suffolk, England—then with the Quakers in **Chuckattuck**, Isle of Wight Co, Va,—then later in Wayne Co, NC. (560-16)

By the beginning of the 13th century rising costs of military activity led the Knights of St. Edmund to insist that they were not obliged to serve outside England. Warfare was becoming more expensive and more professional, so the crown took the opportunity to switch from using part-timers, like the Knights of St. Edmund, to demanding cash payment or scutage from the Abbey of St. Edmunds. Consequently following the 13th century the Knights of St. Edmund adopted a more ceremonial, legal and advisory rather than practical role.

However, the Knights continued to have a practical role in the defense of the town because they were required to help maintain the defenses around Bury St. Edmunds. Originally this consisted of earth work ditch and bank and timber palisade which was replaced in the 12th or 13th century by a new stone wall. Due to the obligation and duty required of the Knights to defend the town of St. Edmund, the campaign has adopted the name the Knights of St. Edmund to once again defend a town from the most sinister threat to the town for almost as thousand years. Info from www.knightsofstedmund.com

A candidate for knighthood might well be the son of a knight, though it was possible for a burgess to place an aspiring child in training which began when about 7 to 10 years old. Often the boy would be sent away to learn his trade, commonly to the household of a relative such as an uncle, though the sons of noble houses might well find themselves at the king's court. As a page, the new recruit would be taught how to behave in polite society, how to keep ladies company, how to sing and dance and recite poetry. However the boy also needed to begin the tough training that would enable him to survive on the battlefield, and he would start to handle practice weapons, learn to groom horses, and begin the arduous tasks of becoming familiar with, and looking after, weapons and armour. When about 14 years old, he graduated to the role of squire, the word being derived from the French ecuyer, meaning a shield bearer. The youth now trained in earnest with weapons. He cut at the pell or wooden post, wrestled and practiced against other squires or knights. When pulled on a wooden horse by comrades, or mounted on a real horse, he tried to keep his seat when his lance rammed the quintain, a post on which was fixed a shield. Some had a pivoting arm, with a shield at one end and a weighted sack at the other, if a strike was made the rider had to pass swiftly by in order to avoid the swinging weight. The ceremony of knighting traditionally took place when the young man was somewhere between about 18 and 21 years old. Some squires were knighted much later in life, or remained squires until they died. (560-2, p. 37 & 145)

There is some confusion between Pagham and Pakenham, but one family was named from Pagham on the south coast of England near—Chichester and Bognor Regis in county West Sussex (just a short distance across the English Channel from the tip of Normandy—where Normans have occupied that part of France before year 1000. Some mention of William "The Conqueror", born at Falaise, Normandy, France (1027-1087)(560-14A, p.3) that is connected to this mystery—is offered at the end of this document. It is a constantly changing document and you need to go to the end of this document—if your focus is on the "origin" of the family—that finally adopted the name PAGE.

The other Page school location is Pakenham, in county Suffolk, north of London, about five miles east of Bury St. Edmunds, which is next to Walsham le Willows and seventeen miles north of Sudbury. I am going to devote more attention to Pakenham because that is the location where it appears our Page Family Line "C" popped up—in early 1300 and developed into a very large family. There is probably a sound connection between these two locations, with almost the same names, but whether it is a blood connection or a royal need for these two "knight" schools—remains to be discovered. Let's hope Y-DNA will help us solve this mystery.

It is interesting that Page genealogist **Rick Bentley Page** found a burial monument of **WILLIAM de PAGEHAM**, at **Tichfield** church, in County Hampshire, England. There is "suspicion" that there might be a Y-DNA connection to family **Totten**—that adopted the name of a town, in that area (as last names were forced) that later appeared in North Ireland, then settled in Newcastle-upon-Tyne in the 1870's, when the family—then emigrated to New Zealand after WW II. The other connection to this is "Tottenham Manor" (in London)—that is also a "possible" connection to Robert de Bruce at http://british—which "might" be the same Y-DNA as DNA analysis is "underway" on the "bones" of a **Rollo** relative, in France. Maybe a brief mention of the French DNA process—might be in order. It appears against French Law to do a DNA analysis—**IF** it is for a "paternity question"—is against French law—(protects pregnant girl friends) but genealogical DNA testing—is NOT against French law—and the confusion—over this issue—scares many French individuals—to NOT sign up for this DNA testing.

Another interesting possible connection is the close Y-DNA with the **HUNTER** family that left Normandy, France—just after the 1066 invasion of England by William the "Bastard" and arrived in County **Ayr**, **SCOTLAND**. More on the Hunter family later.

The earliest mention of Pakenham (County Suffolk) occurs in the WILL of Theodred, Bishop of London in 942-951, when he gave the land at Barton, Roughham and Pakenham to "my kinsman Eadulf's son Osgot". During the years 1042-1065 The Abbot of Bury St. Edmunds leased half a carucate of land, in Pakenham to an unnamed freeman, on condition that after the freeman's death the whole of his land there shall revert to the abbey.

Records also indicate that during 1045-1047 King Edward the Confessor, gave the estate of Pakenham, which formerly belonged to Osgot, to the Abbey. It is possible that Osgot, who by then had gone into exile, had been the freeman who had leased the land from the Abbot.

After the conquest of 1066, the Normans began the task of reforming and modernising the English Church, bringing it up to date with the Norman and Continental model. Anglo-Saxon architecture was swept away and a great wave of rebuilding took place. The original Church as recorded in Doomesday Survey of 1086 (was probably a wooden structure built by the Lord of the Manor whose house would have stood nearby. For more information on the origins of the Knights of St. Edmund (see 560-10) because the new King—William the Conqueror—ordered 40 knights be furnished him for campaign duties and garrison duties at Norwich castle on a three month rota.

During the reign of Henry I (1100-1135) a Walter is recorded as founding a new church at Pakenham. Over the next few hundred years, many additions were added. (560-5)

The family Pakenham was holding the Manor at Netherhall in Pakenham, Co. Suffolk, by the end of the 11th century, (this must be the William de Pakenham family from the Castle of Pirou, Normandy, France) (569-13, p.350) as Vassals of the Abbey of Bury St. Edmunds, according to Burke's Peerage and Baronetage under the name LONGFORDE, the 6th Earl of Longford (Edward Arthur Henry Pakenham) and Baron Longford of Ireland. (399, p.32)

This pedigree was registered at the College of Arms shows that this Pakenham family was holding the Manor at Netherhall in Pakenham, Co. Suffolk, by the end of the 11th century, as Vassals of the Abbey of Bury St. Edmunds." About the year 1100, the church at Pakenham was founded by WALTER, who had, with various other children, an eldest son named PETER. The latter left no legal issue, but on his death his illegitimate son, ANSELM, seized the manor to the exclusion of his father's sister, and succeeded in passing it on to his eldest son, (by Ingrethe his wife), MASTER ROBERT DE PAKENHAM, the first bearer of this surname. He granted lands to his sons in 1252, and was father of MASTER JOHN DE PAKENHAM (d.1158). He was the fourth bishop of Worcester, England from 1151-1157 and probably a native of Pakenham, Co. Sussex. He assisted at the consecration of Roger to the See of York on 10 October 1154, and at the coronation of Henry II, on 19 December 1154. He died at Rome, on 31March1158. He was also known as John le Clerk who married Muriel ? and had son Sir John, who died before 1305, and that male line became extinct in the 14th century. Another son, was Sir William de Pakenham, Justice of the King of Ireland. He added largely to his estates in Norfolk and Suffolk, and married Joan ?? and on his death divided his lands among his four sons. His eldest son, Sir Edmund de Pakenham, who on 23Apr1305 granted to John, son of William, who was son of John de Pakenham lands in exchange for lands at Pakenham, (Suffolk), Belagh Manor, (Norfolk) and Henneshurst (Kent). That family genealogy goes on and on and I will not pursue it. (399, p. 32)

Let us look at Pakenham in more detail. Pakenham is just under 5 miles east of the centre of Bury St. Edmunds, in rolling arable land. The village is just over half a mile long, running from Pakenham Manor in the west to the church at the east end. The village lies in the shallow valley that runs from Grimstone End in the north to Bartonmere in the south, and St. Mary's church stands on a promontory overlooking the village. Land at Pakenham, Roughham and Barton was given in the will of Theodred, Bishop of London, that had a cathedral church at Hoxne, and was probably a German by birth. (506-1, p.437 & 444) (A.D. 942-51), to his kinsman Eadulf's son, Osgot.

The Pakenham estate was given to St. Edmundsbury Abbey by Edward the Confessor. In 1086, the estate included a church with 30 acres of free land in alms.

The names of **WALTER PAGE** and **JOHNNES LE PAGE** (from the vicinity of Northamptonshire) appear in the Close Rolls in 1231 and the name Serlonem (Serlonis) Page appears in 1234. In the reign of Henry I (1100-1135), one WALTER PAGE founded a new church at Pakenham, and the 12th century work recorded above belonged to WALTER's church. In 1199, Abbot Sampson allocated one third of the demesne and tithes to St. Saviour's

Hospital, Bury, and in 1256 Abbot Walpole appropriated the church to the maintenance of hospitality in Bury. The vicar was allowed to retain the church manse and the land and tithes from it together with other tithes and altar dues, but retained no income from crops. (399, p.28)

Sir Hugo's "supposed brother", Sir William de Pageham, was granted letters by King Henry III to become a Commander of the Crusaders in 1270. He returned to Sussex in the southern part of England, after four unsuccessful years of holy wars with Prince Edward, who became King Edward I. Sir William served as one of King Edwards's knights, and his record, as obtained from the book Knights of Edward I, is as follows: Sir William was the Assessor, etc, of Subsidy fees, in county Sussex, on 12Nov1294, and Justice of Goal Delivery for Chichester, Guilford, and Arundel at various times from 16Oct1294. He served as a knight enrolled in the defense of the coast during the rape (siege) of Chichester in 1296.

In 1297 the Christians lost Palestine and left. He was summoned from Sussex to serve against the Scots on 25May1298 and taxed as having 40 English pounds in lands in Hampshire on 24Jun1300 and 1301. (399, p.30)

In the autumn of 1304, Sir William of Pakenham, knight, began to make disposition of his property to his sons. Sir William's eldest son, Edmund of Pakenham, was to succeed his father in the majority of his lands. It is clear that Sir William also wished to provide for his other two sons, Thomas and William. Pakenham manor of **NORTON**, 6Oct1304, William, son of Sir William, quitclaimed to his father for himself and his heirs all rights that he had in the manor (120 acres) of **IXWORTH**. (a few miles above Pakenham and a few miles west of Walsham le Willows). The next month, after Sir Williams death (22Jan1305), Edmund of Pakenham granted to his brother and his heirs, a fishery, that their father had bought from William de Criketot. For this grant, Edmund paid 100 marks cash. Thomas of Pakenham was able to use the manor of **IXWORTH THORPE** to support himself and his family. (560-9) (see 60 & 60A)

Sir William de Pakenham, was sometimes Sheriff of Sussex in January 1294 and he died 22Jan1305. A grant was made in March 1305 to Mary, the daughter of King Edward I, who gave "custody of lands and heir of William de Pageham, in minority, with marriage of heir" It" seems" that this nun was unmarried and "maybe" Sir William's mother. Also that year, the king sent an order that caused a dower to be assigned to Margery, late wife of William de Pageham. William's son and heir was also named in Close Rolls to receive his father's lands. On 8Dec1312 John de Pageham, son and heir of William de Pageham, knight (deceased) in connection with land in Chichester, County Sussex.

October 13, 1307 French King Phillip IV called a "meeting" in Paris of all **KNIGHTS TEMPLARS** and arrested 620 and imprisoned them. Sixty were executed. (560-176, p. 150) Many escaped by ship to Scotland and stayed with **Robert de Bruce**. At the Council of Vienne in 1312 King Phillip of France forced Pope Clement to dissolve Knight Templars. By 1314 the last Grand Master Jacques de Molay was burned at the stake and all traces of Knights Templars in France were gone.

The Knights Templars, had developed (what was later, the Swiss banking system) and by 1150 were issuing letters of credit, written in code, which later became the banking system of the Champaign Region of France and headquarters of the group. They developed how to loan money at high interest rates. Many of the fleeing Knights Templars took refuge in the Swiss and German Alps, in the early 1300's and we have two of our DNA Page Line "C",—John Flaig and Magnus Schiller—that traces their lines back to the Black Forest area of Germany, just above Switzerland, which "could" tie this line to the Knight Templars, as they were seeking a hiding place. More on Flaig and Schiller in my SAXON document.

In 1315 King Edward II, mentioned **THOMAS de PAGEHAM,** of Suffolk, as a son of William de Pageham, Knight. (399, p. 30)

In 1323, in the village of **Ingham,** Co. Suffolk, England—the name **BRUCE PAGE** appears. Robert de Askeby, Parson of Ingham church vs. Bruce Page of Ingham. (560-22C)

The abbot's manor house at **Pakenham** was one of 13 **burnt** by disaffected townsmen and tenants during the so-called **Great Riot of 1327 (**see more on page 22)—a protest against the abbey's bad management of their estates and their alleged failure to meet their commitments. At the Dissolution, the manor reverted to the crown, and in 1545, it was granted to Robert Spring of **Lavenham** and his son Thomas. It remained in the direct line until the death of Sir William Spring, 4th Baronet Pakenham, in 1735, (source: St Mary Church, Pakenham, Suffolk, (560-5) www.crsbi.ac.uk/ed/sf/paken/index.htm.

DEVELOPMENT OF THE PAGE FAMILY "C"

I have attempted to put together a family history of this Pakenham family in County Suffolk in an attempt to see how the Y-DNA line that developed into one line of Page's, that finally adopted the surname PAGE. Much English history was occurring at this time that probably influenced the below and I have inserted a few events that seem related.

942-951 Theodred, Bishop of London gave land to my kinsman Eadulf's son Osgot

1041-1065 The Abbot of Bury St. Edmunds leased half a carucate of land to Osgot

1066 Norman Conquest—new ruler gave lands to his followers.

1118 Original Templar Knights established in France. (560-168)

1128 Knights Templar established in Scotland (560-169)

1100-1135 Walter leased to Sir William Pakenham, knight, that began to dispose of his property. (560-9)

1199 English King John (b.1167-d.1216) became King—who then taxed everyone for the THIRD Crusade—(he was younger brother of King Richard the Lion Hearted)

1215 English King John forced to sign Magna Carter (foundation for US constitution)— and died the next year.

1304 Sir William of Pakenham, knight, began to dispose of his property (560-9)

```
        Sir William de (of) Pakenham, Knight, d.22Jan1305
             Margary
   |           —|          —|        This Pakenham property is not far from
Edmund      Thomas       William         Chris (UK) Page year 1711 family.
 Rose                       |
          John de Parkenham, d.1312
```

The Manor of Nether Hall is partly in Pakenham and partly in Thurston and was under the Lordship of the Abbot of St. Edmunds in 1086 and in the time of Henry III was vested in John de Pakenham.

1253 John de Pakenham who was steward to the Bishop of Ely in 1265 had grant of free warren (royal game license). (560-17)

1270 William de Parkenham to Palestine (8th Crusade) then back to Co. Sussex the same year.

1271-1272 Ninth and last Crusade. William de Parkenham on this Crusade.

1275 William de Pakenham (son of John) held Bishopscroft, near the church in Pakenham

1281   legal action was brought against William by Henry de Pakenham relating to common pasture in Pakenham.

1292   William de Pakenham died and John de Pakenham, who was son of William, who was son of John de Pakenham settled the Manor on his brother Edmund de Pakenham and his heirs. (560-17)

1297   Scottish William Wallace and Andrew de Moray rebelled against King John in his rule.

1306   February 10—Robert de (the) Bruce killed John "Red" Comyn on the altar in Greyfriars Church in Dumfries, Scotland. During the Battle of Grey Friars Kirk. This event resulted in his excommunication by the Pope. This event later produced the Declaration of Arbroath in 1320. It announced that "kings could be chosen by the population rather than by God alone". This document is without a doubt, the most famous document in Scottish history. Like the American Declaration of Independence, which is partially based most of it, and is seen by many, as the founding document of the Scottish Nation. It was drafted on April 6, 1320, a day the U. S. has declared to be "Tartan Day".

Those interested in this MOST IMPORTANT document should "Google" "Declaration of Arbroath". This important RARE PRINT of the 700 years old Declaration of Arbroath—has been donated—by the Scottish Government—to the National Archives in Washington, D.C.—because of the inspirational status for the authors of the American Declaration of Independence. More than one-third of the signatories of the US Declaration were Scots and the link between the two documents formed the basis of calling April 6 day—Tartan Day.

1307   October 12th—Eighteen ships of Knights Templars arrived in the harbor of La Rochelle, France and were GONE the next morning, with all their possessions. (560-170) For more on this demise of the Knights Templars—see previous page. It appears the ships divided and some went to Portugal and some to Scotland.

A Scottish friend of mine Victor Duddy, from **AYR** had a grandfather that grew up in the sparsely settled penisular of Ardnaiurchan and as a young lad—he discovered "about" 10 graves—with clearly "Knight Templar" symbols engravings with Swords (with unreadable names) on a "small unnamed island" on Loch Shiel (fresh water)—(Latitude 56 degrees -45' 6.11 N and Longitude 5 degrees 40' 43.01 W) not far the very small town of Dalelia—which is near the larger town of Acharacle. (see 560-167, p.140 A2) Victor's other grandfather (mothers father) Duncan McIntyre, bc. 1890 was raised in the nearby town of Shielfoot, just north of Acharacle. The University College, London, generic survey for Viking DNA found over 30 grave-finds from about 850-950 on the Isle of Man, in the Irish Sea. (551F, p.78)

Another Scottish friend Fraser Laurie, from Glascow, supports the above information. Could this be part of the missing Knights Templar fleet—that fled La Rochelle, France, with all their possessions, including the so called "Holy Grail and jewels and diamonds being "held for security" on loans?

Another contributor to FTDNA that has—Y-DNA 67 (PAGE line "C" results) is Oliver **HUNTER,** oliver@thehunterfamily.co.uk whose family line is from **Hunterston** in Ayrshire, Scotland (near Preswick), and **AYR** (560-167—p.3H) This family worked for the **ROLLO** family in Normandy, France but left France in 1068, (just after the 1066 invasion) and moved to Ayrshire, Scotland—then later to **Crichton Dean, Scotland**. (560-167, p.129 G3) which is very near Roslin (**Rosslyn)** Castle, which is just south of Edinburgh, Scotland. This Hunter family was closely connected with William Wallace and Robert de Bruce family in 1374 and DNA seems to connect with the ROLLO line and maybe Robert de Bruce line—which "seems" to be connected by Y-DNA to the PAGE Family Line "C".

Those in training to become Knights, start out as Pages, learning how to wait at tables and how to look after horses. At the age of about 14, those that have done well became esquires and would be assigned to a knight, when their military training with armour and weapons began in earnest. They accompanied him to the HUNT, in itself good physical exercise that had the bonus of bringing additional food to the table. They were taught how to break a freshly killed deer, but the use of the bow was limited to the hunting field. (560-2, p. 99) For more info on **HUNTER** clan—see Wikipedia.org/wiki/Clan Hunter.

Others that have Joined FTDNA and feel their male line backs up to Scotland (or next to) and have gotten test results that indicate they probably belong to PAGE line "C" but do NOT have Surname PAGE. They are: Alan Alls (Y-DNA 64 match of 67)—James Jefferson Taylor (match 61 of 67) from Northumberland, England (which is next to Scotland)—Peter J. Roberts (DNA 67) "maybe" connected to Clan Robertson. See below for more info on the Roberts connection.

1314   Knights Templars have by now disappeared from France and some flee to south Germany, near Switzerland and many flee to Scotland and join King Robert De Bruce of Scotland—that appears born at Writtle—small village next to Chelmsford (Co. Essex) where Abraham Page line "C" lived.

1314   The battle of Bannockburn (Scotland) occurs on June 24, 1314 and Bruce's Army has about 5,000-7,000 troops and the English has over 20,000 troops—but were defeated by Bruce. How & WHY? (see 560-171)

1320   Declaration of Arbroath—is a declaration of Scottish Independence that Robert the Bruce had delivered to the Scottish nation. (560-172)

One of our Page DNA Line "C" members is Peter J. Roberts (Is this the Robert de Bruce line?) who has backed up his line to Scotland, and maybe Clan Donnachaidh (AKA Clan Robertson).

1323 The name Bruce Page appears in Ingham (Co. Suffolk) England—who was sued and fined by Robert de Askeby, parson of Ingham Church and was awarded a fine. Info: Calendar for the Feets of fines court, by Walter Rye, 1900. (560-22C)

1329 Scottish King Robert the Bruce—lay dying & asked Sir James Douglas to take his heart on Crusade against the enemies of Christ—into battle against the Moors in Spain, in 1330—before it was returned to Scotland and finally buried at Melrose Abbey in Scotland. (560-173)

1332 Sir Edmund de Pakenham died and Manor passed to Widow Rose, and on her death to son and heir, Sir Edmund de Pakenham who died, without issue.

1350 Shroud of Turin discovered.

1360 Widow Rose died. Rose's second son, Sir Thomas Pakenham gave the Manor to his mother who gave it to Richard de Pakenham, cousin to her son Thomas. Richard died and leaving an only daughter and heir, age 11 years, so the limitation of the Abbot took effect. (560-17)

1367 Henry de (Breton) Pakenham inherited land including Pakenham Manor (Norton) which is 18 miles north of Walsham le Willows and Ixworth. He left this land to his son, Henry.

1408 Son Henry got more land and lived at Pakenham Hall but Henry de Pakenham, died 1445

Son Robert Pakenham, b. 1415-d.1463 buried St. Peter's church, Shropham

Son Henry took over and died 1495. (560-8)

Charles Nash Page's chart #1 (November 1957) gives the following genealogy: There has been much criticism of this genealogy—and many errors found—but I have presented it with this WARNING. Ruthanne Page has devoted years of re-writing and correcting his published works, and she "might" comment on some specific issues. She has recently released a Christmas message to all of her **PAGE LINE "E"** FAMILY—that I have filed under my (560-175) (11 pages).

This is a detailed analysis of the genealogy of C.N. Page book on Page history and how it seems to have been motivated by politics and his desire to show his ancestors—as great or famous people. Her attention seems focused on one John Page/Phebe Payne marriage on 5June1621 that occurs in Levenham (Co. Suffolk), England and is well documented. One of their sons is Ruthanne's line. (see 560-68)

C.N. Page reports that John Page, d. 1543 of Wembley, Middlesex married ? Daniel of West Wolsey, Surrey and in 1536 received from King Henry VIII, a large amount of land formerly church property. Estate divided between his two sons which were Henry Page, b. 1492, Wembley and Sir Richard Page, d. 1558, who lived at Sudbury (24 miles south from Walsham le Willows).

Sir Richard Page was called "Ye Noble Richard" by King Henry VIII. He married Alice ??. Sir Richard became possessor of a large estate besides his father's. His children were:

Rowland Page	Thomas Page	Agnes Page	Dorothy Page	William Page
Received real	d. 1574	mar:	mar: ?? Gerard	
Estate from father	mar: Annie ?? ??	Thornton		
1549 Owned	lived Sudbury			
Bedfont Manor	Court			
Alive in 1593				
l	l			
Children	Children:			
Garrett Page	Francis – d. young			
Richard Page	Henry – buried Sudbury Court farm			
Alice Page	Richard Page			
	Thomas Page			
	John Page			
	Dorothy Page			

Charles Nash Page notes that he made an extended search but could find no further record of descendants of this branch, except the statement that practically the entire estate (**Great Page Estate**) (see 282) passed into the hands of Mrs. **Mary Herne**, mother of **Ann Herne**, who married Richard Page and was willed by Mrs. **Mary Herne** to her grandson, Richard Page (b.20Jul1747-d.6Dec1802), Wembley, thus uniting in him the estate of both branches of the family. He does not appear to have married or have any heirs. His father was Richard Page, of Wembley and his 1st wife was **Ann Herne**. Herne is in bold print because the name **Herne** appears in Co. Suffolk, England and then later in Isle of Wight, Va. and was closely associated with the Thomas Page/Alis Garrett Y-DNA line "C" that is the subject of this research.

Another from County Essex was Philip Page, in the time of King Edward 1st, then John and William le Page of the year 1300. (281-1, p. 2)

Also before 1490, Nicholas Page was living in Co. Essex, and had a son named Henry, who made his home in County Middlesex. Henry had a son, John I, who was married in 1553 to Audrey Reading, and they had two sons, John II and Richard. Richard Page and wife Frances Mudge, had John, Richard and Thomas Page.

John Page moved to London, and then to Co. Essex and married Phoebe Paine in 1620 later emigrated to New England in 1630 and settled in Watertown, Mass. This is DNA Page Family **Line E,** which is Researcher Ruthanne Page's line and is on my chart MASS 5, footnote (12) and on my chart MASS 5C footnote (3) which reflects a conflict. Wray Page says Thomas Page, b. 1597 is not the father of John Page, b.1627.

The other son, Thomas Page, had son John Page, b.1627, Belfont, England—d.1692, Williamsburg, Va, (see my charts VA 5 & ENG 15) who moved to Virginia in 1650, married Alice Lucklin, b.1618, Co. Essex, England in 1656 and made his home in Williamsburg, Va, This is Page Family **Line F**. (281, p. 3) & (281-1, p.3) I guess by now, you have noticed that the Y-DNA is NOT the same.

Because British colonists made up so much of early America, first-name traditions from back in Merry Old England often continued in the colonies. This scheme was common especially in the 18th and 19th centuries. (see 560-166)

> First son was named after the father's father
> Second son, after the mother's father
> Third son, after the father
> Fourth son after the father's eldest brother
>
> First daughter, after the mother's mother
> Second daughter after the fathers mother
> Third daughter after the mother
> Fourth daughter, after the mother's eldest sister

Most of the many Page descendants connected by Y-DNA to Page Family Line "C" "appear" to go back to **THOMAS PAGE, B. 1640, HUNSTON** (Co. Suffolk) married to Alice Garrett on a ship from England (mid-Atlantic) and both appeared in Perquimans Dist, N.C.—in 1659. (560-181) It was thought that Thomas "may" have been born in Virginia, but gone back to Co. Suffolk, England to dispose of some inherited property, and married Alice (Alis) Garrett while returning to Isle of Wight, Va, area just before **1680** with the Garrett family—when a son, Thomas Page was born in 1680. This Thomas Page, b. 1640 was first thought to have left from the small town of Walsham le Willows, in County Suffolk, England, but a very comprehensive search finally located his birth date/ birthplace as Hunston, England. (560-183) It also has been discovered that Thomas Page was married to Alis and they are recorded as being in Perquimans, Dist, N.C. in years 1659, 1663 and 1684. (560-181) It is definite that some of this Page family "C" had also moved to County Norfork, England—and later they did emigrate to Isle of Wight, Va area. (560-148)

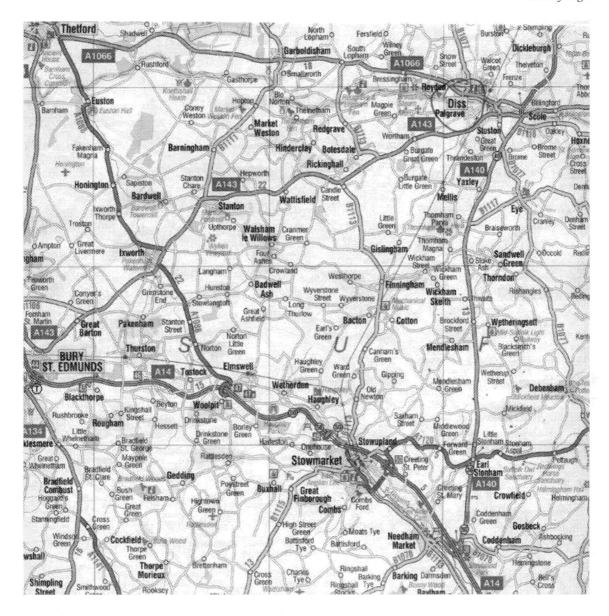

There are four other Page's of Page Family Line "C", (Robert E. Page, Harry L. Page, Fred A. Page and James C. Page) that trace their line back to one Abraham Page, bc.1704, (location not known for sure—but "appears" to be County Suffolk, England. The Y-DNA connection and paper trail is clear—but where this Abraham Page connects to the Thomas Page, b. 1640, Hunston line is still NOT clear. Probably is a nephew or cousin to Thomas Page, b. 1640 Hunston, England married to Alice (Alis) Garrett. It is now becoming clear that many in PAGE line "C" descend from ABRAHAM PAGE because the clear line of ascent back to Thomas Page, Isle of Wight, Virginia is under question and appears broken. Much focus is on this ABRAHAM PAGE line and how he fits into the scheme of family history.

This **Abraham Page**, b. early 1700, England and married to Mary ? (probably Lamb). More mention of ongoing research on this **Abraham Page** will be made at the end of this narrative. (see Appendix A & chart AD1 & AD1B) Further research in England has led our research group to believe our Isle of Wight, Virginia—Thomas Page b.1640, Hunston, England family originally came from Walsham le Willows "area", in Co. Suffolk, England, with some of the family—later living in County Norfolk, England before they emigrated to Virginia. The Quaker church was just getting established at that time in Virginia—so there was a void of good records until they got organized and later developed very good records. The many families from County Suffolk, England formed the core of the Quaker Church movement, in Virginia.

In the Subsidy Returns on **Burials** in Co. Suffolk, England for year **1327**, the following were reported: Hundred de Cleydone, was **De Willmo Page (**Westleton, Lackford & Felixtowe**), De Johanne Page (Sudbury)**, De **Waltero Page**, (Risby) De Galfrido Page, De Henrico Page (Chediston), De Alexandro Page (Brampton), De Radulpho Page, De Georgio Page (Bradfield St. Clare), De Rogero Page (Saxtead & Hintlesham), De Stephano Page (Sudbury & Wyverstone), **De Roberto Page** (Otley), De Ricardo Page (Stradbroke), De Juliana Page (Barton Mills). The use of "De" means "of" in English. Subsidy returns were taxes from 12th to 17th centuries on moveable personal property and sometimes on land and buildings. When one died, his heirs had to pay a tax. (see 560-12B)

There were many land transfers and deeds on residences that had the following named Page men that signed the documents, as witness, in the towns noted, that were father to son relationships for the period beginning 1324 and ending in 1513. All of these documents were within a few miles of each other in the area, just west of Bury St. Edmunds. It seems that part of the Page family C line moved the east side of Bury and the first recorded Thomas Page (1) was Rector of Hinderclay church from 1391-1399. The next is John Page (2), b.1398-d.1452 married to Agnes (2A) and they lived in Walsham le Willows, a few miles south of Hinderclay.

It is the Field Book of Walsham le Willows of 1577, (560-28) which provides the first firm evidence of who lived where and what lands each held. For this part of Walsham we are clearly told: **Lacy, Thomas**—the said customary crofte with a tenement at the easte ende thereof in the tenure of **Thomas Lacy, gentleman** was (as yt seme the sometymes three parcels, and lyeth toward the este between ye Brooke Land in parte and a decayed cottage in the tenure of Richard Reigneberd in parte, and toward the weste between ye foresaid crofte and ortyarde of **John Robwood,** the yonger, in parte and the foresaid cottage of Andrew Curtes in parte/ and abbuttinge northe upon ye Churche way and sow the uppon ye Brooke Lane and conteyne the 3 acres 3 pedrchesae. Today this corresponds to the site of the Memorial Village Hall, the car-park, bowling green, telephone exchange and the Institute. (info from Walsham Village History Group Quarterly Review, Number 9, April 1999) The family name Lacy and Vincent were very large families in County Suffolk, England that were connected to the Page family, by marriage and all three families immigrated to Isle of Wright, Va in the 1600's. (original English language-not corrected)

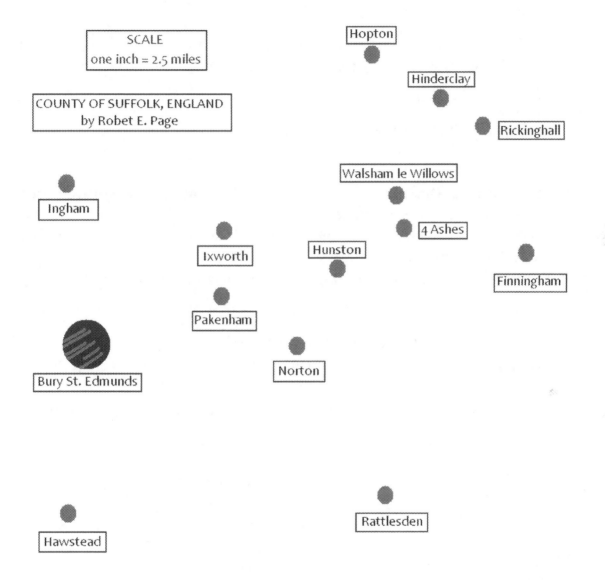

GENEALOGY OF PAGE LINE "C"
IN ENGLAND

The following genealogical information was taken from various records in or around Walsham le Willows, is an attempt to connect all the Page Family names to marriages, when known, and show the children, when known.

Robert Page (0-1) of Sapiston
Olivia Patel of Walsham le Willows

1341—Order to attach Olivia Patel (of Walsham le Willows) because she married Robert Page,(0-1) of Sapiston, without leave.
1344—Olivia Patel (of Walsham le Willows) pays three shillings and four pence fine for leave to marry Robert Page of Sapiston.
1345—Robert Sare essoins (excuse for absence) of common suit by Robert Page.

Info from Walsham-le-Willows Court Rolls 1303-1350.

(0-1) 29Jun1391 William Page and his pledges amerced 3 pence because they did not have him reply to John Cokerel, the skinner, of Westthorpe, in plea of a debt.

Info from manorial Court Rolls of Walsham-le-Willows (1351-1399)

```
          Thomas Page (1)
          l
      John Page, b.1398-d.1452 (2)—a mason—Walsham le Willows
          Agnes (2A) — ale brewer
          l
      —l                                —l
Richard Page (3)—baker          William Page (5) yeoman
b. 1478-d.1557 as a wealthy man  bc.1490—d.1543
—Wife 1 Joanne Merchant (3A) – ale brewer   Marion (5A)
—dc.1463 mar:27Oct1549               bc.1500 –d.Jan1559
          —l
  —l         —l      —l        —l     —l-
—John Page (elder) William  Julyan   Alice  Agnes (3-5)
—(3-1)            (3-2)   (daug)(3-3) (3-4)  Sandy
```

—Wife 2 Joan Merchant (3B) Mar: 27Oct1549

—Richard Page, d.1478 (3)—baker
—Wife 3 mar: 1463 Margaret Oversath, d.5Oct1550 (3C) of Bury St. Edmunds.

John Page (younger)(4A)	Thomas Page (4B/15)	Edmund, d. 1503(4C)(561-16)
	Mary (4B-15-1)	Isabel (4C-A)
		John Page (4C-1)

1)   Thomas Page was Rector of Hinderclay Church from 1391-1399. **HINDERCLAY** is 4 miles north of Walsham le Willows.

7May1400, there was a large land transaction near **Pagefeld** (now called **Lowenstoff**) which is near **Somerleyton**, (560-14) Co. Suffolk, and Thomas Page was mentioned as previously owning several parcels of land near the Jernigan Manor. (560-15)

1407   Thomas Page mentions deed at Suffolk record Office, Bury St. Edmunds branch, held by Thomas Page, for land abutting on land late of Nicholas Wilbeye and on land of Thomas Page, in **Lackford** near Ingham.

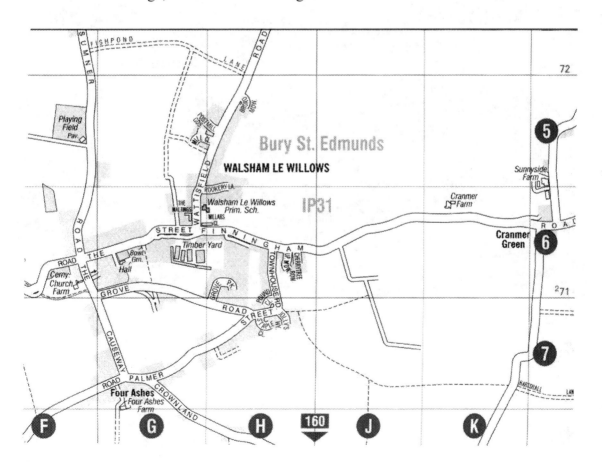

(2)   Dec 1399 **Culford**—John Page 2 shillings per annum for the tenement in which he lives.

(2)   John Page, a mason (2), was living opposite—the **St. Mary's church**, in Walsham le Willows during the time the church was being rebuilt—the house was called "**Dages**" (see YOUR HOUSE, p. 28) (medieval name **Coggeshalls**) occupied the "**Clipper Cottage**" (old name Cooks & Copperlows) (see 560—p.102) from 1426 to **1441**. It was William Cook, early 1300's, then John Freeherd in 1388, then in 1426 John Page (2) until 1482, Thomas Page (3B), and in 1487 William & Alice Waller (6A) (see p.29) and widow Alice, d. 1617 (6A) in 1509. Not until 1676 did bro/sis Samuel & Ann Page (19) regain possession, and in 1698, Samuel Page Jr. (19A) took possession and sold it. (560p104)

Clipper Cottage built in 1351 and was a Page residence 1426-1487 and 1675 to 1698.

St. Mary Church, Walsham le Willows.
Robert Page IV and History Group member Brian Turner.

This is the period that **St. Mary's church was being rebuilt in Walsham le Willows. (see photo of Church as completed by 1441)** The manor accounts show that John(2)/Agnes (2A) Page leased "The **Dages**" (the "P" looks like a "D")—"Medieval name (**COGGESHALLS**) **(560, p27)** tenement paying 7s 6d per annum rent. Beginning in 1389 John/Alice Coggeshall owned the residence, then in 1426, it was owned by Thomas Hereward of Bardwell, then 1428 John(2)/Agnes Page took possession, then 1455, it went to Richard(3)/Joan Page (3A), then in 1463 to Richard(3)/Margaret Page (3C) who owned it until 1479, when John/Margery Saye took possession. (560p.32)

2A)   Agnes Page brewed and sold ale—"an ale wife".

2)   John Page was elected as the ale-taster several times, checking the quality and measures sold. Ale was the most common drink and appears to have been brewed in two or three properties near the cross-roads.

1431   he overstocked the common with his cattle, grazing more than allowed and fined 6d.

1442   John Page, chaplain and Thomas Crystemasses received power of attorney by Bertram. (560-11)

1445   he was elected reeve (Sheriff) for Cooks tenement and the 1475 Rental stated that he held the tenement formerly held by the heirs of John Cook.

1448   John Page (2) surrendered (sold by Court) the cottage with one rood of land to Thomas Berne and wife Margaret. Info: Walsham Quarterly Review #3, Oct 1997.(560-28K)

1437/38 Item paid to Thomas Page (3A), the miller, for cogs and staves and laths for mending the mill this year paid 13d.

1445/46 Repair of Mill in Walsham was underway and Thomas Page (4B) and Peter Umfrey, sawyers, were hired for two days to saw planks of timber for the sail openings of the mill. Paid 12d. (see 560-28 I) The mill post was fetched from **Hinderclay** (4 miles north of Walsham le Willows) at a cost of 7d. This is interesting because the Rector of Hinderclay Church in 1391 was a Thomas Page (1) probably the father of John Page, b. 1398, (2) who was a mason. Walsham had two medieval windmills both belonging to the main Walsham Manor.

1452—(7 Nov) John Page (2) of Ixworth had his will probated, mentions Agnes (2A), wife of the deceased and John Wedirhogge, as executors.

1455   John Page's (2) son, Richard, b.1478(3) & wife Joanne (3A) acquired the house and 3 roods. John Page (2) had apparently used the whole premises for his masonry business.

1489—The "late" John Page, d. 1452 (2) is mentioned in documents as living in Bury—**CHEVINGTON**.

4C)   1476 Edmund Page (4C) of "**Hall House**" died 1503 (see YOUR HOUSE, p.18)-**WALSHAM** le Willows—Will index p.3. "Edmund Page, Walsham—**WILL** dated 7Oct1503, proven 22Dec1503, (561-16) gave to his wife Isabel (4C-A), the tenement on **CHURCH STREET**, Walsham le Willows, and all my utensils, household stuff and to her heirs. Executors named: wife Isabel, and son John Page (4C-1). Witnesses: Stephen Rampoly, Walsham & Richard Page.—probably (3) (see 560-42C)

1476   Edmund Page (4C) granted 1 acre site with hall and stable named "**Hall House**" and was then known as "**Pages**". (see 560, p18)

1488   Edmund Page (4C) and Thomas Page (4B) surrendered "**Avenue Cottage**" (see book YOUR HOUSE, (560 p. 122) (Leves/Poyes/Randes) to Richard Deye Senior. In the past the Avenue Cottage had been occupied by Thomas Norwold that in 1478 had been elected Hayword for the tenement Leves alias Poyes. That was the house that was divided into two when Edmund Page, d.1503 (4C) and Thomas Page (4B) occupied the house—before surrendering it the next year.

"**Hall House**" (medieval—Pages/Pykards) (See YOUR HOUSE, 560, p.18) dates from late 17th century. Its name reveals its history. It is on the site of the medieval manor house known as **WALSHAM HALL** that stood on Hall Green. The manor site was known to contain a hall, garret, knights chamber, bailiff's room, long-house, dovecote, sheepcote, barn and numerous other farm buildings. Edmund Page, d.1503 (4C) was the first tenant of the one acre site with the house, which became known as "**Pages**". (560p.18)

Sep 1482 Thomas Page (4B/15), probably John Page's (2) grandson owned "ploughings" for the tenement of John Page. In 1487 Thomas Page (4B) surrendered two tenements "**Cooks**" and "**Coppelowes**" containing 20 acres of land and meadow to William and Alice Walker.

One of the greatest things missing, for the peasant in the Middle Ages, was the lack of freedom to grind his own corn. His produce had to be taken to the Lord's mill to be ground. Walsham had two medieval windmills—both belonging to the main Walsham manor. East Mill was situated along Mill Lane, north of Riding Farm and the other was West Mill in what is now a small plantation west of a footpath called Rottells Lane. They had a pointed roof, a stepladder to a door at the back of the mill and a long pole to turn the structure into the wind. The sail-yard was the wooden backbone or arm of the sail, the clamp reinforced the centre of the sails and the bords were weather-bording on the floorboards. Info from Walsham Village History #18, July 2001. (560-28 I)

In 1446 Richard Page (3), a baker, acquired the "**Four Ashes**" house and 3 roods.(3 ½ acres) (560, p.104) Richard died in 1450 and in 1454 it went to John/Margaret Vincent. There is a will on file in Bury.

Four Ashes House. Page owned from 1448 to 1454 then 1509 to 1695.

1509, William (5) & Marion(5A) Page owned it until 1542, when William Page(5), d.1543 and wife Marion (5A) took ownership. In 1562 Thomas Page (4B) inherited "**Four Ashes House**" in Walsham (see YOUR HOUSE (560) p106). In 1618 it went to Thomas Page, b.Jan1557 (4B-1) widow, Mary (4B-1). In 1638, it went to Thomas Page (15) then in 1670 to John Page (15A).

In 1672, Elizah Davy and Robert Harding were partners, and in 1677, it reverted back to a John Page, and not clear which one (maybe 15A), then in 1695, it went to Francis Asty. (560, p106)

The Dages built in late 1300's. Page family took possession in 1428 to 1479

In 1428, John/Agnes Page (2) took procession (5Sep1478 Court hearing)—Richard (3) and wife #2 Joan Merchant (3B), were admitted to **Dages** or old name "**Coggleshalls**" messuage with 3 roods of l and. (560, p. 27) Next year, 1479, the two Johns (Elder (3-1)(8D) (59) and Younger (4A)(59-1) surrendered the house and 3 roods of land to John and Margery Saye, and then disappear from Walsham records, probably joining Margaret (Oversath) Page (3B) in Bury. (See 560, p 32)

THOMAS PAGE (4B) or (33) on reaching 21, and living in **Bury**, quit claimed his right in **1479** in the (Dages) "**Coggleshalls**" property to John Saye. (560p.32) Margaret Oversath Page (3C) paid fee for brewing and selling ale 14 times between 1463 and 1478. Richard Page (3) was the baker and sold bread. He held other houses that he rented out, and it was known as a house, which was of the "Separatist Brethren" (dissenter from the Church of England and later in Virginia became strong Quakers). John Freeman, who was admitted in 1689, probably built the present house. For another Edmund Page, d. 1553, Wareham, Co. Norfolk, England—see ENG 9-1.

TIMELINE—Question: Is Page Family line "C" of **VIKING** origin and is it tied to our line? Currently underway is a French Y-DNA examination of bones of two relatives of ROLLO—which will settle the question of our PAGE line "C"—ARE we connected to the Viking line of **ROLLO**—which William the Conqueror is a descendant? The French move very slow with DNA and it seems to get treated as a political issue.

380   Saxons in north Germany are hired by Romans as soldiers.

436   Romans leave Britian and the Britians (Pics) take over—who then hires the Saxons.

800   English Channel coast invaded by Vikings

820   French Seine Valley laid waste by the Vikings

830   Christians persecuted in the Cotentin region of France

856   Edmund crowned King (560-3)

858   Bayeux (France) devastated by the Vikings

866   Danish Viking's arrive in force in East Anglia (England)

869   Viking's capture and kill King Edmund, near Hoxne, Co. Suffolk (560-3) (560-1, p.236 & 248)

875   Further persecution in the west of Normandy, France

885   Paris, France besieged by Vikings

899   Anglo-Saxon King Alfred, (b. 849), "The Great" dies after defeating the Danes (Vikings)

900's   Danish language spoken in East Anglia—Bury St. Edmund, Sudbury and Dunwich appear

911   Treaty of **St. Clair**-sur-Epte: **ROLLO** (Robert 1) became the first Duke of Normandy

942-951 Pakenham is mentioned in **WILL** of Theodred, Bishop of London, when he gave the land at Barton, Rougham and Pakenham to "my kinsman Eadulf's son Osgot". (560-5)

1000's Viking attacks continue

1045-1047 King Edward the Confessor gave the estate of Pakenham, which formerly belonged to Osgot, to the Abbey. It is possible that Osgot, who by then had gone into exile, had been the free man who had leased the land from the Abbot. (560-5)

1042-1065 The Abbot of Bury St. Edmunds leased half a carucate of land, in Pakenham to an unnamed freeman, on condition that after the freeman's death the whole of his land there shall revert to Abbey. (560-5)

The following excerpts are from Reformation and Civil War published by St. Edmundsbury Borough Council. (560-33F)

1000-1100 The Abbey of St. Edmund at Bury St. Edmunds was built.

1044   Bury St. Edmunds was established by Edward the Confessor and remained under the control of the abbot of Bury St. Edmunds until 1539.

1066 September—King Harald of Norway invaded northern England.

25Sep1066—King Harald (Norway) killed by English King Harold.

28Sep1066—William of Normandy invaded England—assisted by Knight **Robert de Bruce**

14Oct1066—Battle of Hastings where William killed English King Harold.

1066   Surnames became necessary—when governments introduced personal taxation, which was known as Poll Tax but it was a slow process and did not really effect the bulk of the population until the 1200's.

1068   The **HUNTER** family—Page family "C" moved from Normandy, France to Scotland.

1086   1,485 settlements named in Domesday Book.

1086—After Norman Conquest in 1066, three Manors emerged. Walsham, High Hall, and Church House.

1086   The Domesday survey records a church holding 30 acres in alms of free land at Pakenham. The original church was recorded as probably a wooden structure built by the Lord of the Manor whose house would have stood nearby. (560-5)

1094   Norman Knight **Robert de Bruce** I—from Bruis, (Normandy) France died

1095   Knight Godfrey de Bouillon, b.1060-d.18Jul1100 (from Lorraine, France)—1st Crusade

1096—May 1097 Crusade Knight (Duke) **Robert I** of Normandy (eldest son of King William I (d.1087) of England)—arrives in Constantinople along with his brother **Robert II** of Flanders.(560-169B, p14/49/53/55)

1097 June—Robert of Flanders defeats Nicaea-marched across Sultunate of Rum.(560-169B, p16)

1097 Dec—Robert of Flanders defeat a Turkish army. (560-169B, p. 14)

1099 August—Robert of Normandy and Robert of Flanders left Jerusalem for Constantinaople and conquered Syrian port of Latakia. (560-169B, p77)

1099 Dec—Crusaders ruled Jerusalem—but Robert of Normandy and Flanders departed for Europe. (560-169B, p83)

1100   Roslyn Castle in Scotland built

1119   Knights Templars created (560-168)

1100-1300 Knights Templars create earliest European wide banking system.

1100-1135 During the Reign Henry I, a Walter Page is recorded as founding a new church at Pakenham. (560-5) Is this the Walter Page family in Risby (Bury) in 1300?

1128 Knights Templar created in **Balantrodoch** (now Temple on River Esk), Scotland. (560-169)

1199 King John, b.1167-d.1216 became King of England (younger brother of Richard "The Lion Hearted". (560-172)

1215 King John signed Magna Carta

1216 King John died.

1231 Walter Page and Johnnes Page (from Northamptonshire) appear in the Close Rolls

1234 Serlonem (Serlonis) Page appears in the Close Rolls.

1240 William le Page appeared as a witness in the Court of Fines for Essex.

1258 Global catastrophe by Volcano eruption causes death of 15,000 Londoners out of 50,000 population. (560-71B)

1270 Knight Robert de Bruce was in 8th Crusade

1274July11—**Robert de Bruce** (House of Brix—Normandy) was born—died 7June1329.

1295 **Robert de Bruce** retires to Estate in County Essex and died 1304 near Carlisle Castle

1250, 1272, 1277, 1283, 1292—Little ice age—began in Europe—and effected Europe

1303 Walsham le Willows records began

1306 Scotland no longer part of Catholic Church

1306 Robert the Bruce fought and killed "Red" Comyln in Battle of Grey Friars Kirk (560-172)

1307 King Philip IV of France orders arrest of every Knight in France—620 arrested and rest of 3,000 Knights fled.

1307 October 12th—Eighteen Knight Templars ships in harbor at a La Rochelle, France—but gone the next morning, with all their possessions. (560-170)

1307 Robert the Bruce won lands in the SW of Scotland. (560-171)

1311 Walsham le Willows records began

1312 Knights Templars disbanded—as the Knights scattered to countries of refuge, one small group settled in the Swiss Alps, and began using the "coded credit" system developed by the Knights Templars, which seems to be the beginning of the "secret" Swiss banking system.

It is interesting that John Flaig and Magnus Schiller have Y-DNA 67 that their oldest ancestors lived in the Black Forest area just north of where the Knights Templars settled in what is now Switzerland. Their Y-DNA 67 scores are almost identical and their oldest ancestors were there in the early 1600's, only a few miles apart. Their non-Page names puts them in the middle of a large number of PAGE family "C" members.

1314 Knights Templars fled France to England and then some took refuge in Scotland under King **Robert de Bruce**, who died in 1329.

1314June24—**Robert de Bruce** defeated English Army at battle at Bannockburn of 20,000 British army with only 5,000 Scottish troops. It is believed the Knights Templars played a large role in the fight. And could be the source of Page Line "C" Y-DNA from those that trace their line back to Scotland and hit a brickwall. (560-171)

1315-1317 Great Famine—all of Europe—resulting in 50% decline in population.

1320—Declaration of Arbroath to Pope John XXII—intended to confirm Scottish Independence. (560-172 & 172A 172B)

1323 **Bruce Page** of **INGHAM** (Co. Suffolk) fined and Robert de Askeby, Parson of Ingham Church awarded the fine. (see 560-20)

1324 Walter Page (91), of Risby (next to Bury St. Edmunds) appears as witness to land transactions.

1327 Reign began January 25th of Edward the 3rd and he died 21June1377.

1327 Great Riot at **Pakenham**, Co. Suffolk and the abbot's manor house was burnt down. (560-1)

1328 Knight Templars fleet of ships disappears and appears to have traveled to America.

1329 **Robert de Bruce—King of Scots**—died (1274-1329)

1329 Bruce asked James Douglas to take his heart on next Crusade against the Moors in Spain, before it was buried in Melrose Abbey. (560-173)

1330 James Douglas was killed in Spain and both Douglas and Bruce's heart were returned to Scotland where they were buried. (560-169B, p232)

1334 English taxes changed from individuals to communities and the lord of the manor decided how much each individual in the village should pay in tax (lay subsidy) (560-174)

1340 Walsham le Willows population 7,150, falling by 1440 to 3,000; but up to 7,000 by 1540.

1347-1380 Plague (Bubonic) covers all of Europe from China to all Europe. The invading Mongols expanding their trade routes—also brought rats with fleas which quickly spread the plague.

1348/9 Black Plague hit Walsham le Willows—population 1,000—119 heads of household died—did not count wives and children but about 50% of the population died. King Edward fled large towns for the country to escape the plague. More plague in 1361, 1368, 1479.

1377 King Edward III changed the tax system to fund the army to attack France called a poll tax on every adult (15 or older) 4d to the king.

1381 Peasants uprising in Suffolk.

1391-1399 Thomas Page (1), Rector of Hinderclay Church, 4 miles north of Walsham le Willows.

1400—8 Oct-5Aug1402 Thomas Page (1) Priest at Dickle Burgh church, town of **Semere**, Co. Suffolk.

1440 Walsham le Willows population was down to 3,000

1441 St. Mary Church, Walsham le Willows finished rebuilding.

1446 Special building next to Roslyn Castle built.

1479 Plague in Walsham le Willows strikes again.

1509 King Henry VIII takes the English throne.

1536   Edmund Page, (Kent) Gentleman, served on Grand Jury that convicted Anne Boleyn, wife of King Henry VIII. Richard Page, Gent, was connected to this incident. (399, p.109-111)

1539   the monasteries were abolished.

1540   Walsham le Willows population gained back up to 7,000.

1547   King Henry VIII died, age 56, after a reign of 37 years. His only son King Edward VI became king, at age 8.

1564   Pakenham Church began to keep burial records and over 4,000 have been recorded.

1580 6 April—Earthquake in England felt as far as Germany. See Walsham Quarterly #2

1584   Colonization of Virginia

1589   Plague broke out at Bury St. Edmunds

1606   Plans made to take a group from Co. Suffolk and sail to Va.

1607   Three ships from Suffolk, England arrive in Virginia, 50 miles up James River, & establish James Fort.

1608   Great fire of Bury St. Edmunds swept through the town. (also in 1644) (560-3)

1612   (30Nov) Thomas Page married Elizabeth Springall in Great Yarmouth, Co. Norfolk.

1616   (25Mar) Rebekka Page married Thomas Leader, (d.28Oct1663, Boston, Mass) in Finningham, Co. Suffolk, and she died 16Oct1653, in Boston, Mass.

1620   Pilgrims landed in America

1622   Harvest in Walsham was very poor. The old cloth trade was ruined. Broadcloth was out of fashion. Bury's clothiers had large stocks of cloth, they could not sell, and were described as much decayed in their estates by reason of the great losses they had received.

1626   War began with France and ended in 1629.

1630   112 people left Co. Suffolk to join Winthrop fleet to Mass.—probably Page Line E.

1631   West Suffolk harvest failed. 800 people fled Suffolk in 11 ships to Virginia

1635   (4Jul) William Page, age 18, transported to Virginia—see VA 8.

1632-36 Bury St. Edmund—old Roman town was hit by the Plague. (560-3)

1637   Bury's population was about 6,000 but suffered the 7th and worst plague ever.

1637   Thomas Page (30) died in Co. Suffolk, England

19Feb1637 Edmund Page, b. 1582, Bury St. Edmund, requested permission to visit his son (no name) for one month, in The Hague, Holland where his son is servant to the Prince.

1638   **Thomas Page**—grocer (23A) surrendered his rights to a property in Walsham le Willows because he **moved to North Walsham,—Co. Norfolk**, in 1638, where he was a grocer and he died in North Walsham in 1647.

1638   six to eight hundred left Co. Suffolk for Virginia. Twelve hundred from Co. Norfolk. Religious zeal and a desire for freedom of worship characterized some of the emigrants.

1642   The English Civil War began. 1644 Great Fire of Bury St. Edmunds swept through town. (560-3, p.434-436)

1647   **Thomas Page died**, (23A) "Grocer" in North Walsham, Co. Norfolk, England.

His **wife was Joyce (23A-1)**, and they had a son Thomas Page (23B-1), who died in 1656 and a son William, b.30May1640, N. Walsham, Co, Norfolk (23B-2) which might be the William Page, that shows up in 1677 in Lancaster Co, Va, that co-owned an Estate with one Thomas Page, who appears to be from Bury St. Edmunds, Co. Suffolk, England which could be our connection. On chart VA 8 William Page, b.1662-d. 1716, Stafford Co, Va had a daughter Mary Page that in 1740 married Anthony Linton, at house of John Remy, in Westmoreland Co, Va which had become Stafford Co, in 1664.

1649   Civil War over and King Charles I beheaded.

1649   King Charles II was forced into exile.

1652   Thomas Page arrived in Lancaster Co, Va (484) (VA 10) probably the John Page, bc.1627, Bedfont, (Co. Middlesex) England mar to Alice Luckin, b. 1625 that moved to Williamsburg, Va in about 1650. (see VA 5-3)

1653   Robert Page arrived in Lancaster Co, Va (484) (VA 10)

1655   Elizabeth Harris (Quaker) sails from London to Virginia

1659   Thomas Page and wife Alis Page recorded as being in Perquimans District, N.C. (560-181)—LDS IGI)

1660   King Charles II came back to England as King again.

1662   Parliament passed the Act of Uniformity which made the Church of England the official religion. All others were forced underground.

1663   Mrs Alis Page and husband Thomas Page recorded in Perquimans Dist, N.C. (560-181)

1665   The Great Plague of London broke out—over 68,000 died. Plague reached as far as Bury.

1665 13 June—Naval battle off-shore of Port of Lowestoft (Co. Suffolk) in which 109 English ships engaged in a battle with 103 Dutch ships which the English won the battle. Lowestoft was formerly called "Pagefield". (See page 20 and 53) This appears to be where many from County Suffolk left England for the American Colonies.

1666   Great Fire of London. 13,200 homes and 87 churches gone.

1672   George Fox (Quaker) visited Virginia.

1674   Large numbers of PAGE names buried in County Suffolk, England (see 560-12)

1674   21 September—**ABRAHAM PAGE** and 8 others (see VA 8-1) transported to **Goucester Co. Va by William Grymes (see VA 5) and Grymes was awarded 450 acres of land. (VA 4-2) This is probably tied to the Gov John** Page **family because he had several ships that regularly traveled back and forth between England and Virginia. (See Appendix A)**

1674 **Thomas Page** (30A) **arrives in Stafford Co, Va** (Maryland border) with wife Mary Newton (30F) and Thomas Locke (30F-1) This is a connection to Page family Dan Page is researching. Capt Robert Caulfield, d. 1691 from Surry Co, Va transported the group and is tied to the Lacy Family (tailors) and the Blackborne family, of County Suffolk, England (VA 8-1)

1674 Bury St. Edmund has 1224 houses and 6,190 people. In Co. Suffolk, there are 28,400 houses and 142,000 people. (560-12)

1675 Thomas Page emigrates to Maryland

1675 Alice Page emigrates to Va. Not clear where Thomas landed but Maryland is only a few miles from north Va. where maybe Alice landed, and not far from Stafford Co, Va.

1677 . . . Gravestones entered the scene and the earliest at Pakenham Church was for John Ager, Gentleman. (560-5)

1679 **WILL OF HENRY RENNELLS FILED, ISLE OF WIGHT, VA & HENRY RENNELLS D. 1681. (SEE VA 52)**

1684 Thomas Page and wife Alis Page recorded in Perquimans Dist, N.C. (560-181)

1685 Catholic James II becomes King of Great Britain.

5Nov1688 Prince William of Orange lands at Torbay and marches to London to take the place of King James II (560-12). There was one Edmund Page (4C) of Bury St. Edmunds had son (no name) that was "servant" of Prince William of the Hague, Holland.

1689 Hearth tax repealed (560-12)

1699 William Page was witness to marriage of Matthew Jordan and Dorothy Bufkin in Chucatuck, Nansemond Co, Va (VA 8)

1700 22March-John Page, d. 1701—married to Ann had **WILL** recorded Isle of Wight, Va

1701 His children appear to be John and Elizabeth (VA 8)

1713 John Page, Nansemond Co, Va was granted 123 acres (VA 8)

1714 Thomas Page, Nasemond Co, Va was granted 284 acres of land (VA 8). But tied to this is Thomas Page married to Joyce ? (23A-1) had a daughter Joyce Page, b. 23May1643, North Walsham, Co. Norfolk, England (23B-5) (see 560-148) that later married 1746 **WILL** of William Page, Isle of Wight, Va mentions his wife Ann, then Betty Fort, Joshua Fort and "granddaughter" Mary Page. (VA 8)

1851 Bury St. Edmund population was 13,900 (560-3)

1861 Bury St. Edmund population was 13,316. (560-3)

1861 Walsham le Willows population was 1,290 and consisted of 2,800 acres. (560-4)

To look at a more detailed history of West Suffolk (mainly Bury) go to web site:
www.stedmundsbury.gov.uk/sebc/visit/865-1066.cfm.

The below is from many sources—trying to tie this Page family together.

1324-1335 Walter Page (91) of Risby (Waltero Page buried 1327—see (560-12C)
                    l
1358-1369 James Page of Risby (91-1) White Lion (see page 39 for another White Lion)
                    l
1458-1482 Roger Page, d.c.1510 (91-2) of Risby (west side of Bury St. Edmunds)
            l   l
Thomas Page (91-3) of Lackford (moves to Westley)   John Page (91-4) Gent of Westley
            l   l   1512-1513
Elizabeth Page   Elizabeth

I THINK I MUST STOP and issue a warning at this juncture—This has been a long and exhaustive search for the truth—often taking—bits and pieces of information—and like a puzzle—one by one—taking each piece and joining—it to another piece. Often conflicting documents arose and which one—do you believe? I am hoping that did not happen often—but Chris (Ark) Page will jump on any "alleged" error to support his carefully focused effort—to disallow any connection to ABRAHAM PAGE, that the "Line "C"—David Page Family Bible says was his father.

So I wish I could say the below is "error free"—but I cannot—at this time. It is still a "research in progress". So with that warning—please read and feel free to challenge any connection (with documentation)—as we work our way to the final movement of this PAGE family "C" to the American Colonies in the 1600's.

There is much documentation gathered over the last 30 years—but we still need some help. Chris (Ark) Page has been very critical of my publication "CAROLINA PAGE's" published in 1990—trying to get others interested in this Page family research effort, long before DNA arrived.

So with that warning—please try and follow the complicated genealogical picture of a very large PAGE family—as it expands—and moves around County Suffolk, England—as it is growing and becoming prosperous—while all the political, religious upheavals, plagues and weather issues are taking place—as they prosper—and make plans to leave England for the American Colonies.

I did not give much attention to the Page family—in this document—once established in the Colonies—because that is another complicated and contested issue by Chris (Ark) Page. Chris did offer his research on the Page family "C" as they grew and became prosperous and started their journey in the southern part the Colonies. What makes the research difficult—was the bunch from Goochland Co, Va—(PAGE Line "P") also traveling the same southern trails—at the same time—using almost the same names. Weak genealogist just seize on a name—if—it fits and the time period about right—and once reported—it becomes "TRUE". I have had the pleasure of working with Art Klinger (Page line "P") and we have tried to separate the two lines.

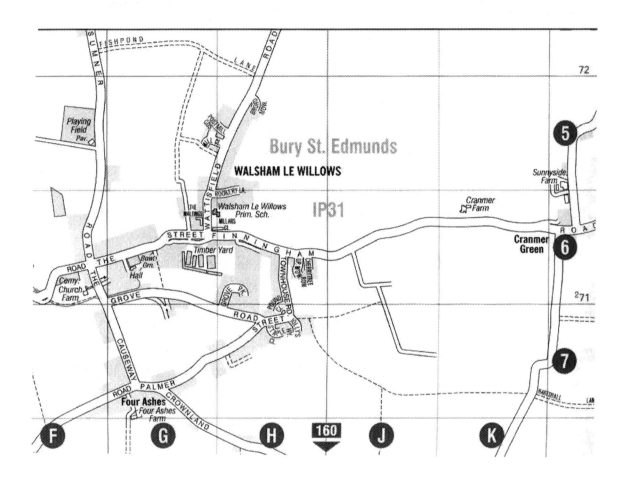

Thomas Page (1) Rector of Hinderclay Church 1391-1399 (4 miles from Walsham)

l

John Page,1398-d.1452 (2) mason—Walsham le Willows
Agnes (2A) – ale brewer

William Page (5) yeoman	Joane(2B)	Richard Page, d.1Jul1550 (3) wealthy baker (561-12)
bc1490 (560-33A)	b.10Nov	Wife #1 Joanne Hawes(3A)mar:2Nov1539 ale brewer
d.18Jan1543 (W)	1565	wife #2 Joan Merchant,(3B) mar:27Oct1549
mar: Marian (Marion/Maryon)(5A)		wife #3 Margaret Oversath,(3C) d.5Oct1550 mar:1463
18Jan bc.1500		l
1542 d.Jan1559 (W) Will dated 8Oct1558		l see page 19 & 22 for more on above family
Buried 2Feb1559		l

John (younger)(4A) Thomas (4B)   Edmund, d.1503 (4C)(561-16)
b.Jan1557   Isabel (4C-1
Mary(4B-1)   l
4 Ashes House   John Page (4C-2)

|--

Thomas Page (6)	Elizabeth Page	John Page (8)	Alice(9) l	William(10)	Richard(11)
bc.1530–d.22Aug1618	b.1525 (7)	d.16Mar	Cook l	d.17Nov1600	Sibbill
Mar: Alice Waller (6A)	d.	1605	l	—l	Cook
30Sep Bc. 1534 (W)	mar: Richard Hawes		Kateryn	Agnes Elizabeth	mar:
1556 d.20Oct1617	23Oct1547 b.1521 (7A)		9-1	Grene 9-3	1595
(560-28) l (W)	Six children			9-2	

(6A-1)   (99)

Thomas	Agnes	William	John	Elizabeth	William	l	Maryon	Anne	Thomas l	Alice	Thomas
b.Jan1557	b.15Apr	10May	3Dec	14Apr	16May	l	19Mar	17Nov	22Jan l	22Jan	2Dec
Mary	1560	1563	1567	1571	1577	l	1591	1594	1597 l	1597	1599
l	(99-1)					l			l		

John,b.2Nov1589 (560-28)   Richard

"the tailor"

Thomas Page(12)	Richard(8G)	William(8B/43)	Henry	John	Ann(8E)	Alice (8F)
bc.1567 (W) Yeoman		d.11Aug1621	8C	(Elder)	John	d.21Feb1598
d. Aug 1618(560-28A)		Mary(8B-1)	Sarah 8D	Johnson	Smear	
mar: ThomazinVincent (12A)		Vincent	8C-1	mar:26Sep1585	
3Sep Bc.1563 (W) (560-7E)	d.26Apr1640 mar:14Oct1595 maybe (59)			
1587 d. Jul 1620 (W)		l	(see 23)		

l —see (560-148 & 561-5)

```
l                          l
l          _____l_____
l          Thomas   Mary     William  William  Catheren  John    Edward
l          b.10Feb  b.27Nov  b.27Apr  b.8Nov   b.4Dec    b.1Jan  b.12Feb
l            1594     1591     1600     1607     1603      1605    1608
l
l (see 560-40B)
l          —l        —l         —l        —l      —l -l —l      —l
John (14) l Thomas l  Thomas (15)  William(16)  Katherine  Agnes l Alice   Richard(15-2)
b.1590    l b.1597 l  b.1599     b.13Jun1602    l       —l  l— l    —l
          l        l  d.1644,Hunston d.Mar1628  Dorothy Thomazyn Marie(17E) Susan (17F)
 Maryann(12B) l    Mary(Marie)    Joan (16A)  b.1610  b.1Jan1604 Daniel   bc.1598
 b.1591       l    b.1620(15-1)   Knopwood 17C          17D      Clarke   John
 d.24Mar1597  l    d.1694 l                               l         mar:     Hammond
        /          l                               l            7Oct     mar:
       /    l--------------------------l           l            1620     26May1619
      l John,b.1617 (15A/20) THOMAS(15B/20A) l                           (560-28A)
      l d.1667,Gent          b.1640 Hunston  l                  Susan signs
      l  Ann(15A-1)          d.1720,IOW,VA   l                  Hawstead petition
      l     l                                l                  with Thomas Page
      l   ANN     Sara    MARY Elizabeth (15B)  l                  in 1670
      l   b.18Jan b.23Mar b.9Jan b.30Sep        l
      l    1609    1612    1615   1618          l
      l   (560-183)       (560-183)             l
      Ann (17) see ENG10-1A                     William Page , (16B)
      b .1594                                   Susan Vincent (16C)
mar:21Sep  #1 Thomas Hawes (17A)                     l
   1616    bc.1588—d. aft 1629(W)– no will      Elizabeth,b.13Jan1637

Mar:19Oct  #2 William Chapman (17B)
    1631
```

see ENG 10-1A has Eliz, b. 1672 (41) who is daug of John Page (15A/20) & Ann (15A-1)

Thomas Page (6), bc.1530
l
Thomas Page, b.1567—yeoman—WLW (12)
mar: Thomazin Vincent (12A)
3Sep bc.1563—WLW
1587 d.Jul1621—WLW
l
Thomas Page (15) b.1599-d.17Aug1644—Ingham– Co. Suffolk (see 560-25)
Mary (Marie) (15-1) (560-159D)
l
_____l_____

Rebecca (15C)	John-Gent (15A)(63)	Susanna (17F)
b.Oct1609	b.1599 (560-25)	b.1598 (560-28A & 32A)
d.5Feb1613	d.1667-Ingham	d.1653
l	/ — #1 Phyllis Webb	John Hammond,b.1594 (17F-1)
l	/ mar:17Jun1592	mar:26May1619, Ingham
l	/ l	l
l	l Thomas John Thomazyn	l
l	l b.May1592 b.Feb1593 b.May1597	l
l	\ d.1676 (560-22)	l
l	\	l

Rebecca (74) --- #2 Mary Nunn (15B) (560-22)
b.1649   Mar:26Oct1628   l
Henry Turner   l Ingham   John Hammond   Susan
Mar:12May1670   l b.9Jun1620 b.14Apr1646
                     l

Marie   Susanna   Sarah   Rebecca   Chris
b.1628   b.1630   b.1634   b.1638   b.4Jul1639
                              d.21Mar1634

See (42) John Sparke mar Elizabeth Nunn, b.1717-d.1770 (Sparke family has **THE LAWN)**

William Page, d. 8Jul1636 (60) – Ingham, Co. Suffolk, England
Susan Holte (60A) – mar Jun 1594
_____l_____

60-3	60-4	60-1	60-2	60-5	60-6		60-7	60-8
Mary	Susan	John	Philip	Joseph	Rebecca		Thomas	Martha
b.1594	b.9Oct	b.19Dec	b.23Sep	b.8Mar	b.16Oct1609		b.13Jun	17Apr
3Aug	1597	1599	1604	1606	Robert Wiffin		1612	1615
d.1653	d.1676			d.17Mar1674	mar:24Aug1637			

William Page (60) Yeoman, d.1636, Ingham—**WILL** (561-7) gave wife Susanna and son Philip 20 pounds each, and son Joseph L20 and Thomas L40, daug Rebecca and Martha L30, and daug Susan Harmont L40 and daug Mary Jernigo Ll5. Son John is executor and will pay wife L8 quarterly.

Rebecca Page(60-6)/Robert Wiffin had daug Ann, b. 8Dec1681. Rebecca Page was also wit: to **WILL** (560-33) of Thomas Page-(Hawstead). Chris Page say Wiffin family were tailors, but I have nothing supporting that.

Thomas Page, (61) – Ingham – probably Thomas Page (30)
l   whose wife #1 was Susan, d. 13Sep1631
Susanna John   (see 560-183)
b.1614 b.1617

Rosary—built in early 1400's—Page owned from 1516 to 1644.

5)   1516 William Page, d.1543 (5)—yeoman—built "**The Rosary**" sometimes called "**Page's**" (old name Echemans/Pakkes) along with John Hawes, the tailor, who probably built the earlier house. William Page (5) was a yeoman, often appearing at the manor court to buy and sell land.
        William/Marion Page (5) and John Hawes,(tailor) took possession in 1516, then in 1543, widow Marion (5A) took possession, then in 1577 John Page (8), then 1606 Thomas Page, (15) and 1644 John Page, Gentleman (15A) until 1644 when Stephen Vincent bought the place. (see 560p.82)

10Jun1537 William Page (5) received a lease from the Crown for 21 years for the Manor of Walsham and a parsonage with lands called "**Esthous londes**". In July 1538 Richard Codington and wife Elizabeth, sold his rights in the Manor in Surry for the Priory of **Ixworth** and its manors, lands, and tenements in Co. Suffolk, which included the reserved rent and a reversionary interest in **Church House**. In July 1541 Codington sold his manor rights to George Wright, who purchased the lease of the Manor from John Page (8), son of William Page (5) before selling the Manor to Henry Chitting.

William Page (5) died in 1543. His **WILL**, 6Dec1542, (561-4) and executors were his wife Maryon (5A), and Richard Page (3), his brother. He was buried 18Jan1542/3, proved 13Feb1542/3, probated 13Feb1542/3 left his property to wife (Marian) Marion (5A) for life, if she remained a widow and then to sons Thomas (6A) John (8). Sons William (10) and Richard (11) received money, as did daughters Katherine, Agnes and Elizabeth. Another daughter, Alice (9), was given some leased land and married a Cook. William (10) had been living at the "**Rosary**" (560, p79) (medieval name—Echemans/Pakkes) since 1516 with John Hawes, tailor, then in 1543, it went to widow Marion Page (5A) then in 1577 his eldest son John (8) inherited. The following year Marion (5A) was elected as Hayward and in 1606, she surrendered the tenement to Thomas Page (15). The WleW Field Book of 1577 gives Thomas Page (15) as the tenant and the 1581 Terratorium called the tenement "sometime of Robert Potenger". In 1644, it went to John Page (15A), Gentleman, until later that year it went to Stephen Vincent. (560p79)

John Page (8D), the elder, seems to own **Ladies Wood Lawn** of 18 acres (WleW Field Book of 1577). John Page (8D) received a Legal Brief in 1617 in the case of Christopher Smeare vs. John Page (560-49C) sent to Mr. John Page at Walsham le Willows, Co. Suffolk. John's sister Alice was married to a Smear. John Page's (8D) **WILL** of **1668**, included a capital messuage and close called **Coldham Park** and owned a messuage and shop in Bury. William Page (5) also owned a gravel pit, which adjoined his "**Four Ashes House**" (medieval-Kembalds/Sextons). The "Four Ashes House" (560, p.104) has had a house on this site since 1326.

1446   **Four Ashes** was sold to Richard Page (3) who owned it until 1454, when it passed through many hands until 1509, William (5) and Marion Page (5A), owned it until 1562, it went to Thomas (4B) and Mary Page (4B-1) until 1638 it went to Thomas Page (15), then in 1670, to John Page (15A) and in 1672 it was owned by Elizah Davy and Robert Harding, but in 1677 John Page (15A) resumed ownership. (560, p.106)

Richard Page (3) **WILL** 1557, proven 1March1557 (561-12) gave to wife #2 Joan (Merchant) Page, (3B) all tenement and all lands in town and fields of Walsham le Willows, and **BADWELL** and one close called Hodgans lying in **BARDWELL**. If Joan Page cannot occupy the tenement then son William (3-2) shall occupy. Upon death of Joan (3A) son William and to his heirs upon condition that he shall pay to daughter Julyan (3-3), L6 13s 4d. If son William die without issue, then son John gets the lands. Son John gets my close Hodians in **BADWELL** after death of Joan. The WILL (561-12) goes into great detail giving money and property to many people. Thomas Vincent named supervisor and witnesses were: Edmund Wright, Thomas Vincent, Robert Vincent and others. Probate: 1Mar1557. Note on **WILL** that Richard Page married Joan Merchant 27Oct1549.

The **Rosary** was owned by William Page (5) & John Hawes, tailor in 1516, then widow Marion Page, (5A) took ownership in 1543, then to son John Page, (8) in 1577, then to Thomas Page (15) in 1606, then in 1644 to John Page, gentleman (15A) when it passed to Stephen Vincent same year. (560, p.82) The "Rosary" (Page's) **remained in the Page family until 1644**. "What" happened in 1644 that caused the Page family to loose the "**Rosary**"? I think the **death of Thomas Page (15) in 1644**, and the need for travel money for Thomas Page, (15B) so he could **emigrate to Virginia.**

1659   **One Thomas Page with wife Alis**—is reported in Perquimans District, N.C.—again in 1663 & again in 1684. (560-181) The Isle of Wight, Va Thomas Page begins buying land in 1682. (VA 50)

By 1817 the "**Rosary**" was part of three cottages owned by William Day, a carpenter and beer retailer.

Thomas Page (12) late of **Thornham Magna** or Great Thornham is mentioned in document dated 29May1638, by Wyseman Bokenham, of Weston Mercat, Suffolk and Thomas Byshopp, his heirs, and assigns, one tenement or "ancient cottage" in Great Thornham, lately in tenancy of Thomas Page, between "Slay Street Way" and "Garnons Garden" and an acre and half of land held of the Chief Lord of the manor by ancient suit and service.

1577   Field Book described the manor property as a well-built messuage with a little orchard and back yard adjourning dwelling house of John Page (8) (561-1). The 1595 Rental showed him holding the tenement "**Pages**" (medieval name Pakkes) later called The **Rosary**. (HOUSE, p. 79)

Thomas Page (6) probably built the present house. He was born in 1530 and died in 1618 and **was buried on 22Aug1618, (560-40B) the entry in the parish register notes that he was the bailiff.** He is described as a Yeoman in his will (561-9), leaving his tenement called "**Kembalds**" and one pightle called **Clay Pightle and Brokeyard & Great Meadow,** to Mary, d.1626 (15-1), his daughter-in-law, widow of his son **Thomas Page, b. 1599-d.1644 (15)**, from **Rickinghall** (N.E. of Walsham) until her son **Thomas Page (15B)** was 27. (560-183)

This appears to be the Thomas Page, **b.1620** (15B) that in 1636 married **Mary Newton** in Hunston (Co. Suffolk) (see 560-183) and they emigrated to Stafford County, Virginia in **1674** or before (see my chart VA 8-1).

William Page (8B & 23) got **Clay Pits,** formerly owned by William Page, my father (5) and that he pay Richard Page (8G), my son, 32 pounds. Thomas Page (15B), grandson, son of Thomas Page (15) (late of Rickinghall—deceased) my freehold lands lying in **meadow field and 2 half acres in close called Lendell** and that he pay to 3 sisters, Marie, Doreysey & Susan Page 4 pounds when they reach 21. Richard Page (8G) owns **Nicholas Pightle & Barrow Field.** William Page (8B), my eldest son, and Richard Page, (8G), my son, the profits of said tenements and lands to pay the funeral and probate expenses of my will. Witness: Thomas Fulcher and Rainold Page. This Rainold Page might be (21A).

William Page (8B & 23) "the Tailor" in his **WILL** (561-5) dated 20Jan1621, proven 21Jun1624 gave to wife (Executrix) Mary (Marie) (23-1)the tenement, and all lands and 1 piece of pasture called **ROBBELLS,** (purchased from William Harrison). Upon death of Mary, tenement and lands go to son Thomas Page (23A) (for him to pay to son William (23C), L60, when he reaches age 24. Son John (23B) gets 1 acre of meadow in Great Meadow when he is 25. Son Joseph (23D) gets pightle called **CLAYPETTS** given to me by my deceased father Thomas Page (22), of Walsham. Son Joseph gets the rents and profits when he is 21. Jane (Page) Hawes and then to her son John Hawes—1 acres 3 roods of pasture called **BRECHE.** My daughter Katherine (23E) 19L within 4 months or the mansion house where I now dwell, if the fail to pay the L19. Daughter Sara,(23F) L30 to be paid by son Thomas at age 21. Son Thomas gets framed table and one back chair.
Witnesses: Stephen Vincent and George Complin. Probate: Bury St. Edmunds 21Jun1624. See William Page (8B & 23) for family tree. (**WILL** is 561-9)

The **Four Ashes House (see 560, p.106)** in 1670 had a new owner John Page, d. 1667 (15A/63) who took possession (but 1672-1676 other owners), then in 1677 regained ownership by John Page (maybe 30D) which **stayed in the Page family until 1695,** when he surrendered the tenement to Francis Asty.

1674 Hearth Tax Returns (560-12) shows John Page (15A) with Sam Page and Vinsent family living in a house with 3 fireplaces. **Thomas Page (15B)** living in house with 7 fireplaces. William Page (16B) house has 4 fireplaces.

Four years later in 1678 **John Page** (15A) **surrendered the entire tenement** to Robert Harding except the one small house in which Elizah Davy lived. (560-p.105)(This is the time period when **Thomas Page (15C)** b. 1640 Hunston, is believed to have returned to the Isle of Wight, Va between 1674 and about 1679).

There is **Thomas Page and wife Alis** recorded as being in Perquimans Dist, NC in **1659, 1663, and 1684.** (560-181) The site was rather crowded and divided by palking which John Page, b.1590 (14) was to keep repaired. Elizah was to have access for carts and swains. (560-p105) Later that year Robert Harding surrendered back to John Page (8D), oldest son, one messuage "**Four Ashes House**" also called "**Kembalds**" with a yard, orchard and half a pond.

1546   Elizabeth Page, b. 1525 (7) married Richard Hawes, b. 1521.

15May1555 Suffolk Court records say: "Thomas Page to skore his dyche against the said watercourse on this half Hallowmas next comynge under the payne of 3s 4d.
See Walsham Quarterly Review #12—Jan 2001.

12)   **WILL** of Thomas Page, d.1618 (12), on page 15 of 54 pages. Both Thomas Page (12) and Robert Page (13) apparently lived in **Hunston**, which is 2.7 miles southwest of Walsham le Willows. (560-183) Robert Page (13)(34A) had daughter, Margaret Page b.19Jul1607, and daughter Briget Page, b. 9Dec1609, and son Robert, b.12May1611. and maybe Henry Page(18A) born 24Apr1614—d.1670. Info: (12 & 13) from **Hunston**, Co. Suffolk,—St.Leonard Shoreditch Baptisms (1558-1640) (560-183B)

Thomas Page (15) served on the enquiry of the manor courts and was a church warden in 1606 and 1615. On his **death in 1644**, his son John, Gent (15A) inherited the messuage and 18 acres of land and immediately surrendered it to Stephen **Vincent**. The Page family and Vincent family were joined in marriage many times. John Page, d.1667, Gent (15A) was by now living at the "**Lawn**" (since 1612 (John #1) and calling himself a "Gentleman". (In 1640 John Page #2, (must be his son) took possession and he also was a Gentleman., then in **1668, Thomas Page (15)** took possession of **The Lawn.** He was a trustee of the Game Place, Guildhall and town land, was a town warden in 1676 and on the enquiry of both manors. The 1674 Hearth Tax (560-12) shows he had seven hearths and survey of 1695 held the messuage free containing 3 acres and 2 roods. In 1699, license was granted to demolish the long-house called a cowhouse or le Stoverhouse (560, p.132) The next entry of this property is on Parish map #323, in 1817, that the owner/occupant was John Sparke (42) until 1842, when John Hutton Munro took possession. In Isle of Wight, Va area, the Page and **Vincent** family were Quakers and remained very close.

The Lawn—built early 1400's and owned by Page family from 1612 to around 1700.

49

Prior Close—built in early 1500's and owned by Page family 1576 to 1633.

The **Priors Close** was previously owned by the Vincent family since before 1504 until 1574 when they sold it to Henry Rogers and then in 1576, John Page (8) took possession. (560p.95)

1576   John Page, d. 1606 (8) bought "Priors Close" (560, p.95) when the Field Book stated he held a customary tenement with a yard and orchard and half a pond from **Church House Manor** containing 1 rood 10 ½ acres. John Page (8) lived at the "**Rosary**" and before his death in 1605/6 when in 1606, he surrendered Priors Close to his son William Page, d.1628—yeoman (16) wife Joan (16A), together with land along Summer Road and in Clay Street. (560-, p.96)

John Page, d. 1606, (8) WILL describes him as a "yeoman" and left all of his property, "**Church Way Pightle**" and one acre of meadow, that his father, William (5) had left him the property, to his son Thomas Page (6) John Page, d. 1605/6 had acquired the house now known as "**Priors Close**"

Belonging to "Church House Manor" that he left to Wiliam Page, d.1628 (16) and wife Joan (16A), who sold the property in 1633 to William Rainbird. Son John (8D) and daughters Alice (8F) and Anne (8E) received money. Both sons Thomas (12) and William 8B) were executors of the WILL.

WILL of Thomas Page, d. 1618 (12) on page 15 of 54 pages. Both Thomas Page (12) and Robert Page (13) apparently lived in **Hunston**, which is 2.7 miles southwest of Walsham le Willows. (560-183) Robert Page (13)(34A) had daughter, Margaret Page, b. 19Jul1607, and daughter Briget Page, b. 9Dec1609, and son Robert, b. 12May1611 and maybe Henry Pge (18A) b. 24Apr1614-d.1670. Info: (12 & 13) from Hunston, Co. Suffolk,—St. Leonard Shoreditch Baptisms (1558-1640) (560-183B)

William Page, (16) d. 1628, (the Elder) called himself a yeoman, took possession in 1606 and made his **WILL** (27Feb1627) (561-6) leaving his wife, Joan (Knopwood) Page (16A), (executrix) in 1628, but in 1633 sold it to William Rainbird. (560p.96) Joan Page (16A) also got his messuage in **Church gate Street** (The **Causeway**) with all the yards, gardens, orchards, barns and stables and buildings and in 1592 the land "The **Lawn**" (old name Outlaws) and a pasture called **Childerswell**, next to Summer Lane. In 1612, John Hawke surrendered the Greens tenement and **The Lawn (560p.131)**, to John Page, d.1640 (15A/20). Also one pasture called **Knights Close**, lying on Clay Street., she had from his father, IF Joan (Knopwood) (16A) remained unmarried.

After her decease OR remarriage, the property was to go to their ONLY son, William Page (16B). She remained a widow and together she and son **William** (16B) and his **wife Susan VINCENT** PAGE (16C) lived in "**West Cottage**" (Ebells) from 1633 until they **surrendered their land and finally the house** to John Cobiron in **1679**. William Page (16) Will was proved at Bury on 1Apr1628 and he was buried 8Mar1628. The Page and Vincent family were close in Co. Suffolk, England and also in Isle of Wight, Virginia, beginning around 1680. (560, p.15)

Is this William Page, bc. 1620's (16B), somehow connected to the William Page married to Ann? in Isle of Wight Co, Va (see chart VA 54) that died 16Oct1746. William Page, d.1621 (8B) was married (in 1595) to Mary Vincent (8B-1).

There was a **Thomas Page, b. 1640, Hunston** married (560-178) on a ship in mid-Atlantic to Alice Garrett (Yarrett) that arrived at Isle of Wight Co, Va in or before 1659, and appears to be the root of the FTDNA Page Family **line "C"** in Colonial America administered by George W. Page. The goal of this research was to find the parents of Thomas Page, b. 1640, Hunston, England (560-183) that appears in Isle of Wight, Va before 1680, when some children were "maybe" born in Va. in 1680 and later. (see VA 50)

The 1509 Rental gives Alice Waller Page (6A), as the tenant of a tenement, recently held by John Page, Gent, d. 1667, (15A), formerly held by the heirs of John Cooke and tenement called "**Coppelowes**". Years later, she surrendered it to her son, William and his wife Margaret, both tenements, that then contained 16 acres 3 roods of land and meadow, parcel of the original 20 acres.

1616 Ann Page, (17) b.1594 married Thomas Hawes, b.1588,(17A) WleW-d.1629, 4 children (see 560-28F) Walsham Quarterly Review #8, Jan 1999. Ann Page was daughter of Thomas Page,(12) bc.1567-d.Aug1618, who was married to Thomazin Vincent,(12A) bc.1563,—d.Jul1620.   Dorothy,(17C)   b.5Apr1610,   WleW,—d.25Mar1645   in Barringham, daughter of Thomas Page (12) mar:1630 to John Plummer.

Susan Page (17F) mar John Hammond (17F-1)26May1619, Ingham, Co. Suffolk. Susan signed 6 person petition to Hawstead Church with Thomas Page (40) in **1670**, other signers were Edward & John Sparke. John Sparke (42) mar Elizabeth Nunn, b.1717-d.1770. This connects to John Page (15A).

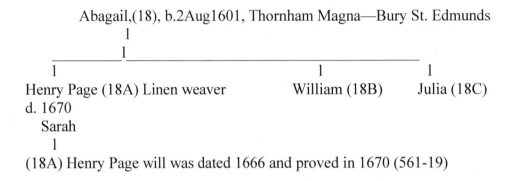

Abagail,(18), b.2Aug1601, Thornham Magna—Bury St. Edmunds

Henry Page (18A) Linen weaver   William (18B)   Julia (18C)
d. 1670
  Sarah

(18A) Henry Page will was dated 1666 and proved in 1670 (561-19)

See ENG 10-1A for one Henry Page (48) mar to Elizabeth ?. First son John Page, b. 1653 and son Henry Jr, b.1671 (48-1), then another Henry b.1690 (48-2) from Baptism records at Walsham le Willows, Co. Suffolk.

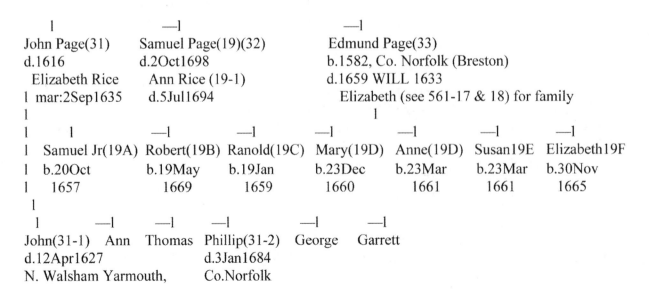

John Page(31)   Samuel Page(19)(32)   Edmund Page(33)
d.1616   d.2Oct1698   b.1582, Co. Norfolk (Breston)
 Elizabeth Rice   Ann Rice (19-1)   d.1659 WILL 1633
 mar:2Sep1635   d.5Jul1694   Elizabeth (see 561-17 & 18) for family

  Samuel Jr(19A) Robert(19B) Ranold(19C) Mary(19D) Anne(19D) Susan19E Elizabeth19F
  b.20Oct   b.19May   b.19Jan   b.23Dec   b.23Mar   b.23Mar b.30Nov
  1657   1669   1659   1660   1661   1661   1665

John(31-1) Ann Thomas Phillip(31-2) George Garrett
d.12Apr1627   d.3Jan1684
N. Walsham Yarmouth,   Co.Norfolk

Samuel Page, d.1696, (19/32) married Ann Rice (19-1) at "**Pages**" and "**Coppelowes**" (560, p102) around 1695. Samuel Page Jr (19A) lived at **TITLED HOUSE** (medieval-**Smith's tenement** (560, p39). Samuel Page,(32) was, on three occasions, ordered to repair his house. He was the tenant in 1695 survey. He died in 1696, leaving the property, **TILED HOUSE** (old name Smiths & Taylors) & ("**Four Ashes House**") (medieval—Kembalds/Sextons) to Samuel Page (19A), his son, who sold it in 1698. There had been a house on this site since 1326. Most of this info was from **WILL** of Silvester Howlett dated 13Mar1676, who was buried 16Mar1676. In 1674 Hearth tax has Samuel Page (19) living in house with John Page (15A) and Vinsent family with 3 fireplaces. (560-12, p.295)(560p.104) William Vincent— the tailor (560, p.38)

Edmund Page, b.1582 (33) living in Co. Norfolk in 1637, seems to be the Edmund Page that wanted to travel to The Hague, Holland to visit his son (no name), a servant working for Prince of Orange, who was William II of Orange-Nassau (1326-1650). William II was also the Count of Nassau that in 1641 married the daughter of King Charles I, of England, Scotland and Ireland. One child William III was born 8 days after his father's death. William III married his cousin, the eldest surviving daughter of King James II of England, Scotland and Ireland.

John Page (31) died 1616 and had a **WILL** dated 1616 at Walsham le Willows, Co. Suffolk.

It is believed that most of the Page family had died or left the Co. Suffolk, England area for America by the years 1674 to 1679 or moved to Co. Norfolk (see MAP) and then some emigrated from there to America.

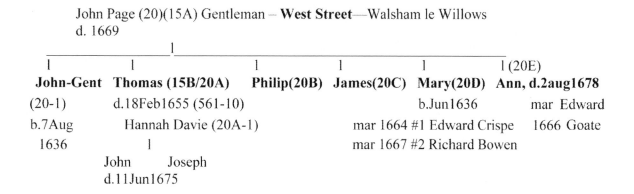

John Page (20)(15A) Gentleman – **West Street**—Walsham le Willows
d. 1669

| John-Gent (20-1) b.7Aug 1636 | Thomas (15B/20A) d.18Feb1655 (561-10) Hannah Davie (20A-1) | Philip(20B) | James(20C) | Mary(20D) b.Jun1636 mar 1664 #1 Edward Crispe mar 1667 #2 Richard Bowen | Ann, d.2aug1678 (20E) mar Edward 1666 Goate |

John   Joseph
d.11Jun1675

John Page, Gent (15A)(20) **WILL** (561-2) dated 3Jan1667, buried 18Jun1669. Proved 17Dec1667, Wit; Edward Goate, Ann Bucher, Joan Grocer, Bro John Page (20) gives to oldest son Thomas, (20A) his "**Capitall Mesuage**" where he lived and all other houses in Walsham and all his lands, pastures and mesuage on south side of Kings highway leading from Walsham to **Ixworth**. Also all the parcells of Meadow in the great meadow in Walsham and one acre and half of meadow sometimes **Gewings** and his close called "**Coulsham Parke**" and his close called "**Nunnes**", To sons James Page (20C) (maybe moved to Co. Norfolk) and Philip Page (20B), his estate rights. James Page (20C) gets my mesuage and tenement in **Bury** St., Edmunds with all the shops and appurtenances and belonging known as "**Smythes Grounds**" and "**Lacies Close**". In Walsham or **Bardwell**. Also James (20C) gets close "**Wicken**" in **Stanton** with four acres. James maybe moves to Co. Norfolk. Phillip (20B) gets several parcels of lands and grounds in **Walsham** on north side of highway leading from Walsham to **Ixworth** known as "**Lakins**" (30 acres) Will witnessed 17Feb1667. Thomas Page (15)(20A), son, to be executor.(560, p. 132) Thomas (20A) **WILL** of 9Sep1654, (561-10) gives **WEST STREET** to Wife Hannah(20A-1), until son John is 24. Names kinsman John Page of **Hopton**, as executor.

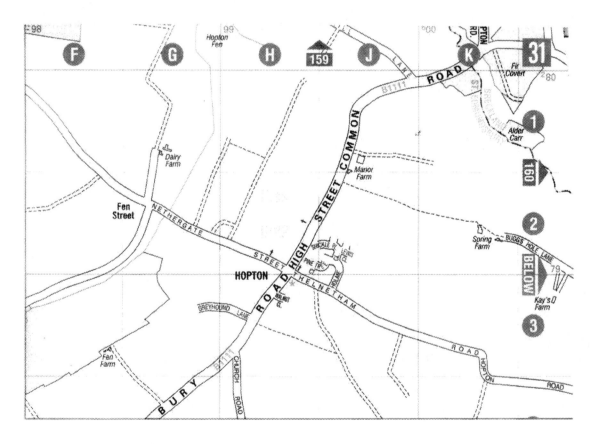

20) 1612 John Hawke surrendered "**Greens**" tenement to John Page (15A)(20) and presumably "the **Lawn**" (560p131) because when the Herbage Book was made in 1625 John Page (20) of **West Street** paid a total of one pound, 11s and 512d in tithes on cows, calves, wool, lambs, geese, pasture, orchard, hearth and plough. He was a "gentleman" and was

probably responsible for building the first stage of "**The Lawn**", as well. The 1662 house "**Greens**" tenement, and no doubt, entered the free tenement, "the Lawn", as well. The 1662 Hearth tax shows he had seven hearths, so he may have extended the house. He was a town warden in 1650, 1661, and 1662. He served on the enquiry of both Walsham and Church House manor courts. He died in 1668 leaving a very detailed will. (see WILL Page 51 of 54) He left his son, Thomas Page (15B)(20A), a linen weaver, on West Street, Walsham, the capital messuage that he lived in and a close called "**Coldham Park**" so he had probably been responsible for laying out the park land surrounding "**The Lawn**". Thomas Page (20A) married Hannah Davie (20A-1) in 1652. After Thomas Page (20A) died in **1655**, (561-10) she later married George Stratton on 21Dec1658.

There is another Thomas Page, Gent, that in 1657, bought a mansion house called the "**White Lion**" in "**Rickinghall**", which is 4 miles from Walsham le Willows. (maybe 15B or 29 or 30). James Page of Risby (91-1) also had house named **White Lion** (page 28)

9Sep1654 Thomas Page (20A)—wife Hanna gets my tenement and ground in WEST STREET, until son John is age 24. Sons John and Joseph, got bibles and other books and my two brass pots each to have one. Thomas died on 18Feb1656, **WILL** probated 20Mar1655, proved on 9Sep1655, (561-10)—buried on 19Feb1656. **WILL** witnessed by relative **John Page** (executor) from **Hopton** and Robert Baker. (561-10)

There is another Thomas Page—not (20A)—that married Dorothy Gosling in 1684 at **Ickingham**, Co. Suffolk, which is 17 miles from Walsham le Willows. Another son, Phillip (20B) was left land, with permission to sell the trees, that were already marked for sale. It appears that Phillip (20B), son of John Page (20) got married on 23Sep1657 to Anne Cheeswright, at **Market Cross** (maybe Market Weston) Phillip appears to be from **Acton** (near **SUDBURY**). Another son James (20C) received property in Bury St. Edmunds and money, but is believed he moved to Co. Norfolk.

Thomas Page (20A) was a trustee of the "**Game Place**" Guild hall and town land, was a town warden in 1676 and on the enquiry of both manors. The 1674 Hearth Tax (560-12) shows that he had seven hearths. The survey of 1695, stated that he held the messuage free containing 3 acres, 2 roods. In 1699 a license was granted to demolish the long-house called a cowhouse or le Stoverhouse. He left his son, John (20-1), b.7Aug1636, also a "gentleman", his copyhold property including half a long-house in "**Greens**" tenement and no doubt, entered the free tenement, **The Lawn**, as well. John (20-1) had 4 fireplaces according to 1674 Hearth Tax Return. Reviewing the Walsham Village History Group Quarterly Review #27 (Oct 2002) reports that on July 15, **1853, The Lawn, a desirable and compact Mansion House in Walsham le Willows.** was sold at auction to Mr. Richard Martineau, age 49, a partner in the Whitbread's Brewery, in London, that wanted to move his family to the country.

560-185

Robert Page

From:	"Robert Page" <flkeybob@terranova.net>
To:	"Robert Page" <flkeybob@terranova.net>; "Robin Page" <Robin_Page@mac.com>; "Robert Page IV" <robertpageiv@gmail.com>
Cc:	"Jo Church Dickerson" <JochurchD@aol.com>; "James Clyde Page" <golfdad84@roadrunner.com >; "Harry L. Page" <Return1809@aol.com>
Sent:	Saturday, January 26, 2013 1:27 PM
Subject:	Suffolk Why I'm giving 12 of my cottages to charity - Features - East Anglian Daily Times

Thanks to my son, Robert E. Page IV for finding this update on THE LAWN in Walsham le Willows that we visited in 2008.

The Lawn - medieval name "Outlaws" was built on the former site of the "Outlaws" by Robert Lister, who was the reeve (Sheriff) in 1434/5 and was bailiff between 1441 and 1452. It is a freehold tenement and therefore difficult to trace in early documents.

The Lawn is described in great detail on page 131 of the book "Who Lived in Your House" - People at Home in Early Walsham le Willows, Suffolk, (2007) by Audrey McLaughlin.

The Lawn was surrended in 1612 to John Page, gentleman (see page 57 in "House of Pages" (30) & (40) - then to his son John Page Jr, d.1667 (15A/20), gentleman in 1640 and then in 1668 to Thomas Page, (15B/20A) gentleman, (b.1640, Hunston (Suffolk), England-d.1719, Isle of Wight, Va), and later to his daughter Elizabeth Page, b.26Mar1672-d.9Oct1740, who on 21 April 1702, married John Sparke, b. 1675-d.16Jan1745. Both Elizabeth and John Sparke are buried at the St. Mary Church cemetery in Walsham le Willows. See photo of cript of Elizabeth and John Sparke. The property later in 1817 was still in the name of the Sparke family.

January 26 2013 Latest news:

EAST ANGLIAN DAILY TIMES MAY 26, 2011

MODERN PHILANTHROPIST: Richard Martineau, from Walsham-le-Willows, who comes from a line of men who did good work for the community

Suffolk: Why Iâm giving 12 of my cottages to charity

By Steven Russell
Thursday, May 26, 2011
5:17 PM

A Suffolk landowner is donating a dozen cottages to charity -- homes built for villagers by his philanthropic ancestor about 100 years ago. Steven Russell hears about this latest step by a benevolent family

1/26/2013

The properties owned by the Martineau family includes much property in Walsham le Willows and they are donating one property to charity each year. The newspaper East Anglian Daily times (26May2011) has an eight page story on each property to be donated. Most of the properties were owned by the Page family in previous times. You can google the story or contact the author for a copy.

Another Page family—**LINE "K"**—is in Rickinghall and difficult to separate these families. This is Philip I. Page—line K. (Oxford Y-DNA 10) (later research says this is really line "C"—NOT line "K" which means a "possible" NPE occurred somewhere—only on this one line—after this time period. Only more Y-DNA research will reveal this confusion. Philip Page only did Y-DNA 10 and he must do at least Y-DNA 37 to even get close to the true results.

In 1888, Disclaimers of Persons, who were disclaimed as Gentlemen of Coat-Armoury John Paul Kylands, F.S.A. Guildford, printed by Billing and Sons, reports that John Page (20), **IXWORTH THORPE**, Suffolk, in 1664 and his two sons John Page (20-1), of **WALSHAM** le Willows, and Philip Page (20B) of **Gedding**,(560-49B) were disclaimed as "Gentlemen". The effect of this is the herald—who made the visitation in 1666 was not persuaded by the evidence presented by the three named Co. Suffolk "Gentlemen" and use of the social status symbol, was NOT awarded. There is also a remote possibility that they "refused" to pay the necessary fee to the crown for the title and arms, and were denied the social status, reports George W. Page. It should be noted that in the 1600's, there were mass emigrations from Co. Suffolk to the Colonies and other places.

Info from Christine (Page) Barnes—very conflicting info—need more Y-DNA research

```
DNA          Richard Page (21) - yeoman              See ENG 10-2 and PA 50
Family C     d. 31 May 1639                          for extended family history
Walsham le   Sibell Cook (21-1)                      of this line, "maybe" line K.
Willows      d.27Feb1641                             Philip I. Page, is living
             |                                       in England

|—        |        —|      —|      —|     —|        —|       —|      |
Reignold (Raynold) (21A) John  William George Dorothy(21E) Thomas  Mary   Eliz
b.28May1600       b.2May  b.27Feb b.9Aug b.5Apr      b.2Nov  b.9Jan d.1679
d.1688            1603    1604    1607   1610        1613WW  1615
Margaret          (21B)   (21C)   (21D)  Richard     d.1626  (21G)  (21H)
d.1685                                   Cooke       (21F)
|

|        —|      —|     —|      —|            —|      —|
Mary (21A-2) Hannah Mary  Samuel Elizabeth(21A-3) Joseph  John (21A-1)
b.15Feb1623 b23Oct b.18Oct b.27Jun b.24Mar1632    b.13Sep b.14Jul1639
d. 2Mar1626 1625   1627    1630   d.17Sep1679      1635    d.1714
Coke                                                       21A-2 #1 Elizabeth
                                                           #2 Mary Alder,d.1710
```

1627—Admission of Robert Grocer on surrender of Richard Page (21) & (maybe (8G) to grove of 5 acres. (560-11) Richard Page, (21) yeoman of **WALSHAM** le Willows signed his **WILL** on 19May1639, and it was proved on 10Jun1639. (561-13) He was buried 31May1639. Witness: Henry Smith and Thomas Lister. He named his wife Sibell as executrix and Raynold (21A) his son as executor. His wife got the **Wicken Close and all the meadow ground in the Great Meadow, during her natural life, then it goes to Raynold Page, son. appears to be Page Line "C" not line "K".** There seems to have occurred a Non-Paternal Event (NPE) which further Y-DNA testing of males can reveal that the event took place, but not females, but it does not inform us how many generations in the past the event took place. Additional testing of many males of this line might narrow down the NPE. There are many reasons an NPE takes place and should not be considered an embarrassment.

21-1) Sibell Page WILL dated 21Feb1641, probated 22Mar1641 and Sybil Page, widow buried 27Feb1641. (561-13A) Names her sons, Reignold Page and Thomas Page as executors. Wit: Austin Godbit and Stephen **Vincent**. See page 17, (6).

*   *   *

Reginald Page (21A) son of Richard Page/Sibell Page b.28May1600—d.1688 (see 560-28J)

Blue Boar—built around 1420 and **Reginald Page, b.1600** took possession from 1629 to 1695.

The "**Blue Boar**" (Pyes/Bays) built around 1420 belonged to John Bindes, a grocer. He in turn surrendered it to Reginald Page, d.1688 (21A) in 1629. (560p.127) The year before Reginald (21A) had acquired the messuage with a garden and orchard from John Harte, so he now had the main house and the shop and stayed there for about 50 years. He was a church warden and regularly served on the jury of the now combined manors of Walsham and Church House courts and also was the bailiff. His wife was paid by the town wardens to teach a local child. Cottages built at the front of the house were first used as shops but they were demolished within living memory. His name appears in the Hearth tax lists of 1662 and 1674. He paid tax on three hearths. **Reginald Page** died in 1688 and was 88 years old. In 1693, Thomas Youngman, a tailor, was the occupant. By 1817 it was a public house called the "Boar", where local auctions were held. (see 560-8J)

Another Richard Page/ Dorothy (21B) (561-23)

21B) 1618 Richard Page, Gentleman (21B), married Dorothy Cooke, widow of Thomas Cook, a rich vintner from London. Dorothy was first married to #1 John Robwood, **WALSHAM** le Willows, Co. Suffolk, England of the Robin Hood fame and one of the earliest families recorded in **WALSHAM**, that died in 1599. Next Dorothy married Thomas Cooke, d. 1616, Gentleman from London, (see 561-23) then in 1618 along came husband #3 that was Richard Page. (Is this Page line "k"? Not clear, where this Richard Page fits into the Page family. It appears that most of this Page Family line had either died or moved away by 1680. See Walsham Quarterly Review #16, Jan 2001. (560-28H) In the Bury Post of 4Mar1801 reported that Richard Page of Walsham le Willows, blacksmith, assigned over his affects to Mr. Nathaniel Gilson of that town for the benefit of his creditors.

Joyce Page, b.1643, (23B-5) North Walsham, County Norfolk, England (560-148) shows up in Isle of Wight, Va—as a widow of **Henry Rennells** (Reynolds) on 9Jun1681 when presenting the appraisal of ESTATE (see VA 52) (173A, p.21) which means she got married to Henry prior to 6Apr1679, when Henry filed a **WILL** in 1679 in Isle of Wight, Va and named his wife as Joyce. The children of Henry Rennells (Henry & Sarah) were probably from his former wife, Elizabeth. When Henry died in 1681, Joyce (23B-5) went back to her family name because of the large Page families in the area.

Joyce was appointed extx by (Henry Reynolds) **WILL** on 9Jun1681, Security was by Thomas Ward, Henry Clark. (see 173A, page 71) Henry Rennells property was appraised by Hodges Council, Epenetus Griffin, Joseph Bracher and was recorded on 23Jun1728. (see 173A-Wills and Administrations of Isle of Wight Co, Va, page 106) The Rennells family traveled to Sampson Co, N.C. then on to Marion Co, S.C. with David Page, b. 1744 family (son of ABRAHAM PAGE)

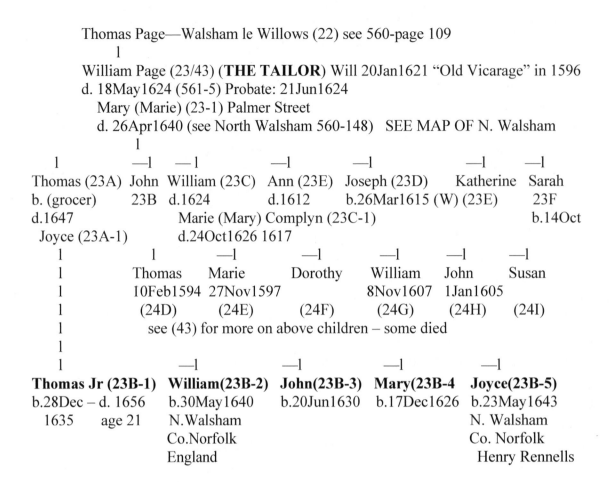

Thomas Page—Walsham le Willows (22) see 560-page 109

William Page (23/43) (**THE TAILOR**) Will 20Jan1621 "Old Vicarage" in 1596
d. 18May1624 (561-5) Probate: 21Jun1624
  Mary (Marie) (23-1) Palmer Street
  d. 26Apr1640 (see North Walsham 560-148)   SEE MAP OF N. Walsham

Thomas (23A)	John	William (23C)	Ann (23E)	Joseph (23D)	Katherine	Sarah
b. (grocer)	23B	d.1624	d.1612	b.26Mar1615 (W) (23E)	23F	
d.1647		Marie (Mary) Complyn (23C-1)				b.14Oct
Joyce (23A-1)		d.24Oct1626 1617				

	Thomas	Marie	Dorothy	William	John	Susan
	10Feb1594	27Nov1597		8Nov1607	1Jan1605	
	(24D)	(24E)	(24F)	(24G)	(24H)	(24I)

see (43) for more on above children – some died

Thomas Jr (23B-1)	**William(23B-2)**	**John(23B-3)**	**Mary(23B-4**	**Joyce(23B-5)**
b.28Dec – d. 1656	b.30May1640	b.20Jun1630	b.17Dec1626	b.23May1643
1635 age 21	N.Walsham			N. Walsham
	Co.Norfolk			Co. Norfolk
	England			Henry Rennells

The John Page, b.20Jun1630 (23B-3) is probably the John Page on my chart VA 52—when John Page married Felicia Hall, from Nanesmond Co. Va on 13July1719. I also have a note that John Page was a foot soldier in Surry Co, Va in 1687 and would guess that is the same John Page. On my chart VA 54, I have John Page with WILL dated 22Mar1700, Isle of Wight, Va with children John and Elizabeth Page. This pretty much ties together the English bunch to the Virginia bunch.

There were a few allied families, that continued to stay close with the Page family that moved with them, as they slowly moved south from Virginia, then westward. One was the Rennells (Reynolds) family. On my chart NC 202, Thomas Page, Sr—began to dispose of land he owned in Sampson Co, NC beginning in 1782 to 1794.(Is this Thomas Page Sr, d.1838—son of ABRAHAM PAGE) Much of the land he sold to the Richard Runnels family. On many of the properties Dredzell Runnels and Francis Boykin/Ann Marshall (173—Marriages in Isle of Wight Co, Va. p. 4) & Bius Boykin were the chaincarriers. (see 173A, Wills of Isle of Wight, page. 323 & 359. The Page, Runnels and Boykin families traveled together in the U.S.—state to state for over 100 years.

The Old Vicarage—built in early 1300's and owned by Page family 1496 to 1679.

In 1591 the "**Old Vicarage**" (medieval-Spilmans) (560p.108) property went to Stephen Spilman and in 1596 Stephen and wife Thomasina surrender the property to **William Page, d. 1624** (23 & 43) (561-5), **the tailor**. William Page (23) was a church warden in 1605 and 1611. He made his will in 1621, leaving his property to his wife Mary (Marie)(23-1), until his sons, Thomas, John, William and Joseph reached full age. Daughters Katherine and Sara were to receive money. William (23) stipulated "that if Mary died while the youngest children were still under sixteen, **Thomas (23A)** (grocer) was to maintain, educate, bring up and keep my said children in good and decent manner of diet, lodging, apparel and schooling. He left Thomas (23A) the long framed table which standeth in the hall and my form which belongs to the said table and also one back chair." William (23C) died in 1624 and Mary (Marie) 23-1) was admitted to the property. Thomas Page (grocer)(23A) moved to North Walsham, where he died in 1647. (560-148)

1624 widow Mary (23-1) took possession, until 1640 when she died, and son Thomas (23A) and Joyce (23A-1) Page took possession, then in 1647 widow Joyce took over until 1658, when son William Page (23B-2) took possession until **1679**, when it went to Edward Rye. (560p.110) (23C-1) Wife Mary (23-1) also was given land purchased of Stephen Hawes, and one piece of pasture called **"Robbells"** which William Page (23) had purchased from

William Harrison. (same name later shows up and in 1720 ans dies in Isle of Wight Co, Va.) **WILLIAM HARISON'S WILL** was probated in 1595 at the Prerogative Court of Canterbury, England) For details of the division of William Page's property see the Will (561-5) of **William Page, d.1624 (23)—tailor** of Walsham le Willows, dated 20Jan1621. Witnesses: Stephen Vincent & George Complin—Probate at Bury 21Jun1624. Thomas Page (23A) (oldest son of William Page and Marie (23C-1) his wife).

The entry in the 1625 Herbage Book shows widow Page (23-1) on Palmer Street, paying tithes on 6 cows, 1s, calve 5s, lambe 1/2d, and ort 3d, mowing 6 acres 61/2 d, goose tithe put to Goodman aowplyn, hopes due, wall 11/2 d. and a fole 1 d". Mary died in 1640 and her son Thomas (23A) was admitted to Spilmans in Palmer Street, parcel of 28 acres with a garden and various parcels of pasture adjoining. (560p.108)

Thomas Page (23A) also owned **Four Ashes House (560p82)** that in **1696, was acquired** by **William Baker.** and had also acquired "Kembalds" messuage **in 1638** but **had moved away from the village of Walsham le Willows (not clear which year—but between 1638-1647) to North Walsham in Co. Norfolk, where he was a grocer.** (A comment must be made at this time that a BAKER family has appeared in the Y-DNA results) After William Page's (23) **death in 1647**, his widow Joyce (23A-1), now married to William Wilgress, a gentleman, was admitted to all of his property with custody of their son Thomas, b.28Dec1635 (23B-1), aged twelve. Thomas Page Junior, b.28Dec1635-d.1656 (23B-1) (aged 21) and his brother William Page, b. 30May1640 (23B-2) was admitted. By 1679 Edward Rye had bought the house and surrendered it to his son Thomas, who immediately passed it on to John Eastling. John Eastling died in 1689 leaving daughters Ann Rainbird, Sarah Osborne and Hester Page. **WILL** of Marie Page (23C-1) 21Oct1626 and probated 21Nov1626 and buried 24Oct1626 (see very long Will on page 22 of 54) Marie Complyn (23C-1) married to William Page (23C) who died in 1624, later remarried to John Musket. Her brother George Complyn, is seen on many Page wills as witness. (560, p. 109)

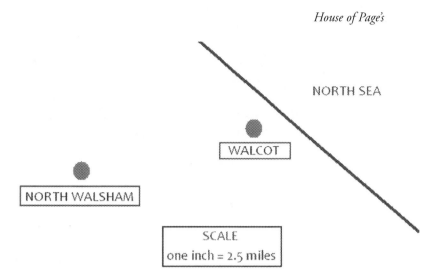

NORTH SEA

WALCOT

NORTH WALSHAM

SCALE
one inch = 2.5 miles

COUNTY OF NORFOLK, ENGLAND
by. Robert E. Page

FELTHOPE

John Page (25) grocer - Will 1670
Elizabeth
l   —l   —l   —l   —l
Marie   Elizabeth   Robert   John   Sara

John Page (25)—Grocer—**North Walsham, Co. Norfolk. WILL** of 1670. (561-3) Again Will very hard to read. Wife was Elizabeth, daughters were Marie and Elizabeth, sons were Robert and John. There was a **Thomas Page** (23A) that had acquired "Kembalds" in Walsham le Willows in 1638 had **moved to North Walsham** and he died in 1647.

John Page (25 and 118) – North Walsham, Co. Norfolk
Mar: 17Oct1596 Elizabeth Baude
|

Joseph	Marie	Elizabeth	Maria	John	Elizabeth	Robert	Sarah	Sarah
b.4Dec	b.2Sep	b.15Mar1600	b.27Mar	b.18Jan	b.26Feb	b.26Feb	b.23Nov	b.8Nov
1597	1599	d.23Jun1602	1602	1604	1606	1608	1610	1612
						d.1611	d.1611	

Thomas Page (119) North Walsham, Co. Norfolk (560-148)
|

Thomas	Elizabeth	John	Joseph	Samuel	Anna
b.1624	b.1628	b.1629	b.1630	b.1632	b.1633

John Page (121) North Walsham, Co. Norfolk (560-148)
Mary
|
John Page – bap 26Dec1722

Thomas Page (122) North Walsham, Co. Norfolk had son John Page—bap 13Feb1628-d.26Dec1640

Thomas Page (113) – Walcott, Co. Norfolk (560-146)
Margaret
|

Margaret	Thomas	Edmund	William	Nicholas	Cicely	Myles	Katherine	Margaret	Rebecca
b.31Jan	b.8Apr	b.9Mar	b.1Jan	b.9Nov	b.13May	b.9Mar	b.25Mar	b.25Mar	b.20Feb1606
1563	1565	1566	1568	1572	1571	1578	1600	1603	d.10Mar1607

|
Martha, b. 20Sep1591

Edmund Page (114) Walcot, Co. Norfolk (560-146)

Edmund Page (114) Walcot, Co. Norfolk (560-146)
Dorothy
l
Edmund   Elizabeth
b.Mar1609   b.1Nov1613

Edmund Page (115) Walcot, Co. Norfolk (560-146)
Sarah
l
Edmund   John   Anne   Richard   Dorothy
b.4May1631 b.14Feb1635 b.5May1633 b.27Jan1634 b.19Aug1638

Edmund Page (116) Walcot, Co. Norfolk (560-146)
Amy

John Page – Hunston (560-159A)
l
l   —l   —l
Lawrence Page (27)   George Page (28) Yeoman - in Walsham   Simon (29)
Ann(Hunston)   d. Feb 1619   l
Iscop – d. 1615   mar: Agnes Wrighte   John   Thomas   Phillip   Marie
                     1576 d.1615
                     l
        John (28A) Executor – this is John Page(15/Ann15A-1)(see p. 30)
_____l_____
l   l   l   l   l
John   Anne   Sara   Marie Elizabeth

WILL of George Page (28) signed on 8Jan1618 (561-15) (see page 16 of 54 pages).
Witnesses. Thomas Page, George Complin Probate: 8Mar1619 Buried: 2Feb1619
(see WILL 561-15 for more into)

Thomas Page (29) – Hawstead – Co. Suffolk—see (15B) for possible connection
Audrie (29A)
l
l
30-1   30-2   30-3   30-4   30-5   30-6   30-7
Thomas   Martha   Martha   John   Joseph   William   Isaac
d.1639   d.1639   d.1642   b.4Oct1644 b.15Jun1645 b.3Jun1647 b.16Dec1648

Thomas Page (15B) or (29)
Audrie
1 —
| |
Thomas Page (30-1)   Martha
b, 14Feb1639, Hawstead—lived only 3 days d.3Mar1639
d.17Feb1639, **Hawstead**, Co. Suffolk, England

Thomas Page, b. 1599-d.17Aug1644 (15) (560-183)
   Mary (Marie),d.1626 (15-1)
      1
      1
Thomas Page, (30) – **d.1672**—yeoman (Hawstead) see VA 8—maybe (30) is same as (40)
wife #1 Susan – b.?—d.13Sep1631—Hawstead (560-32)
wife #2 Mary Newton, b.1620—mar: 1636 – Hunston, Co. Suffolk (560-183)
   1   wife #3 Elizabeth Frere, mar:7Mar1670, Finningham, (30-1)
   1   **d.23Feb1680**, Rickinghall—buried 2May1680, Finningham.
   1
— 1 —

Thomas (30A)	Mary (30F)	William(30B)	Susanna (30C)	John	Joseph(30E)	Robert(30G)
b.6Dec1640	b.31Mar	d.1664	1Jan1622-1690	(30D)	b.27Aug1622	b.1Jan1627
Hunston	1620	Anna Goose	Thomas Gleason		b.1644 d.17Mar1674	
d.1719-IofW	Thomas	d.1686	1607-1686 (30C-1)		(560-32)	
Alice Garrett	Locke		1		Mary (30E-1)	
(30A-1)	(30F-1)(560-32)		1		Clayden	
1	mar:11Jun1635		Susanna,b.1639 (30C-2)		mar:1651	
See VA 50			Thomas Pratt		1	
560-181			(30C-2A)		Susan(30E-1A)560-32A	
560-183					b.1663-d.29Sep1681	

Thomas Page and wife Alis are recorded as being in Perquimans District, N.C. in 1659,1663
and 1684. (560-181)

WILL of Thomas Page (30) of **Hawstead**, Co. Suffolk, England—yeoman—(see 560-32
series)
Will dated 15Jan1636/37-d.1639 (561-8)—see Abraham Page & Alice Garrett-also in
Hawstead

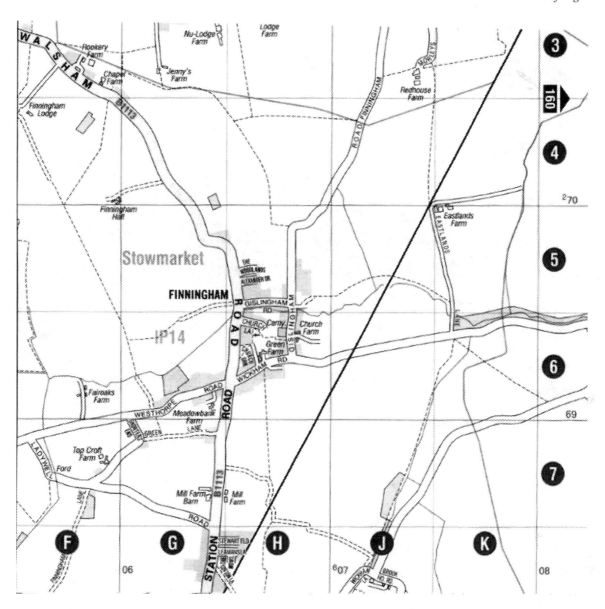

(30) Archdeaconry of Sudbury Will—witness: **Rebecca Page b.1609 (560-6 & 560-30)**, Thomas Page, b.1612 (560-7) and George Scarpe (d.Dec1644)(560-32A), at **Ixworth** on 11July1637. Will Proven: 11Jul1637 (561-8) Will mentions that he owned land and two tenements in **Finningham**. Thomas Page (30A) was executor. (30-1) Will says wife #3 was Elizabeth Frere (30-1), who married Thomas Page (30) of **Walsham (maybe Hawstead) on 7Mar1670) (560-22A)**, but IGI mentions 1st wife was Susan. Elizabeth Page (30-1), died 23Feb1680, Rickinghall—but buried in Finningham on **2May1680**. Joseph Page (30E), son of Thomas/Susan Page is mentioned in 1674 Hawstead Hearth tax with 2 hearths. (560-12) There were two Joseph's born, 1st died 1622 and 2nd born 1624, which is in 1674 Hawstead Hearth tax. Joseph married Mary Clayden.

Brook Farm Cottage—built in middle 1500's. Page family took possession in 1652 until 1672.

Thomas Page (6) bought **Brook Farm Cottages** (medieval-Cooks) in 1552, (see 560-60 & 60A) then Robert Page, single man, of **Norton**, (next to Woolpit) gained possession in 1553 and in 1572 Thomas Page (6), father of Robert Page (34) Yeoman of **Hunston**—took possession, then Robert Page (34A) then sold to Thomas Goodryche of **Wyyerstone,** in 1599, a "close" in **Norton**, and Thomas Page was attorney. In 1622 it was sold again with Alice Page, widow of Robert Page (34A) the right of dower.

Another Thomas Page's (30) son John Page, d.**1672** (30D) took possession in 1656 (from Anne Neale, widow of Robert Neale) until **1672** when kinsman John Page (20-1) of **Hopton**, owned it until James Hawes family bought it in 1672. In earlier years, the Hawes family had owned it. Later in 1817 John Sparke (42) owned it. (560, p.16)

SPECULATION Could this Thomas Page (30A), son of Thomas Page/Elizabeth (30) be the Thomas Page, b. 1640 **Hunston** (30A-1) (560-183) that married Alice Garrett/Yarrett prior to 1659 (Both recorded being in Perquimans Dist, N.C. in 1659) on a ship mid-Atlantic and arrived in Isle of Wight Co, Va (VA 50) It was assumed that they came from England but wondered—if they just moved from north Virginia to southern Va, because William Garrett

(Yarrett) (who died around 1650) and wife Francis Whittington, in 1650, owned land on N. Side of Rappa River, in Rappahannock Co, Va. One of Thomas Page's,(b.1640), daughters was named Rebecca, b. 1682, and a son named Thomas Page, b. 1680, also had a daughter Mary (no DOB), and a son John, b. 1685. ANSWER: Probably yes . . . and had a son, named Thomas Page (30A-1), then that Thomas Page appears to be the Thomas Page, b 1640, **Hunston**—d.1719, Isle of Wight, Va. **Thomas Page and wife Alis** were recorded as being in Perquimans Dist, N.C. in **1659, 1663 & 1684.** (560-181)

There is another Thomas Page, b.1638, that attended King Edward 6th Free Grammar School in Bury, then admitted to Magdalene college in 1657 (age 19-DOB 1638), graduated in with BA in 1661, which probably rules out any Virginia birthplace. Another "slight" possibility is Thomas (30) might be the son of Joseph/Mary Page (30E)—but I doubt it.

Info says Thomas Page (30) is from **Page Family line C** This Susanna Page (30C) that married Thomas **Gleason** (30C-1) (see page 33) and her brother William Page (30B) both emigrated to Watertown, Massachusetts prior to 1664 and appear to be from Page Family Line C (info from Dan Page, Okla—email—depage@ipa.net) Dan Page is a descendent of the Gleason line but gets his Page name from the Axilheath Page—**LINE P**—from Goochland Co, Va. Further research reveals, the Thomas Gleason (Leason), that emigrated to Massachusetts, was from Sulgrave, (Co. Northampton), England and the Page Line C is not known to have any relatives in Northampton.

The Thomas/Susannah (Page) Gleason marriage had Susannah, b. 1639 and Thomas, b. 1637, in Sulgrave, County Northampton, England—which would fit the above Thomas Page, b. 1638—with his college education. They later moved to Massachusetts and I have not pursued that possible connection.

Information reveals one Thomas Page, (30A) entering **Stafford Co, Va** in **1674** with wife **Mary Newton—Hunston** Parish records (560-183) reveals they married in 1636 in **Hunston** (Co. Suffolk) England (560-183) and Mary Page (30F) married to **Thomas Locke, b. 1641** (30F-1) in 1635 (560-32) They were transported by Capt. Robert Caulfield. (see chart VA 8, VA 8-1 and VA 54) Thomas Locke (30F-1) is grandson of John Locke, d.1621, (elder) yeoman, of **Alpheton**, Co. Suffolk., and son of Randolph Locke, d.1624. This is the same family **Dan Page** is chasing BUT his search centers on the other daughter, **Susanna Page** (1616-1690) (30C) that was married to **Thomas Gleason** (1607-1686) (30C-1)(see 560-159A) (see 221 at end of this document) This Thomas Page (30A) must be Thomas Page (15B). In ENG 10-1, there is a Thomas Lock, b.1774—d.8Mar1823, from Walsham le Willows. (see 560-7) There are a lot of Lock's in **Hunston** (Co. Suffolk), England. (See 560-183)

Isle of Wight, Va is a very close religious community—tied close to the Quakers. William Brasie, of Levy Neck, died 22Jan1699, his **WILL** mentions the John Harrison family, Samuel **Newton** of Lawnes Creek, **THOMAS PAGE** (taylor), Nansemond Co, Hugh Brasie, Isaac Ricks, Thomas Jordan, Robert Lacie of Lawnes Creek in Surry. These families all came from around Walsham le Willows, Co. Suffolk, England. (173A, p.40)

Interesting info comes from Virginia Cavaliers and Pioneers, Vol 2, (483) that reports on page 165 that on **4October1675,** Henry Aubry got 5,100 acres in Rappahanock Co, Va for transporting 102 persons, and on that list is Alice Page, William Vincent, Howell Powell. On page 232, Thomas Powell, got 480 acres for transporting two persons on **20Apr1682,** and also Charles Savage (page 231) got 570 acres in Surry Co, Va for 12 people, including one Thomas Page, and on page 237, Robert Caulfield of Surry Co, Va got 2250 acres in Surry Co, for 26 people including **Mary Newton, Thomas Locke and Thomas Page.** (This sounds like the above 1674 Stafford Co, Va. arrival info—Is it a 2nd trip from England or just a movement from northern Va to southern Va? Or just a duplicate filing to gain free land—which seems to happen often)

It is interesting, that there is a William Page, (VA 8) who died 1716 in **Stafford Co, VA** and he had a daughter Mary Page, that in 1740 married Anthony Linton at house of John Remy. On my chart VA 54, Isle of Wight Co, Va. there is William Page Jr, b.1662 that has a daughter Mary Page. This Isle of Wight Co, Va family are Quakers and William Jr, b.1662 was the son of William Page/Mary, who was the son of William Page that died 14Oct1746 in **Isle of Wight, Va** and was married to Ann.

THE BELOW THOMAS PAGE ARRIVED IN ISLE OF WIGHT Co, Va circa 1674/79
THOMAS PAGE (15C) or (30A) (see 560-159A) (see VA 50)
b. 6Dec1640, Hunston, England – d. 20Feb1719, Isle of Wight (Nansemond Co), Va
Alis (Alice) Maybe Garrett/Yarrett (30A-1) (married Mid-Atlantic 1659)

				see 560-181A for below
Mary,(E)	Thomas Jr	Alice	Rebecca	John
William	b.7Feb1680(B)	b.7Feb1680(B)	b.8Nov1682	b.19Feb1685 (C)
Powell	d.1744 (B)	Henry	Thomas Gay	d.13May1740 (D)
b.1665	Isabell	Autry	mar:11Nov1699	mar Hanner(Hannah)
d.1734, (A)	Lawrence		(A) 1707	b.1687
mar:14Feb(A)	mar:15Jan(A)			d.1725(D)
1700	1702			

(A)Isle of Wight Co, Va (B) Nansemond Co, Va. (E) Hunston, Eng
(C)Perquimans Dist, Albermarle Co, NC. (D) Bertie Co, N.C. (560-159)

On July 24, 1645, one Michael Masters, received 413 acres for transporting 9 people to Virginia. One of these was a Thomas Page. Twelve acres of this land was next to Samuel Jordan, the father of Thomas Jordan, of the Quaker group in Isle of Wight. The Page family and the Jordan family were very close in Co. Suffolk, England and in Virginia.

There was a Thomas Page, (15) b.1599-d.17Aug1644 **Walsham** le Willows, Co. Suffolk that left his tenement "**Four Ashes House or earlier Kembalds**" to his wife, Mary, (is this Mary Newton married to Thomas Page in 1636) until his son Thomas, born 1640, **Hunston**) (15B) was 21.(560-183) Thomas (15B) could have left for Virginia, right away, and was part of the group of 9 that—Michael Masters received land for transporting 9 people before **1645**. Thomas Page (15C), was born circa 1640. Probably his father, Thomas Page (15B/30A) died in the 1660's and now, his son Thomas (15C) returned to Co. Suffolk, England, as the eldest son, to dispose of his English property, along with his brother John Page (15A). While in England, Thomas Page (40) who had married wife #1 (maybe Susan ?, had one daughter Mary, (Elizabeth), b.1672-d.1740, (41) who later married John Sparke, Gentleman b.1675-d.1745, at Walsham le Willows, and by **1676**, all the property was disposed of by then.

What is confusing—is that it appears than this Thomas Page (40) (also maybe 30A-1) married **Mary Newton** wife #2 in 1636 in **Hunston** (Co. Suffolk) (560-183) then wife #3, **Elizabeth Frere**, on 7Mar1670, **Finningham** (30-1) who died 23Feb1680, in **Rickinghall** but buried 2May1680 in **Finningham**. (551G, p.17)(560-30A)—see page 49A, 49B and 49C

John Frere, b.21Oct1569—d.15Dec16 33, Finningham—Gentleman—owned Green Farm
    Elizabeth (Ann) Sandwich, d. 1628, Finningham—daug of John Sandwich
       l
John Frere, b.13May1606, Finningeham,
          d.6Mar1679—see 560-30A
       l
John Frere, Gentleman—Purchased Finningham Hall in 1664
b.6May1644-d.14Jan1709
mar: Elizabeth Sheppard, d. 9Mar1679—see ENG 10-1, p.46
         ___l_____
    l   l
Elizabeth Frere,(30-1)   John Ferer, b.13May1606, Finnningham, d.6Mar1679 see 560-30A
d.23Feb1680, Rickinghall-buried 2May1680, Finningham
Mar: **THOMAS PAGE (30)** on 7Mar1670 (see 560-30A)

Some of the above from "Descendants of John Frere"—of Sweffling and the Barbados.

John Frere, b.1740 delivered a paper to the Society of Antiquaries of London on 22June 1797 of his observation of flint hand-axes in the brick pit at Hoxne, which he reasoned had been made by people "who had not the use of metals and who lived in a very remote period. He has been called the father of scientific archaeology and has been honored. A plaque was erected by the Finningham archaeology society on 8August1999 at the Finningham church.

JOHN FRERE

Plaque installed during August of 1999 at **Finningham**, Suffolk, England, near the now famous site of **Hoxne** in Suffolk. *(photo courtesy of <u>John Frere Scott</u>, one of the individuals involved in erecting the Plaque). The Plaque was sculpted by the Cardozo-Kindersley Workshops at Cambridge founded by the late David Kindersley. The Finningham Church is the resting place of many early Freres. There is much there of interest to family members.*

John Frere was the father of John Hookham Frere, who was a British Diplomat during the Peninsular Wars and Writer. John Hookham Frere retired to Villa Frere in Malta which still exists. Sir Bartle Henry Frere was John Hookham's nephew. John Frere was a Memeber of Parliament (MP), as well as FRS. John Frere also had a son George of "Lincoln's Inn" who was one of the founding partners of the lawyers Frere Cholmeley and a founder of the Law Society. More information can be found on these individuals at <u>"Additional Information on Freres"</u>**. As an added footnote there were a few Freers who served as Officers under the Duke of Wellington in the Peninsular Wars, including** <u>Colonel Arthur William Wellington Freer</u>.

The brief, but defining, article below written by Antiquarian **John Frere** in 1790 set the stage for Paleolithic Archaeology as we know it today. It challenged Archbishop James Ussher's Creationist doctrine made in the early 1600s that pinpointed creation as beginning at 9:00 PM on October 23rd in 4004 B.C. Among the tools first identified by Frere was the *Acheulian HandAxe* which has become a basic "Horizon Marker" of the Lower Paleolithic cultures studied by archaeologist today. (Stan Freer, Ph.D. - Archaeologist)

****

("The Beginning of Paleolithic Archaeology" John Frere from Man's Discovery of his Past:

Literary Landmarks in Archaeology edited by Robert F. Heizer, PrenticeHall, Inc., 1962, pp. 70-71)

THE BEGINNING OF PALEOLITHHIC ARCHAEOLOGY

http://home.cc.umanitoba.ca/~sfreer/jfrere.html

It now appears that Thomas Page was already married to Alice (Alis) Garrett—(which occurred in mid-Atlantic—before 1659)—as they were traveling from England to Virginia with his wife's family Garrett, (they are recorded in Perquimans Dist, N.C in 1659—(see 560-181) and when they arrived back in Va.—prior to 1680 when Thomas Jr, and Alice (twins) were born in 1680. They started getting land grants in 1682 and later. (see VA 50) and (560-181).

It is clear that Elizabeth Page's father was a Thomas Page (15C) and John Sparke and wife Elizabeth Page are both buried at St. Mary church in **Walsham** le Willows. (see my photo of cript). More on this genealogical connection of this link between England and the Virginia Page families, which is a vital link for genealogical reasons.

In 1672, George Fox, dc.1691 (Quaker) visited Virginia and this began the Quaker movement.

In **1672**, Thomas Page's (15) brother, John Page (15A) (chart VA 52) surrendered one house (**FOUR ASHES HOUSE)**—(560, p.104) on the tenement to Elizah Davy & Robert Harding, then in 1677, it went to back to John Page (15A) who owned it until 1695, when it went to Francis Asty. (560p.106) Robert Harding, surrendered one messuage in 1677 called **KEMBALDS (NEW NAME—FOUR ASHES HOUSE)** with a yard, orchard and half a pond back to John Page (15A). (560-p.105)

The two brothers John (15A) and Thomas (15)—probably split the money and probably both returned to Va. There is a John Page (VA 52) in Isle of Wight, during this time period, that has not been clearly identified and this is probably John Page (15A) that appears in Isle of Wight, Va by 1677. There is a Joyce Page Rennells, (must be Joyce Page, b.23May1643 (23B-5) (see 560, p110—**THE OLD VICARAGE**), that is—mixed up with this family, that on 9Jun1681, presented appraisal of Isle of Wight, Va ESTATE of Henry Rennells, who d.1681.(see my chart NC 202) The Rennells and Page families were close in County Norfork, England and Virginia.

Also in 1674, one Thomas Page (30A) (page 32 & 47) arrived in Stafford Co, Va (on Maryland border) with wife Mary Newton, b.1620 (30F) (560-183) and Thomas Locke (30F-1) (VA 54), that were from **Alpheton**, Co. Suffolk. This makes a connection to the Co. Suffolk, England that Dan Page is researching. This is when all the property in Co. Suffolk is being disposed of, by the Page family.

Then in 1675, there is one Thomas Page that emigrates to Maryland—also the same year, one Alice Page emigrates to Va and these two places, are just a few miles apart and are a hotbed of the "new Quaker movement". Are they connected? I think YES. See VA 8 and VA 8-1.

The first recorded land transaction in Virginia for one Thomas Page was on 2Feb1662 when he was granted 600 acres on s. side of Rappahannock river in northern Va. next to Howell Powell. (314)—The Powell Families of Va and the South by Rev Silas Emmett Lucas, Jr. One of Thomas Page's (15C) daughter Mary Page, married one William Powell Jr, in Isle of Wight, Va in 1700. (see VA 50) This William Powell Jr, b.1679 married to Mary Page, had daughter Mary Powell, that was born in Holland. (see T1 & VA 50-1, 3A) See above for more info.

In 1686, Thomas Page was given 133 acres by **Henry and Elizabeth Hearne** (560-164) for his transporting three persons: James Doughty, his wife and James Doughty, Jr. (VA Patent Bk. 6: 310 and Bk 7: 528) John Powell married Deborah, daughter of Henry Hearne.(VA 50-1) Henry Hearne of **Ingham** (Co. Suffolk, England) married Elizabeth Peak, of Ingham on 24Oct1665. It seems that part of the Herne family moved to **Cavenham,** Co. Suffolk, and the widow was buried in Ingham after her death. Interesting that Rebecca Page, of **Ingham**, married Henry Turner in May 1670.

The next transaction was in 1688 when Thomas Page was assigned title of land for persons being transported from "maybe England", but now suggests they were living in Stafford Co, Va and moved to Isle of Wight, Va. (source 137—Early Page Families by John Buford Page, who is Page Family C). Thomas and Alice Page were transported "to America prior to 1694", when in 1688 headrights (600 acres) were given to **George Harris**, d. 1719 (source: 173A, p. 82—Isle of Wight Co, Va—Wills and Administrations by Blanche Adams Chapman). Some of Thomas and Alis Page relatives, the Garrett family were also transported with them. The Page family settled in Perquimans District, (Thomas/Alis Page in Pequimans Dist, N.C. in 1659-see 560-181) which was part of Old Albermarle Co, NC. Land Records in Nanesmond Co, Va (1645-1671) show that the following land grants to Page names:

13Nov1713 John Page	—	123 acres (probably brother of Thomas Page)
16Dec1714 Thomas Page	—	284 acres (Thomas Page/Alice Garrett)
17Sep1731 Thomas Page	—	203 acres
2Aug1736 Thomas Page Jr.	—	285 acres

There appears in the (560-155) Virginia Land Patents, book 12; 189: the following Page's were transported to Va by Robert Clark, sometime before 22Feb1724—when Clark received a patent for 425 acres of land in Isle of Wight Co, Va.. Thomas Page, Alice Page, Thomas Page, Rebecca Page, Mary Page, John Page. There was a Robert Clark in Isle of Wight Co, Va during those years. Looks like two individuals, **George Harris** and Robert Clark "maybe" got paid twice for transporting the same Page family, which is not too uncommon. "Maybe" the Page family went back to Co. Suffolk, England on a visit, to take care of ESTATE affairs and this was the return trip?

There is a time period when Thomas Page and family seem to "disappear" from the records, during those critical years, so maybe shipping records out of Port of Bristol, England might confirm those dates and they actually went back to Co. Suffolk, England for business reasons. There was a lot of activity during this time, in this Page family around Bury, St. Edmunds, Co. Suffolk, England. Another option says they were living in Stafford Co, Va and moved to Isle of Wight, Va. Records do show that Thomas Page on **20Apr1682** was transported to Va by Captain Robert Caufield. (560-155A) and Thomas/Alis Page were recorded being in Perquimans Dist, NC in **1684**. (560-181)

To check on Virginia land grants and property transactions go to:
http://www.1va.lib.va.us/whatwehave/land/index.htm

Who was **George Harris?** William Harris (d.1697) was living in London with his wife Elizabeth (b.1629), when she sailed from England in late 1655 or early 1656. She left her husband William and baby in London, at the same time that Col. John Page, Gent, merchant from London sailed to Tidewater, Va and built a magnificent brick home outside of present-day Williamsburg, Va. John Page owned portions of several ships used in the tobacco trade with London, and Elizabeth "could" have sailed with those ships. Elizabeth Harris was a Quaker and **George Fox** (1624-1691), founder of the Quaker Society, had just written from his cell in Cornwall's Launceston Jail, "Let all nations hear the sound by word or writing. Spare not tongue or pen . . . be valiant for the truth." Elizabeth Harris was the messenger and arrived in Hampton Roads, Va. where she helped establish five Quaker groups along the western shore of Chesapeake Bay from Chuckatuck Meeting House up to Annapolis in Maryland. This Quaker movement was not well received by Virginia government and ordered that all Quakers be imprisoned till they depart the Colony. It is not clear what the relationship was between George and William Harris and Elizabeth, his wife. **George Fox** visited Virginia in 1672 on a missionary journey to North America and preached to Lower Norfolk County people at the Elizabeth River plantation of John Porter.(560-180, p. 2) Fox died in 1691 in London. Looking at Quaker records at **Chuckatuck Meeting House** reveals many of the same families from Walsham le Willows, England. (560-180A)

Research in Co. Suffolk, England finally revealed **ALICE GARRETT** and **ABRAM PAGE** living in **Lowestoft** (formerly Pagefield) in **1674**—which is a large port. Could this be the port the Garrett and Page family left for the Colonies. Take a look at the next County Norfolk, north of Co. Suffolk, reveals near the town of **Ipswich**, two Garrett's. They are Jacob, iron founder—Ipswich, one Samuel Garrett, a grocer in Botesdale and then one **William Garrett**, a butcher in **Woodbridge, Co. Suffolk**. Looking at hand written documents in the old English script, it is almost impossible to tell the difference between a Y and a G. It is believed Yarrett and Garrett is the same name.

In looking at land records in Isle of Wight Co, Virginia (created 1634) we find one William **Yarrett** granted 150 acres on 3Apr**1641**, upon the branch of the lower bay called Seawards Creek (Book 2, p. 96) This grant was apparently transferred to Thomas Brandwood of London, merchant, on 14May1646. It is possible that one or both of them were still in England, when the grant was made and transferred.

On 29Jul1650 (VA Patent Bk 2:216) William Yarrett & Francis Whittington, 580 acres on N. side of Rappa River, next above land of Robert Bird, 20 acres still due upon last name in certificate. (Cavaliers & Pioneers. Vol 1, p.191)

On 29Jul1650-18Jun1700 William Yorrett of Rappahannock Co, (later Richmond Co.) obtained 580 acres from Gov. Berkley. **Yorrett DIED**—Land Escheated. (Va North Neck Land Grants 1694-1742, Vol I. George W. Page believes Thomas Page, lived and may have been born in Old Rappahanock Co. (now Richmond Co.) where he met and married Alse (Alice) Yarrett (Garrett) (daug of above) before moving south into the Nansemond area. (SEE 560-155)

On 6Jun1657, William Yarrett was granted 500 acres beginning close to Goose Hill creek, and so down the said creek to Seawards Creek. In looking at Quaker documents from "Early Quaker Records in Virginia" (pp 1-64), the family William Yarrett (Elder) is as follows:

William Yarrett (Elder)		Dates are Quaker calendar
d. between 1679 and 1687.		need to be adjusted
Margaret, d. 1687		see 560-180B for details

Katherine	William (younger)	Elizabeth	Margaret
b.1Mar1651	b.5Sep1656	b.15Mar1658	b.1Dec1664
	d. 1676		

It is obvious that the above Thomas Page, bc.1640, **Hunston**, England had to arrive in Isle of Wight Co, Va before 1659 (because they both recorded as being in Perquimans Dist, N.C.in 1659) (560-181) and according to Page Family "verbal history" was married to Alice (Alis) Garrett/Yarrett—in the middle of the Atlantic by the Ship Captain—as they were en route to Virginia.

What has finally become apparent is there is "not a direct line of descent" between the Thomas Page, b.1640 that arrived in Isle of Wight, Va between 1659 (560-181) and 1680 down to ABRAHAM PAGE, that first appeared in Bertie Co, NC on 3Jan1740—as witness to a land sale involving David Jonijend (Jernigan) that appears to later marry Alice Page, b. 1740—daughter of ABRAHAM PAGE. Many "alledged" sons of this ABRAHAM PAGE

(Jesse, b.1742—David, b.1744—Joseph, b.1748—Solomon, b.1760—Thomas, b.1768 line moves from middle North Carolina to the Robeson Co, NC and Marion Co, SC area. All of the Y-DNA results have a solid paper trail from around 8 Page descendants back to ABRAHAM PAGE but there is NO "clear" link to the THOMAS PAGE line. It "appears" that the two family lines are closely related and "probably" connect back—one or two generations. More later on the ABRAHAM PAGE line.

It is also interesting that in 1678, one **ABRAHAM PAGE** was imported to Gloucester Co, Va by William Grimes who was awarded 450 acres (see NC 25-1) Later there was a Grimes/Page marriage.

Is this the ABRAHAM PAGE in North Carolina's father?—or just another trick to get more land awarded?

In **1674** (Hearth tax) (560-12) **ABRAHAM PAGE** (2 fireplaces) and **ALICE GARRETT** (3 fireplaces) were both living in **LOWESTOFT** (Mutford), Co. Suffolk, England. This is a seaport town. Members of the Thomas Page and Garrett family were traveling on the same ship that **GEORGE HARRIS**, d. 1719 was awarded 600 acres of land for transporting them. Property records never reveal where the ship left from, but they probably left from **Lowestoft** (formerly called Pagefield) which was a large English port—only that—they arrived in Virginia and 600 acres of land was awarded for this effort.

The name of the ship or the documents awarding **George Harris** 640 acres is still missing. In 1989 Jo Church Dickerson (Marion Co, SC) interviewed Susan (Page) Bryant, b.18Jan1911—who was in a nursing home in Marion Co, SC. She is from the Abraham Page/Joseph Page, b.1748 line) (see AJ1C chart) She relates Page Family history . . . . as Thomas Page was traveling from England to America—he met Alice Garrett traveling with her family on the boat and they fell in love and were **married by the Ship Captain** in Mid-Atlantic. She said all the Pages in Robeson and Marion/Dillon counties are descended from that marriage. (see 560-178)

Research has revealed that the following ABRAHAM PAGE (3) family has been discovered in County Essex, England and "seems" to be our missing father of 5 sons (Jesse, b.1742—David, b. 1744—Joseph, b. 1748, Solomon, b. 1760—Thomas, b. 1768 and 1 daughter Alice, b. 1740 in NC/SC of PAGE family "C" line. (see 560-179) CAROLINA PAGE's—AD1 for expanded family)

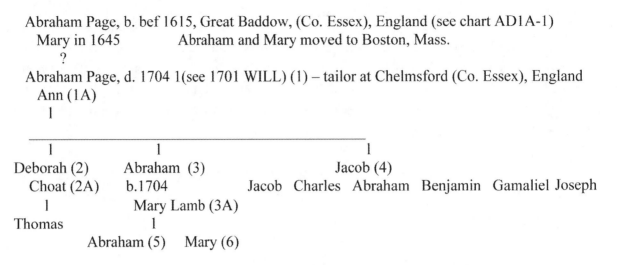

Abraham Page, b. bef 1615, Great Baddow, (Co. Essex), England (see chart AD1A-1)
  Mary in 1645   Abraham and Mary moved to Boston, Mass.
    ?

Abraham Page, d. 1704 1(see 1701 WILL) (1) – tailor at Chelmsford (Co. Essex), England
  Ann (1A)
    1

Deborah (2)   Abraham (3)   Jacob (4)
  Choat (2A)   b.1704   Jacob Charles Abraham Benjamin Gamaliel Joseph
    1   Mary Lamb (3A)
Thomas   1
        Abraham (5)   Mary (6)

1)   14Jul1695 Abraham Page imprisoned at Gaol at Chelmsford for in-arms against his Majesty's royal Father and Brother and had not given testimony of their sorrow for the Government sicne, and all such persons as preach commonly in conventicies at such meetings. He must remain in Gaol until he finds such sureties. (Essex Record Office-Session Rolls, 1685 (see 560-156)

1A)   1718 Anne Page (widow)WILL at Chelmsford, Co. Essex—242 BR 17.

2)   Deborah (Page) Choat, daug of Abraham Page was executor of **WILL** of Abraham Page, dated 22Sep1701.

3)   Abraham Page, b. 1704 (tailor of Halstead), Co. Suffolk, mar Mary Lamb (3A) on 3Oct1727 at **Grundisburgh**, Co. Suffolk (see 29) LDS IGI—this is the one that appears in Edgecombe Co, NC in 1740 (see NC 25) and later raises a family on the NC/SC border.

4)   Jacob Page, in **WILL** of 1701

5)   Abraham Page, b. 1730, **Copdock**, Co. Suffolk—christened in 1732 in Co. Suffolk, England.

6)   Mary Page, b. 1734, **Glemsford** (Suffolk), England.

26Sep1678—Abraham Page transported to Gloster Co, Va by John Collis, Book 6, p.190 (VA 4-2)

5Jun1678—Abraham Page transported to Gloster Co, Va by William Grimes, Book 6, p.185 of the Va Cavaliers and Pioneers, by Nell Nugent. This appears the same ship with 2 people getting credit for the transportation. Not uncommon.

See Chapter Two for more information on the search for ABRAHAM PAGE.

There is evidence that Thomas Page, in Isle of Wight Co, Va is probably related to the grocer Thomas Page (13A) in **North Walsham**, Co. Norfolk, England and it is interesting that William Garrett, might be a butcher in a nearby town.

There are many "Garrett's" in Co. Suffolk, England, according to 560-12, p.379, but no "Yarrett's". There are also Yarrett's (Garrett) in Rappahanock County, VA, during this time period but appears more a father William Yarrett in Va and a son William Garrett in England.

So now it is clear of the connections. Next is a timeline to show what happened.

14Feb1639 Thomas Page (30) Yeoman, (wife #2 Elizabeth), at **Hawstead**, Co. Suffolk dies and leaves **WILL** dated 15Jan1636/37. Thomas Page and Rebecca Page along with George Scarpe are witnesses. Abraham Page is in **Hawstead** (Co. Suffolk), during this time period.

1674 Suffolk Hearth Tax: **Layham**, Cosford, Co. Suffolk—George Scarpe family removed to Layham. Cosford, (Co. Suffolk) is a few miles south and east. Same village houses one Samuel **NEWTON** (see 560-155A) and **RATCLIFF**. These names show up with **THOMAS PAGE (THE TAILOR)** family as fellow Quakers—in the **Chuckattuck** records.

1674 Transported to Stafford Co, Virginia with Thomas Locke, Mary Newton and Thomas Page. Mary Newton is "maybe" the mother of Thomas Page, bc.1640's. (560-183) (see chart VA 54 & 560-155A).

1674—**Chattisham** (Co. Suffolk) Hearth tax—Abram Page living next to Thomas **Newton** (560-12)

1675-79 Thomas Page gets settled in "tailor" trade, "maybe" under supervision of his stepfather, Samuel **Newton**, who is an ardent Quaker. (this is questionable)

1682 Capt. Robert Caufield left property to Samuel Newton, Quaker, in his WILL.(560-155A)

Another family Harrison, is also mentioned, and maybe is the last name of Alice, might be that Harrison,—but doubtful—married Thomas Page, bc.1650 (15C). The Harrison family is seen in Walsham le Willows and sold a large pasture called "**Robbells**" to William Page (tailor) (23) in Walsham le Willows and also in Isle of Wight Co, Va. One William Harrison sold land to William Page, mentioned in 1624 **WILL**. John Harrison married William Bressie's sister Milboran Bressie. William Bressie left 2,000 pounds of tobacco to Thomas Page, (15C)—ye taylor—of Nasemond County, Va. There is a close association of many families from Co. Suffolk, England that associated together, or by marriage, in both Walsham le Willows and Isle of Wight Co, Va.

Interesting info but puzzeling is William Bressie & wife were guardians of two John Cary children (Miles Cary) prior to returning to England for a time. (560-155A) Captain Robert Caufield transported John Cary back to England.

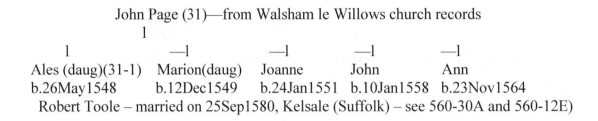

John Page (31)—from Walsham le Willows church records

Ales (daug)(31-1)	Marion(daug)	Joanne	John	Ann
b.26May1548	b.12Dec1549	b.24Jan1551	b.10Jan1558	b.23Nov1564

Robert Toole – married on 25Sep1580, Kelsale (Suffolk) – see 560-30A and 560-12E)

—

Richard Page (32)—from Walsham le Willows church records

Annys	Maryon	John	John	Susanna
b.11Jun1549	b.15Sep1551	b.2Jan1552	b.27May1576	b.9Feb1577

Thomas Page (34) **Hunston** – Co. Suffolk. (560-183B)

Robert Page (34A) (13)

34) 13Feb1552 and 25July1553, Thomas Page (6), Yeoman, of **Hunston** (2.7 miles north of Walsham le Willows) bought from Edward Brooke, of **Hunston**, 5 acres of land, meadow and pasture, parcel of **Hardings** in **Norton,** for total of 28 pounds.

31May1553, Quit claim from Mary Brooke of **Hunston**, Widow of Edward Brooke, to Robert Page, (34A) **Hunston**, Single man, of piece of 5 acres of ground in **Norton**, next to **Woolpit**, sold by Edward Brooke, Gent, late husband of the said Mary, to Thomas Page, father of Robert Page. (560-60A)

This Thomas Page (34) is probably Thomas Page (30A)(see page 46) and I have not added Robert Page (34A) as his son. But he is on page 46 as (30G)—mother was Wife #1 Susan.

20Sep1566 Letters of attorney from Edward Brooke to John Page, of **Hunston**, Yeoman, for delivery of documents. Not sure who this John Page might be.—probably (8D).

John Page (35) Will 7 Apr 1650 **Mundford, Co. Norfolk** (near seaport)
Rebecca Philpps

Anna Page	Robert Page	John Page
	Margaret	

Margaret

(35) Will John Page dated 7Apr1650—Proven on 9May1650. Wit: Richard Philpps Will mentions Ralph Derue?

The following family history data is from St. Leonard—Shoreditch Baptisms (1558-1640) located in **Hunston**, Co. Suffolk, England. They are probably related to Thomas Page (12) & Robert Page (13)

William Page (36) – Hunston—560-183B
1
—1—

Judith	William	William
b.30Mar1562	b.20Oct1566	b. 12Jan1603

Thomas Page (37)—Hunston—560-183B
1

Audy	Francis (son)
b.7Oct1559	b.28May1610

* * *

Salomon Page (38)—Hunston—560-183B
1
1

Margaret	Mary
b.1Nov1613	b.14Sep1617.

Edward Page (39)—Hunston—560-183B
Katherine
1

Anne	Elizabeth	George	Judith
b.18Jul1618	b.6Jan1635	b.24Nov1639	b.5Nov1637

Thomas Page – Gentleman (40)—same as Thomas as (30)
wife #1 Susan –b.?-d.13Sep1631—Hawstead (560-32)
wife #2 Mary Newton, b.1620 – mar: 1636 Hunston (560-159D)
wife #3 Elizabeth Frere, d.**23Feb1680** (30-1) mar: **7 March 1670**, Finningham
1
Elizabeth Page (41)
b.26Mar1672
d. 9Oct1740, Walsham le willows, buried St. Mary Church, Walsham le Willows
John Sparke, (41-1) Gentleman who married 21Apr1702, in Finningham
b.1675   (see 560-30A)
d.16Jan1745, both buried St. Mary Church, Walsham le Willows

Coat of Arms of the Sparke and Page families on this Crypt.

Crypt of Elizabeth (Page) Sparke and John Sparke

St. Mary Church in Walsham le Willows—rebuilt in 1441.

The "above" ground Elizabeth Page (41) coffin, is the "only one" in the large graveyard and next to the Church. Robert E. Page has PHOTO of the "only above ground" coffin and (rubbing by Robert Page IV of the Sparke and Page crest) at St. Mary's Church in Walsham le Willows. The photo and the rubbing of the crest showing the Sparke and Page crest will be provided at the end of this publication. The left side of the Coat of Arms is the Sparke family and the right side is the Page Coat of Arms. It would be interesting—if someone has access to Burke's General Armory—could see if the below Coat of Arms for this Walsham le Willow family will be shown.

Thanks to the **Walsham le Willows History Group** Brian Turner, Kenneth Stockton and Rob Barber for their assistance to Robert Page III and Robert Page IV taking pictures of the PAGE homes and St. Mary Church during our visit in August 2008.

WALSHAM le WILLOWS HISTORY GROUP (left to right)
Brian Turner—Kenneth Stockton—Robert Page—in rear is Rob Barber

To look at the PAGE family crest go to: www.houseofframes.com and type in the name Page.

There are 26 different (but almost the same) Coat of Arms for the many Page lines in the Burke's General Armory. They all seem to follow the following:

ARMS: or a fesse dancettee between three martlets azure within a boarder of the last.

Or, a chevron between three martlets sable.—on a gold field, a black chevron between three black martlets).

CREST: A DEMI-HORSE PER PALE DANCETTE OR AND AZURE. Arms: on a gold field, a blue bar with three points at the top and bottom between three blue martlets (birds), all within a blue border. Crest: The top half of the horse divided by a vertical jagged line, the left side gold and the right side blue.

John Sparke (42)
b.1717—d.29Oct1788
Elizabeth Nunn (42-1)
b.1717—d.19Jan1770

40) Thomas Page could be (15B) which would make him father of Thomas Page, b.1640, Hunston (15C) that returned to Isle of Wright, Va circa 1674 but before 1680. Thomas (15C) had daughter Mary, but no birth date is known and she went to Va with her father Thomas, and later married William Powell. (It is possible that Mary might be sister and not daughter. The Thomas Page, b. 1640 had a sister Mary, b. 1642) Next son, Thomas Jr and Alice (twins) both born 7Feb1680, Va. So Elizabeth, b. 1672 could fit into the time frame. There is a growing record of TWINs in this family. (see 560-183) for more information on Thomas Page (15)

This Thomas Page, d.17Aug1644 (15) (see 560-183) owned **Kembalds (later 4 Ashes House)** in Walshan le Willows (NOT **Rickinghall**), until his son Thomas Page, b.1611 (15B) turned 27, which was 1638. Interesting that one Thomas Page, b. 14Feb1639, died 3 days later and a twin sister Martha Page, died a few weeks later. Meanwhile—wife of father Thomas was Mary (15-1) who maintained the house. It **stayed in Page family until 1672**. Interesting the dates, about this family that was going to arrive in Isla of Wight, Va before 1680. (560p.105) (see 560-183) for more on this family.

THOMAS PAGE, d. 1672 (30) (40) Hunston
Mar:1636 Wife #2 Mary (maybe Newton) (560-183)

THOMAS (30A)	Mary (30F)	This Mary Page could be the one
b.**6Dec1640, Hunston**	b.15Jul1642	in Isle of Wight, Va (VA 50)
d.1719,Isle of Wight, Va(VA 50)		that married William Powell.

Adam Page (43)—Hunston—(560-159D)
Ann Lister

Mary	Thomas	John	Barbara	Agnes	Alice	Edmond	John	William	Francis
b.30Jul	24Oct	25Mar	30Mar	26Sep	15Oct	11Oct	6Aug	6Aug	13Oct
1564	1568	1571	1572	1574	1575	1577	1581	1581	1582

Thomas Page (40)—Hunston—(560-159D)

Nath	Sarah	Thomas
b.30Jul1586	b.14Apr1588	b.16Jul1592

John Page – Hunston – (560-159D)

Lawrence Page (27) (page 41) Hunston (560-159D)
Ann

Hannah	Mary	Lydia	Elizabeth	John
b.24Feb	b.9Feb	b.21Oct	b.23Aug	b.28Aug
1594	1596	1599	1601	1603

It was first speculated that Thomas Page and wife Alice (Alis) Garrett (Yarrett) and the Garrett family "might" have been living in northern Virginia (Stafford Co) and just moved (by ship) south to the Isle of Wight, Va area (to get land awarded for transportation of immigrants)—AND DID NOT TRAVEL FROM ENGLAND—as we had long believed. This has proven to be wrong.

Christopher (Ark) Page cspage@cox.net believes that wife of Thomas Page (15C) is Alice Harrison. I favor Alice Garrett. (see 560-181) is clearly showing Thomas and Alis were already married when they were recorded in 1659 in Perquimans Dist, N.C. (560-181) The father of Chris (Ark) Page—Bobby W. Page agrees that the wife of this Thomas Page is Alice Garrett. (560-181C)

The Quakers church meeting place was at Chuckatuck—Nansemond Monthly Meeting which began just prior to 1672, and met at Thomas Jordan house. The first known meeting house in Nansemond, Va was in December 1674 when Henry Wiggs and Katheren Garret (Yarret) (daughter of William Yarratt were married. (560-180, p. 1)(560-180A, p. 5)

24July1645, Mr. Michael Masers received 413 acres for transporting 9 people to Virginia. One of these was a Thomas Page. Twelve acres—of this 413, was next to Samuel Jordan (173A, p.268/284), the father of Thomas Jordan, (173A, p.40) of the Quaker group in Isle of Wight, Va.

There was a Thomas Page (15), that died 1644, **Walsham** le Willows, that had son #1—John Page, Gent (15A), d.1667 married to Ann (15A-1) and son #2—Thomas Page (15B) (30A) it is believed, this is the Thomas Page (15B), that fathered Thomas Page (30A-1), born b.1640, **Hunston**, England—that later married Alice Garrett, who was born about the same time, but probably in England—not Virginia.

1659   Thomas Page and Mrs. Alis Page recorded in Perquimans Dist, N.C. (560-181)(VA 50)
20Feb1662 Thomas Page granted 600 acres on s. side Rappa River, Va next to Howell Powell
    (137)
1663   Thomas Page and Mrs Alis Page recorded in Perquimans Dist of N.C. (560-181)
1684   Thomas Page and Mrs Alis Page recorded in Perquimans Dist of N.C. (560-181)
    See VA 50 for more land grants for Thomas/Alis Page

1652 Thomas Page (30A), bought **BROOK FARM COTTAGE (560, p 16)**(old name "Cooks"), **Walsham** le Willows and then his son John Page, d.1669, **Walsham** (15A) owned it from 1656 (occupied by John Rice—until he died in **1672)**, and it went to relative John Page, b.7Aug1636 (20-1)(26A)(30D) of **Hopton**, who passed it on to James Hawes in 1672. (info: 560, p.16). It is also interesting that in the 1817 **Walsham** le Willows Parish map of #

199, it reveals that **John Sparke** (42) was the owner, but the occupant was Edmund Sills and Robert Hawes.

1672 the Page residence **KEMBALDS (LATER 4 ASHES HOUSE)** in **Walsham** le Willows (not Rickinghall), was owned by Richard Page in 1446 to 1454 and then the Page family from 1509 until year **1672**, when Elizah Davy and Robert Harding shared the residence—which was the year 1672 Thomas Page's (15B) daughter Elizabeth Page (41), was born, who in 1702, married John Sparke (41-1), in St. Mary Church, **Walsham** le Willows, and both are buried at St. Mary church and I have pictures of the largest cript in the cemetery. (see 560, p. 106 for the long history of the Page family Line "C"). See my charts AD 1—T1 & VA 50 for Mary Page, that marries William Powell, b. 1768-d.1734, Isle of Wight, Va. They were married 14Feb1700, Isle of Wight, Va. It is believed that this above Elizabeth Page (41) that married John Sparke (41-1), in **Walsham** le Willows, where both lived and died and are buried in the church cemetery. Have pictures of cript with the PAGE Coat of Arms. I was always puzzeled by the absence of much information after this marriage.

In **1677** John Page, son of John Page (15A) resumed ownership until 1695, when it went to Francis Asty. (560, p.106)

It is noted that on **29Apr1682** Captain Robert Caufield, Surry Co, Va was granted 2250 acres in Surry Co, Va (next county from Isle of Wight) for transporting 26 persons, one of which was Thomas Page, (maybe Hawstead) with Thomas Lock, & Mary Newton. Thomas Page/Alice Garrett, (see VA 50 & T1), had daughter Rebecca born 8Nov**1682**, Isle of Wight, Va that later married Thomas Gay in1699. Was Thomas Page in **1682** returning from a trip to County Suffolk, England? Answer "probably yes". (see below 560-155A & my source 483)

In the year 1659 (OR before) Thomas/Alis Page were transported to America when headrights (600 acres) were given to George Harris (d.1719) in 1694 (173A, p.82) The Garrett family was among the passengers. The Pages settled in Perquimans Dist, NC which was part of the Old Albermarle Co, NC (137) This location is on the Va/NC border, next to Nanesmond Co, Va.

1674 (Plague year) Thomas Page (30A) (also 15B) was transported to to Va by Capt Robert Caulfield, along with daughter Mary, (30F) and husband Thomas Locke (30F-1) (they had married on 11Jun1635 in **Hawstead**, Co. Suffolk) and arrived in Stafford Co, Va.(see VA 8 & 8-1)

On **2Feb1682**, Thomas Page was granted 600 acres of land on s. side of Rappahannock river next to Howell Powell (source 314) (VA 50) One John Page had been granted 281 acres of land on s. side of Rappa River for transporting six persons on **21Apr1657** (Thomas Page from London (on Thames River port of Deptford, near Woolwich, Co. Kent). Thomas Page and Alis his wife was reported in Perquimans Co, N.C. in **1658, 1663 & 1684**.

The year 1657, is the year (another) Thomas Page, b. 1638 (30A) graduated from public school at Bury St. Edmunds, and got his B.A. degree in 1661 from Magdalene college, so this is NOT the one that caught the boat from London in 1657 and recorded in Perquimans Co, NC.

There was a Thomas Page in **1688** granted 290 acres of land in Surry Co, Va, which is probably Thomas (30A-1) married to Alice (Alis) Garrett. (30A-2) This info came from VA Cavaliers & Pioneers, Vol 2. (560-155A)

Many more baptisms at Walsham le Willows, from St. Mary's church records are listed in ENG 10-1A. I was not able to make family connections—except with a few of them. All towns listed in ENG 10-1 and ENG 10-1A are also found in my "Index of Towns" focused on mainly Co. Suffolk, England, but does contain some of the other Page families, and shows the large concentration of many PAGE lines in this part of England. If you would like a copy of the INDEX or ENG 10-1A—let me know.

CHAPTER TWO

APPENDIX A—TO ENG 10-1 AS OF 1 DECEMBER 2012

Chart ABE 1—(3 pages)—23 Apr 1990—A collection of names ABRAHAM PAGE—hoping to later indentify which is my ABRAHAM PAGE—that is the oldest ancestor of my Page Line "C".

Listing of all ABRAHAM PAGE Inforation   ABE1   23 Apr 90

81)p.1606   1620-1650   ABRAHAM PAGE - Boston, Mass   - Immigration List
23)

141)   1628   ABRAHAM PAGE - bricklayer - Gt Baddow - Will #110 BW 49   - Wills at Chelmsford,Essex, England(p. 262)

98) 25Aug1636   ABRAHAM PAGE, a tailor, had a bond from William Vincent for 20 pounds, when 21 years
100)   from Great Baddow, Essex, England-gave letter of atty 23Oct1645-wife Mary
          (see Colonel Records 1638) - from Pioneers of Mass.

38)p.347 1645   ABRAHAM PAGE, a tailor from Baddow Magna, Essex, England emmigrated to Boston, Mass.
23)(82,p300)   His wife was Mary of Braintree church; had son, Abraham b. 7Mar1646, Boston but died
100)   same month. They moved to ?

29) 27Feb1648 ABRAHAM PAGE born   JOHN PAGE/Elizabeth Gile   Haverfield, England

29) 27Dec1648 ABRAHAM PAGE born   JOHN PAGE/   Essex, Haverfield, England

30)p.215 1665   ABRAHAM PAIGE   - Boston

129) 1674   ABRAHAM PAGE - imported - Gloster Co, Va - by William Grimes

TRANSPORTED means someone other than the person indexed paid for his passage
IMMIGRATED means individual furnished his own transportation to Maryland

129)   1678 ABRAHAM PAGE - imported Gloster Co, Va by John Colles

29) 29Oct1683 ABRAHAM PAGE christened - Father was Abraham Page - Salford, England

29) 18 Mar 1699 ABRAHAM PAGE christened Par: Abraham Page/Elizabeth Page - Surry-Morton, England

141)   1704   ABRAHAM PAGE - tailor at Halstead, England - Will 50 OR 15-Wills at Chelmsford,
          Essex Eng. P. 262

29) 25 Oct 1708 ABRAHAM PAGE christened - FA: Robert Page - Mavendon, England

29) 26 Nov 1709 ABRAHAM PAGE mar Anne Salisbury - Derby Church, Gresley, England

29) 18Oct1710   ABRAHAM PAGE was christened in Morston Parish (Moretaine), England, father was Abraham Page

29) 3Oct1727 ABRAHAM PAGE Mar Mary Lamb - Suffolk Co, Grundisburgh, England

29) 30May1730 ABRAHAM PAGE - christened - Abraham & Mary Page - Copdock, England

29) 30Jun1732 ABRAHAM PAGE - christened - Par: Abraham & Mary Page - Suffolk, Glemsford, England

29) 30Sep1734 ABRAHAM PAGE had a son that was christened at Barton in the Clay, England, wife was Mary Page

29) 13Oct1734 ABRAHAM PAGE mar Mary Kirby, in Bedford, Barton in the Clay, England

72)p. 1735   ABRAHAM PAGE mar Mary Kirby,

29) 30 Sep 1739 ABRAHAM PAGE born - Par: Abraham & Mary - Barton in the Clay, England

129) 3Jan1740 Land sale John Butler to James Manney - ABRAHAM PAGE - wit: to land sale : Bertie Co, NC
          270 acres on SS Indian Creek, adj Richard Holland. now in possession of David Jon?jond at
          "Godfrey Lees Great Branch" - part of tract granted to Godfrey Lee - wit: David Jon?jond, Jurat,
          ABRAHAM PAGE - May Court 1741 - Benjamin Hill? c/c - Bertie Co. Deeds - Vol IV

69)   1741 ABRAHAM PAGE, of Grantchester,(Cambridgeshire), England was a bonded passenger (prisoner)
          to America for stealing ducks

157) 20Dec1743 ABRAHAM PAGE wit sale of 100 a, on n. side of Maherin River from John Barnes to Lydia Barnes in
          Northhampton Co, NC. wit: David Jornagen, James Maney & ABRAHAM PAGE

Continuation sheet for infomation on ABRAHAM PAGE   ABE2 23 Apr 90

2 Apr 1761   ABRAHAM PAGE #135   Dobbs Co, NC 150 acres File #0106 (see 28Apr1768,Henry Page)
                150 acres on N.side of Neuse River, adjoining George Roberts. Surveyed 8 Nov 1761
                (N.C. archives cannot find - no surviving Dobbs Co. Wills either)

25) 25 Apr 1767 Crown grant to William Whitfield, 145 acres on s. side of Nuce River, including a bend
                of Nuce river and the improvements where ABRAHAM PAGE lived. Dobbs Co, NC Book 23-956A, p.

28 Apr 1768 3606 Dobbs Co, NC   100 acres   To HENRY PAGE   File #0107 land between Little river
                and Neuse river acres on Charles branch, adjoining Arthur Coor & Thomas Page.(see 2Apr1761,
                Abraham Page) surveyed 4Apr1768, entry 3606, 28Apr1768, land lays in part of Dobbs Co that
                became Wayne Co in 1799 Little river empties into Neuse river in Wayne Co, just west of
                Goldsboro, NC

16 Feb 1768 #932 Dobbs Co, NC 286 acres,to THOMAS PAGE on s.side of Little River of Neuse.
                This land lays in that part of Dobbs Co that became Wayne Co in 1779, Little river empties
                into Neuse river in Wayne, just W. of Goldsboro NC, co seat of Wayne Co, NC, adjoins
                Thomas Jernigan and Thomas Coar

31)   1789   THOMAS PAGE AND SON HENRY PAGE (negros Dick, Nan, Pat) Dobbs Co, NC   tax list shows
                Lived next to ABRAHAM PAGE

30)   1771   DAVID PAGE OF S.C. TO WILL CLYBURN, planter,Bladen Co, NC(formerly New Hanover) deed dtd 8Sep1774
60)p.779   10 lbs on s.w. side of Ashpole swamp, upper part of 300 acres, Book 37, p. 146
                patent dated 29Nov1771, proved Nov 1774, wit: Richard Grantham, James Grantham

32) 18Apr1771 Crown to DAVID PAGE book 20, page 680 Bladen Co   300 acres s.w. of Tadpole Swamp
                adjoining Alligator swamp near Providence line

129)   1773   ABRAHAM PAGE - wit: to deed - Edgecombe Co, NC - Thomas Wells to Ephraim Lawrence

49) 26 Feb 1776 ABRAHAM, WILLIAM & JOHN PAGE of Dobbs Co, NC Militia Regiment fought at Battle of Moores Creek
                Bridge under Capt Thomas Williams Company. They fought both at the Bridge for 36 days and also
the expedition to the lower Cape Fear for 22 days. New England began the battle for freedom at a bridge at Concord
- the South had its first revolutionary test of arms at a bridge over Widow Moore's creek in the NC swamps. The
fighting only lasted some 3 minutes and ended in a rout of forces loyal to King George III. It lacked the patriotic
impact of Concord on Bunker Hill but the victory by NC militia & minutemen disrupted British plans for a military
takeover of the Southern Colonies.

60)p.366 20Jul1778 ABRAHAM PAGE, Pvt, Bradley's Co, enlisted for 9 months
NC (HIST Archives says ABRAHAM PAGE (ID #1500) Pvt Bradley's Co, 10th Reg, NC Continental (1776-1783), p. 130.
of enlistment 20 Jul 1778, 9 months, died 26 Sep 1778, period of service was 2 months Register prepared at
Philadelphis, Pa 28 Jul 1781. Soldiers who died during service were treated as if he served full length of service
during 1776-1783 and heirs were entitled to one square mile of property. This ABRAHAM PAGE was from Caswell Co, NC
not Robeson Co, NC says NC archives.

60)p.366 26Sep1778 ABRAHAM PAGE died, while in Rev Army - do not know where   (see M42 for more info)

60)p.675 5 Aug 1783 Bladen Co NC court, judgement against ABRAHAM PAGE & JOSEPH PAGE in favor of David Shipman awarded
see M21   67 acres on Ashpole Swamp at Holly branch. This property was bought at public sale on 3 May 1783
                Daniel Shipman) see p. 161 of Loyalist in NC for more info

60)p.677 19 Aug 1783 David Shipman sold his claim for 67 acres of Bladen Co. judgement to Lucy Ellis

60)p.750 20Jan1785 ABRAHAM PAGE Heirs - 640 acres in Tenn (Military Land Grant) given to Heir - WILLIAM PAGE)
                - Capt Tillmon Dixon received warrent.

* 20May1793 ABRAHAM PAGE (ID #1500) Book 81, p. 160 Sumner Co, Tenn 640 Acres land grant (military)
75)p.323   (assigned to Nancy Sheppard by WILLIAM PAGE, heir) (see M41)

160) 8 Nov 1795 Benjamin Wilkinson, Sr, Pitt Co, NC sold to William Wilkerson -
                One negro for 20 pounds - wit: ABRAHAM PAGE, JOHN PAGE

      1810   ABRAHAM PAGE, Barnwell Dist, SC, Fed Census

60)p.192 5Dec1811 JOSEPH PAGE *** ESTATE *** Sampson Co, NC
see P81   brothers: ABRAHAM PAGE, DEMPSEY PAGE and Joseph Lee of S.C. sold to
                John Johnson of NC some land in Sampson Co, NC

Continuation sheet for information about ABRAHAM PAGE   ABE3 23 Apr 90

* 13 Jan 1813 ABRAHAM PAGE SC state plat, Barnwell District, SC - 244 acres on Reedy Fork of
              Garrow branch waters, So. So. Edisto River

* 1 Feb 1813 ABRAHAM PAGE SC State Grant, vol 57, p. 347 Barnwell Dist
              224 acres Reedy fork of Garrow branch waters , So. Edisto river

61) *2 Mar 1818   Marion Co,S.C Wills of JOSEPH PAGE (SR) vol 1, book 1, p. 124(114)
                   mentions Daugs, Elizabeth Floyd, Delilah Floyd, Ann Herring, Susannah Page(youngest girl)
                   sons, Abraham(oldest boy), John, Elias(youngest boy)
                   wit: Edmond Price, Delilah Price

90) 24 Mar 1818   ABRAHAM PAGE sold to John Grainger/Charity Buffkin - 827 a. in Horry Dist, SC
156)   N.E. side of Drowning Creek - must pay by 1 Jan 1820
                  wit: Benjamin Buffkin, Goldsberry Grainger - signed 5 Sep 1818
                  (see Page Bible Record - Goldsberry is son of John & Charity Page)
                  (book C1, p. 68)

       1820 ABRAHAM PAGE - Barnwell Co, SC -   federal census   1-1-1-0-2

90)   1821   ABRAHAM P. PAGE - Probate - Marion Co, SC - Administrator was
               William Hill who got most of $2560 estate

*19 Mar 1821 **** WILL **** - ABRAHAM PAGE (son of David Jr) Robeson Co,NC
                   mentions: William Hill, Lewis Jones, Seria Ayers

       1830 ABRAHAM PAGE   Barnwell Co, SC - owns land

*16Sep 1845 WILL of ABRAHAM PAGE, Barnwell Dist, SC, vol 2, p. 119-120
             mentions: wife Sarah Page, eldest son, William, sons- Jacob 2nd, Matthew Page, Abraham, Joshua
588   Daugs-Selah Stringfield, Eliza Rabb, Narcissa, Matilda, Mary
801   witnesses: Isaac Williams, Joel McLemore, Benjamin Williams

54) 28 Sep 1846   ABRAHAM PAGE - Robeson Co, NC (Alice Page v. Averit Nichols, Admin of Abraham Page estate)
                   Balance due against Averit Nichols of £85. Sale of negro's at issue.

58) 23Sep1852 ABRAM PAGE mar Sarah Ann Rackley

Chart VA 50—15 Jan 1992—(4 pages) produced on the Thomas Page, b. 1640, Hunston (Co. Suffolk), England that arrived in Virginia/North Carolina in 1659 with wife Alis Garrett from information gathered from Robert Davidson and Jesse Page, author of (60) "Page Family in North Carolina", and publication (314) The Powell Families of Va and the South by Reverend Silas Emmett Lucas, Jr.

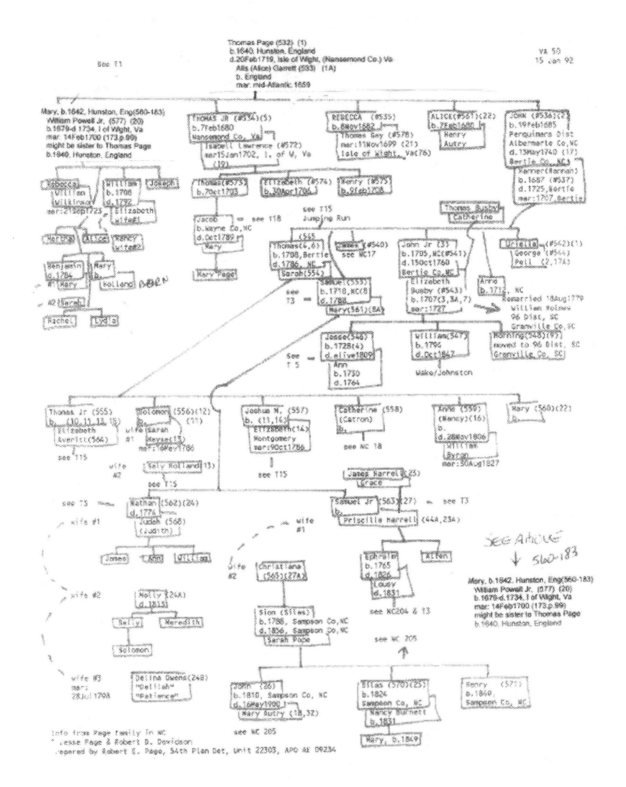

2 of 4

First Page to VA50 15 Jan 92
1) 2Feb1688 THOMAS PAGE granted 600 acres on s. side of Rappe. River in Va, next to Howell Powell - from (314)
    1688   THOMAS PAGE, Nansemond Co, Va - assigned title of land for persons being transported from England - see
              (137)
    13Sep1688 THOMAS PAGE, Isle of Wight Co, Va got land from Henry & Elizabeth Hearne. see (129)
    10Jan1692 THOMAS PAGE was wit: to mar of John Persons/Mary Patredg at home of Thomas Tooke.
    11Apr1692 THOMAS PAGE and Alis PAGE was wit: to mar of John Denson/Mary Brydell at brides parents home Francis & Mary
              Brydell.(137)
    14Oct1699 THOMAS PAGE was wit: to mar of Jacob Rickesis/Mary Exum at Public House in Chuckatuck. (137)
    11Nov1699 Thomas Gay, husband of REBECCA PAGE, daug of THOMAS PAGE, Isle of Wight Co, Va gave land to REBECCA PAGE.
              Thomas Gay was son of Jeane Lawrence of Isle of Wight Co, Va.   (129)
    18JUL1700 THOMAS PAGE was wit: to mar of Richard Rattcliff Jr/Elizabeth Hollowell at parents house, Richard/Elizabeth
              Rattcliff. (137)p.23
    9Jun1701   THOMAS PAGE, a tailor, Nansemond Co, Va was mentioned in WILL of William Brasie (Quaker?) - (129)
    11Mar1700 THOMAS PAGE land grant for 144 acres on s. side of Chowan River & Notaway River. SEE NC 20
    15Jan1702 THOMAS PAGE (534), son of THOMAS PAGE (532) of Nansemond Co, Va mar Isabelle Lawrence (572), daug of Henry
              Lawrence & sister to Michalle & Thomas Lawrence. see (129), & (137)p.23.
    25Feb1703 THOMAS PAGE, Isle of Wight Co, Va bought land from Frank Alsbury of Nansemond Co, Va - 170 acres on Currowagh
              Swamp adjoining Robert Carr & Thomas Marnk - wit: William & Mary Parker, J. Gay. - see (129)
    9Oct1705   THOMAS PAGE, I. of Wight Co, Va express regret "For being a subscriber for Thomas Sikes Cert of Mar."
              see (137)p.23.   *1704 Thomas Page -owns 103 Acres- Rent Roll*
    9Jun1708   THOMAS PAGE/Alis sold to William Powell 170 acres on Currawaugh Swamp, I of W. Son, William Powell was
  executor- for more info on Powell family - see (314)

    16Dec1714 THOMAS PAGE purchased property in Surry Co, Va & later 284 acres in Nausemond Co, Va near NC line but later
              returned to Isle of Wight Co, Va
1A) 20Feb1719 ** WILL ** of THOMAS PAGE(532), wife was Alice (533) - see (129)
    1720   THOMAS PAGE - Craven Co, NC - no TWP
    1720   THOMAS PAGE (532) Died, Isle of Wight Co, Va - his wife was Alis.   see (65)
    1720   THOMAS PAGE (532) ** WILL ** Isle of Wight Co, Va - son JOHN PAGE (536) appointed executor. see (137)p.24.

2) 19Feb1685 JOHN PAGE, Perquimans Precinct, born to THOMAS PAIGE & ALIS, his wife - see (60)p.1.
    1715   JOHN PAGE/Hanner migrated to Albermarle Region, NC after Tuscarrora War of 1715 (163)
    11Apr1720 JOHN PAGE (536), Albermarle Co, NC in Capt Robert Patterson's Company visiting Moherin Creek to Mohering River.
    11Apr1720 JOHN PAGE (536) was member of Capt Robert Patterson's Co. (85 men) explored up Maherin Creek to Mahering River
              in N.C. - providing military protection from Indians and this was later known as Roanoke River region.
              - see (40)(60,p.1)(129) & (137).
    1721   JOHN PAGE - Albermarle Co, NC Tax Roll - 300 acres - (129)
    13Jul1722 JOHN PAGE received 320 acres from Thomas/Catherine Busbee on n. side of Morrattok River on Jumping Run.
              wit: Geo Williams & Thomas Brown - (43) & (60)p.1
    26Mar1723 JOHN PAGE received grant for 320 acres, Bertie Co, NC on n. side of Mahering River at Horse Pasture Creek.
    9Feb1728   JOHN PAGE bought from Henry Rhodes 160 acres Bertie Co, on Cashie Swamp on Busbees line. (60)p.5
              Wit: Peter Cone & Richard Mackling
    9Nov1725   JOHN PAGE (536) & HANNAH (537) sold to Samuel Garland 320 acres - Bertie Co - wit: Thomas Busby, Nedham Bryan
              & Portia Thomas (60)p.3
    29Sept1729 JOHN PAGE Albermarle Co, NC - paid suit rent on 520 acres - (10)
    30Oct1730 JOHN PAGE & Joshua Platt were witness to ** WILL ** of Louis Thomas - Craven Co, NC
    1737   JOHN PAGE - land sale - Bertie Co, NC (9)
    13May1740 ** WILL ** of JOHN PAGE (541) proved - Bertie Co, NC mentions: Samuel (553) & Thomas Page (543). (60)p.7 (93)
    20Jul1740 JOHN PAGE ** ESTATE ** inventory taken - submitted by Uriella (Page) Pell on 6Nov1741 - (60)p.7
    3 May1741 ** WILL ** OF JOHN PAGE (536) Bertie Co, NC - wit: SAMUEL (553), THOMAS (545) & UREILLA PELL (542). (60)p.7
2) 11Aug1742 George Pell gave 500 pds for bond for JOHN PAGE ESTATE.
    19May1748 JOHN PAGE (541) bought from State of NC 300 acres on n. side of Little River, Johnston Co, NC near Robert
              Raifords (see footnote 288) line and THOMAS PAGE line.
    10Oct1748 JOHN PAGE grant of 100 acres on n. side of Little River near Robert Raiford line & THOMAS PAGE
              corner. (60)p.100.
2) Nov 1750 JOHN PAGE/Hannah acknowledges deed to Richard Wilborn - Goochland Co, Va
2) 6Aug1728 JOHN PAGE JR, Bertie Co, NC received from Thomas Busby, his f/law, 170 acres on e. side of Cashie Swamp.
3) 1727   JOHN PAGE mar Elizabeth Busby - all children Jesse, William & Morning born in Bertie Co, NC
    6Apr1728   JOHN PAGE JR received gift of 170 acres on Cashie Swamp from Thomas Busby, his father in law. (60)p.5
3) 11Feb1754 JOHN PAGE sold to THOMAS PAGE 100 acres on Jumping Run wit: Frank Searsin & Edward Hawkins.
3A) 6Nov1758 ELIZABETH PAGE, (543) Adm of JOHN PAGE ** ESTATE ** (541) appointed guardian to WILLIAM & MORNING PAGE.
3) MAY1764   JOHN PAGE ** ESTATE ** court orders William Holmes, new husband of ELIZABETH PAGE, to give security for his
              admin of the JOHN PAGE ESTATE .

3A) 18Aug1779 ELIZABETH PAGE (543), wife of JOHN PAGE (541) & mother of MORNING PAGE (548)remarried William Holmes of 96
              Dist, SC.

See second page of three pages to VA 50

Second Page of 3 pages to VA 50   15 Jan 92

4)   1738   JESSE PAGE in WILL of Catherine Bunby for 1 cow and calf - lives Bertie Precinct on n. side of Roanoake River.
                 source of info - (12) & (60)p.6.
4)   1Dec1762   JESSE PAGE (546) granted 517 acres in Johnston Co, NC on Black Creek (60)p. 101
4)   17Jan1764   JESSE PAGE/Ann sold 100 acres on Black Creek in Johnson Co, NC to William Smith Sr.wit: Look Tanner, Francis
                 Payne (60)p.102
4)   26May1798   JESSE PAGE (546), Wake Co, NC sells to THOMAS PAGE, Johnston Co, NC 200 acres on Great Branch at Johnston/Wake
                 county line. wit: Mark & Aerill Myatt. (60)p.118
     30Jan1795   JESSE PAGE sold to JOHN PAGE 100 acres on Mollys Branch Johnston Co, wit: Mark Myatt, John Powell

     1734   THOMAS PAGE - ferry from w. side of Blackwater to THOMAS PAGE place established.   (10) & (60)p.358
     1737   THOMAS PAGE - land sale - Bertie Co, NC (9)
5)   11Mar1740   THOMAS PAGE land grant 144 acres on s. side of Chowan River & Nothaway River - see (41)
                 wit: JCL Danil, SAM PAGE, THOMAS PAGE
5)   1741   THOMAS PAGE (534) of Roanoka, records his mark. - (60)p.7.
     1741   THOMAS PAGE petition for land - Edenton, Wilmington, New Bern - Dobbs and later was Wayne Co. see (10)
     21May1741   THOMAS PAGE Sr - owned 200 acres in Craven-then Dobbs-then Wayne (60)p.97
     4Aug1741   THOMAS PAGE Sr - owns 300 acres on n. side of Little River - 3 miles below Robert Raiford. (60)p.97
                 For info on Raiford Family - see (288)
     1742   George Pell failed to give bond money so THOMAS PAGE gave bond & is to take possession of land. (60)p.8.
5)   12Aug1742   THOMAS PAGE (534) appointed guardian to orphans of JOHN PAGE (60)P.8
     AUG 1743   THOMAS PAGE sold something to Nathan Rowland.
     1751   THOMAS PAGE sold to Robert Butler(Butter) - Dobbs Co
6)   8Sep1753   THOMAS PAGE(545)/Sarah (564)sold 100 acres in Bertie Co, NC   (60)p.10
     8Sep1753   THOMAS PAGE sold to Aaron Elis 200 acres of the 526 acres granted in Jun 1753.
                 wit: Jas Abington, Micajah Ninton, Needham Bryan.
                 THOMAS PAGE - same one owned land in Craven-Dobbs-Wayne-Johnston Co, NC
     3May1760   THOMAS PAGE land grant for 200 acres on e. side on Great Cohera Swamp on Beaverdam.
     22Dec1768   THOMAS PAGE land grant for 200 acres between Great & Little Cohera on both sides of Bearskin Swamp below
                 Berry's Path.
     17Apr1772   THOMAS PAGE (Duplin Co,NC) sold land to John Sampson - (60)p......
     8Jun1779   Capt THOMAS PAGE - Duplin Regiment of Militia - Col James Kenen - total troops of 54.
6)   6Aug1785   *** WILL *** OF THOMAS PAGE SR(545), Bertie Co,NC - mentions wife Sarah(564), Solomon(556),Joshua(557),
                 Catherine(558), Mary(560) - Bertie Co, NC (60)p.28.

7)   15Oct1760   ELIZABETH (Bunby) PAGE (543) appointed guardian of WILLIAM and MORNING PAGE (60)p.14

8)   6Oct1750   SAMUEL PAGE (553) sold to Edward Harrell, Bertie Co, 330 acres on Cashey Swamp. Wit: THOMAS PAGE & John
                 Harrell (60)p.9
8A) 1792   MARY PAGE (561), Bertie Co, NC, widow of SAMUEL PAGE (553), due dower - Cashy Swamp
8A) 1792   MOLLY (must be Mary,561) PAGE, widow of SAMUEL PAGE (553)that died several years ago without a Will - due
                 dower on 170 acres from her land in Cashy Swamp. James Wood is on her land.(60)p.37
8A) 18Jul1795   MARY PAGE (561) sold to William Ninton, Gates Co, NC 31 acres on Jumping Run, next to Henry Averits land.
                 Wit: Edward Acree, Geo Morriss, Henry Averet.(60).p 39

9)   18Aug1778   MORNING PAGE (548), Granville Co, SC sold to her brother THOMAS PAGE 200 acres Bertie Co, NC   (60)p.21
10) 30Sep1778   THOMAS PAGE (555) mar Elizabeth Averitt (564), Bertie Co, NC   (60)p.21   wit: George Wair
11) 2ONov1786   THOMAS, SOLOMON & JOSHUA PAGE sold to Edward Acree 2 tracts on Jumping Run (1) 31 a. (2) 20 acres. Wit: John
                 Acree, Josiah Carney, Thomas Davidson.
12) 22Apr1786   SOLOMON PAGE bought from Edward Aires 172 acres in Bertie Co, NC (60)p.30 -
                 wit: JOSHUA PAGE (557) & George Williams - Land next to THOMAS PAGE SR (545)   (60)p.30
13) 16May1786   SOLOMON PAGE (556) mar Sarah Wayse - Bertie Co, NC wit: John Dodrill, bondsmen, wit: Thomas Ruyen
                 Butler, (60)p.30
13) 1815   See Will of Joshia Mayse, Bertie Co, NC
     20Apr1830   SOLOMON PAGE mar Saly Holland - Bertie Co, NC - JOSHUA M. PAGE, bondsman

14) 9Oct1786   JOSHUA PAGE (557) mar Elizabeth Montgomery - Bertie Co, NC wit: Jesse Bryan, Bondsman (60)p.32
16) 25Aug1796   ANN (NANCY) PAGE (559) (Father was THOMAS PAGE) sold to William Hodges, wit: John H. King, Jesse Hodges, James
                 Pierce - 200 acres Bertie Co, NC (60)p.40
16) 28Nov1806   ANN (NANCY) PAGE (559) DEATH - Bertie Co, NC
16A)   MARY PAGE named Administrator (60)p.42
17) 13May1742   ** ESTATE ** of JOHN PAGE (536)- George Pell summoned to court in Bertie Co, NC to post bond (60)p.8
17A) 12Aug1742   **ESTATE OF JOHN PAGE ** George Pell failed to post bond (60)p.8
18) 22Aug1847   ESTATE OF Starling Autry - Mary Autry (Sampson Co, NC heir of Starling Autry, some mentioned : JOHN PAGE,
                 John & Jane Autry, Sewell & Charity Sessoms, MARY PAGE, in bad health & unable to appear in court. (60)p.220
19)   Isabell Lawrence 's father was Henry Lawrence of Nasemond Co, Va - see (129)
19) 15Jan1702   Isabele Lawrence, daug of Henry Lawrence & sister of Michale & Thomas Lawrence was wife of Thomas PAGE, (SON)
                 of THOMAS PAGE - Nansemond Co, Va and was married at house of Francis Denson, widow. - see (129)

see page 3 for more data

20)   William Powell's mother was Elizabeth Powell - see (129)
     3Oct1734 Will of William Powell mentions: wife, Mary, Sons: Joseph, Benjamin, William (exec), daug: Martha, Rebecca
               Wilkinson, Mary Hollnad, Rachel, Alice, Lydia, son/law Samuel Riddlehuste, Wit: John Darden, Thomas Powsell,
               Daniel Days.info from footnote (314)

21) 11Nov1699 Thomas Gay, son of Jeane Lawrence of Isle of Wight Co, Va gave land to REBECCA PAGE (535), daug of THOMAS PAGE
               of Isle of Wight, Va - see (129)
22)   Alice Page, wife of Henry Autry, got land grant in Rapphonock Co, Va - see (129) from Sheridan Randolph.
23) 1780   ** WILL ** of James Harrell mentions: wife, Grace, Daug Prisilla, g.sons Ephraim, Silas & Allen, daugs-Sarah,
               Elizabeth, Mary Grace Purvis. - (60)p.23 and W5.1.
23A)   Priscilla Harrell, daug of James Harrell, Bertie Co, NC see (60)p.23/24 - also from John B. Page

24) 20Jun1767 NATHAN PAGE, Bertie Co,NC (562) bought from Jonas Wood, Northampton Co, NC 400 acres Bertie Co, NC NEXT to
               Harrells property wit: Samuel Page (60)p.15
     6Jun1774 NATHAN & JUDITH PAGE, Bertie Co sold to Moses Purvis, Northampton Co, NC 300 acres on Warton Swamp - Bertie
               Co, NC (60)p.16
     1Dmar1783 NATHAN PAGE/Judith sold to John Dodrell-wit:SOLOMON PAGE, Joseph Summerlin, Frederick Holland 280 acres in
               Bertie Co, NC (60)p.24
     1783   NATHAN PAGE (562) sold 200 acres of great grandfather JOHN PAGE (536) land on N. SIDE Roanoke River (46)

     5Apr1786 NATHAN PAGE/Judiah sold to Edward Acree 160 acres in fork of Jumping Run and left area - Wit:THOMAS PAGE(60)27
     Nov1797   Court ordered that power of attorney from Ester, Edith, Cashiah & Delilah Owens to Patience Owens be
               registered on oath of NATHANIEL PAGE

248)28Jul1798 NATHAN PAGE mar Delina Owens, Betie Co, NC wit: Elizabeth Bryan, James Jordan, bondsman (60)p.40
               (something not right with this reported marriage)
               NATHAN PAGE in **WILL of Alice Owens, Bertie Co, NC - mentions Daug Delia Page, g.daug Penny & Patience Page
               son/law Simon Pearce
248)25Nov1807 NATHAN PAGE/DELILAH (Owen) PAGE, PATIENCE, ESTER, EDATH, KAZIAH OWEN, Bertie Co, NC sold to Gabriel Harrell,
               Bertie Co, NC 50 acres on Acres & Youngs property line to Gabriel Harrell's property.
     19NOV1813 ** WILL ** of MOLLY PAGE - Bertie Co, NC (60)p.44 and (46)
               MOLLY PAGE named MEREDITH PAGE as Executor of WILL.
     1814   WILL probated and heirs are: SOLOMON PAGE, son of SALLY PAGE
                                              WILLIAM PAGE, son of JOSHUA PAGE (557)
                                              MEREDITH PAGE, Executor and SALLY PAGE, Executrix   (60)p.44 and

248)26Feb1817 NATHAN PAGE/Patience Owen, Bertie Co sold to Abraham Smith 241 acres Bertie Co, NC on Green Branch. Wit: Wm
               Xinton, Jesse Hodges, John B. Acre. (60)p.44

25) 1849   SION PAGE (570) (Sampson Co. NC) denies charge of bastardy by accuser Nacy Jackson (60)p. 221

26) May1850   JOHN PAGE to serve on grand jury in Sampson Co, NC

27) 6Nov1758   SAMUEL PAGE(563), Bertie Co, NC bought from James Boyte, Northampton Co, NC 280 acres on Wattoss Thorou Fan on
               Poscoson.
     6Dec1772 SAMUAL PAGE (563) bought from Abraham Beman 83 acres on n. side of Swift Creek, Edgecombe Co, NC (60)p.60
     16Oct1774 SAMUAL PAGE bought from Charles Powell, Edgecombe Co, NC 83 acres on w. side of Swift Creek.
27A)18May1778 SAMUEL PAGE(563)/Christiana sold to Henry Harrell 50 acres in Bertie Co, NC (60)p.20

Thomas and Alis Page was transported to America prior to 1694 when headrights were given to George Harris (600 acres) for the
transportation. Some of Thomas and Alis Page relatives, the Garretts were also transportated with them. The Pages settled
in Perquimans District which was part of Old Albermarie Co, NC

Isle of Wight Co is located next to Nansemond Co, Va very near N.C. state line.

Info from Page Family in NC, The Powell families of Va and the South, Jesse Page & Robert Davidson

-Prepared by Robert Page, 54th Planing Detachment, Unit 22303, APO AE 09234

Chart VA 50-1—4 Jan 2004—(3 pages) is a genealogy chart on the Powell family. The Mary Page that married William Page Jr, bc.1665-d.1734, Isle of Wight, Va was thought to be "daughter" of Thomas Page—but now it appears that Mary, b.1665, Hunston, England was a "sister" of Thomas Page, b.1640, Hunston (Co. Suffolk), England.

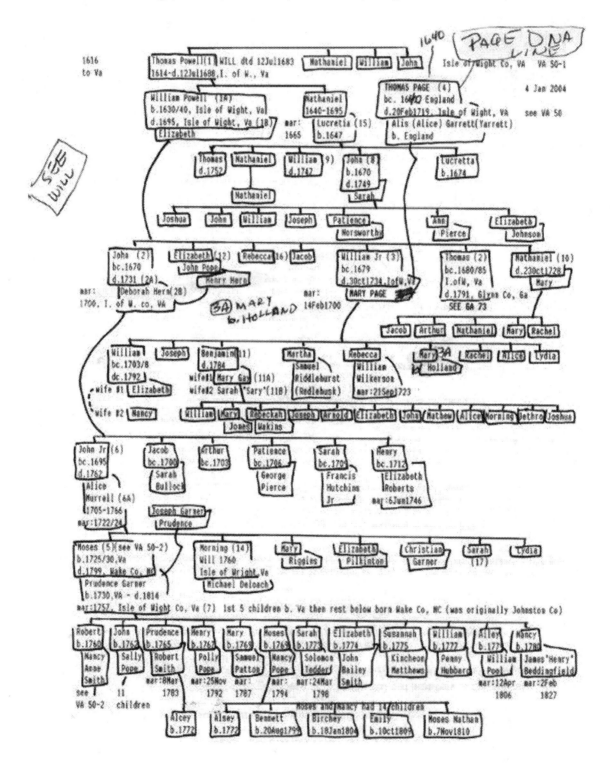

Page Two   VA 50-1   4 Jan 2004

1) Thomas Powell, a yeoman and Colonial immigrant to Isle of Wight Co, Va circa 1616. He bought and sold land there for
    50 years and records of his known children and grandchildren, his ** WILL ** in 1687 and disposition of his land to
    his descendants for over 100 years is carefully followed and proven and properly identifies these families.
    It appears that Thomas Powell had brothers Nathaniel, William and John.
    Will of Thomas Powell dated 9Feb1687/8 legatees, Thomas, Nathaniel, William and John Powell: son William, daug/law
    Elizabeth Powell; daug/law Lucretia Corbett; Lucretia, John, Roberta and Elizabeth Powell. son William executor,
    dated 12Jul1683. Wit: Thomas Griffen, Francis Hutchins.   see (173A,p.27,74)
1A) Apr 1619 Captain Nathaniel Powell, Senior counselor and Acting Governor,
            Captain William Powell, Burgess from James City County
1B) 12Jul1683 William Powell (b.1630) ** WILL ** 11Dec1695 gave children land on Bowsarrow Swamp (173A, page 5)
    wit: Thomas Powell, Thomas Gale, Richard Hutchins.
    Endowment tablet erected in special memory by one of the Descendants of the above individuals.
    as taken from (472) Bruton Parish Churchyard and Church: A guide to the Tombstones, Monuments, and Mural Tablets.
    published by Bruton Parish Church, Williamsburg, Va.- page 81.

2) 7May1712 Thomas & John Powell, St Mary Parish, Essex Co, Va bought from Richard Long, 316 acres (part of 1149 acres in
          Essex Co) See VA 19 for probably the same Long family.
    11Feb1713 John Powell and Jane his wife, Essex Co, Va sells to Machael Lawless 158 acres adj land of Richard Long and
          Thomas Powell.   NOT CLEAR WHICH JOHN POWELL THIS IS
2A) John Powell ** WILL ** 18Feb1730, Isle of Wight, Va
2B) 1700 John Powell, of Nansemond Co, Va and Deborah Horn, daug of Henry Horn. (173,p.38)

3) 14Feb1700 William Powell, son of Elizabeth Powell, widow, aar Mary Page, daug of Thomas Page, both of Isle of Wight.
          Va. (173,p.99)
3) William Powell ** WILL ** dated 30ct1734 - recorded 24Mar1734 (173A, page 121)
    lived on 120 acres on Western branch - Nansemond Co, Va - Isle of Wight, Va - gave son Joseph land at Corrowaugh,
    adjoining Robert Carr. Wit: John Darden, Thomas Powell, Daniel Day.

4) Thomas and Alis (Garrett) (Yarratt in Isle of Wight) Page were transported to America prior to 1694 when headrights
    were given to George Harris (600 acres) for transportation. Some of Thomas and Alis Page relatives, the Garretts were
    also transported with them. Many of the children of Thomas and Alis Page settled in Perquimans Dist, NC which was part
    of Old Albermarle Co, NC
    2Feb1682 Thomas Page granted 600 acres on s. side of Rappa River in Va, next to Howell Powell   see VA 50
    9Jun1708 Thomas Page sold to William Powell 170 acres on Currawaugh Swamp, Isle of Wight, Va.   for the
9Jun1708 Thomas Page/Alis sold to William Powell 170 acres on Currawaugh Swamp, I of W.   Page family
20Feb1719 WILL of Thomas Page. Wife was Alice see (129) Son John Page appointed executor (137,p24)

5) Apr 1762 Moses Powell was appointed by the court as a surveyor
        1766 Moved to Johnston Co, NC with some friends and neighbors, settling near his in-laws and friends. This area
        just southeast of Raleigh was later cutoff to form part of Wake Co, NC. This land stayed in the family until 1890.
        Moses Powell fought in Rev War.
    24Feb1800 Moses Powell ** WILL ** Wake Co, NC
6) 14Jun1760 John Powell * WILL * probated 1 Apr 1762. Isle of Wight Co. Va.
6A) Alice was daug of George Murrell and Mary Walters Murrell, Surry Co, Va. see VA 60 for Murrell family.

7) Moses Powell aar Prudence Gardner in 1760, Wake Co, NC according to NC LDS IGI.

8) Will of John Powell, dated 3Sep1748, recorded 12Jan1748 - Wit: John Darden, William Watkins, William Watkins Jr.
    executor wife Sarah and John Darden. (173A, page 158)

Page Three   VA SO-1   4 Jan 2004

9) Will of William Powell, dated 13Sep1747 - recorded 12Nov1747. (173A, page 155)

10) Will of Nathaniel Powell, dated 23Oct1728 - recorded 26May1729 (173A, page 106) wit: Robert Berryman, James Brown
10) 1729) Mary Powell, wid of Nathaniel Powell mar Robert Berryman. (173,p.4)

11) Will-Benjamin Powell, dtd 11Aug1783-record 1Apr1784 Wit: Michael Johnston, John Watkins, John Darden (173A, page
11A) 10Mar1792 Benjamin Powell mar Mary Gay, daug of William Gay.
11B) Wife of Benjamin Powell is Sary. (173A, page 259)

12) 1695 Elizabeth Powell mar John Pope (173,p 38)
13) 3Mar1739 Jacob Powell mar Sarah Bullock (173,p.102)
14) 1760 Morning Powell, daug of John Powell, mar Michael Deloach. (173,p.11)
15) 1678 Lucretia Powell, widow of Nathaniel Powell, mar John Corbett (173,p.11)
16) 21Sep1723 Rebecca Powell mar William Wilkinson, son of Henry Wilkinson. (173,p.50,100)
17) 1730 Sarah Powell mar Francis Hutchins. (173,p.25)

27Sep1669 James Powell, merchant was Justice and Capt, Isle of Wight, Va married Ann Pitt, daug of Capt Henry Pitt of
I. of W. - formerly Bristol. Gen of Va families, Vol V, Gen Pub Co (1982) (Largo)
Not sure of connection. For possible connection see (173A, page 3, 13, 18, 19, 25, 31, 33, 70,157, 263, 309.

THIS IS A DIFFERENT POWELL FAMILY - see NC 277A
1750 Moses Powell married Mary Williams, Duplin Co, NC
1762 Moses and Mary Powell moved to Edgefield Co, SC
1773 moved to Wilkes Co, Ga Info from (488)

Sources of Info:
129) Letter from Sheridan Randolph.
137) Early Page Families by John Buford Page.
173) Marriages of Isle of Wight Co, Va (1628-1800) by Blanche Adams Chapman, Genealogical Pub Co, (1982)
173A) Isle of Wight Co, Va Marriages (1628-1800) by Blanche Adams Chapman, Genealogical Pub Co, (1975)
314) Powell Families of Va and the south by Rev. Silas Emmett Lucas, Jr.
314A) Powell Records of Va, N.C. S.C. and Ga by Leon Saxon Powell.
413) Old Albemarle and Its Absentee Landlords by Worth S. Ray, Gen Pub co, Baltimore, MD (1977)
472) Bruton Parish Churchyard and Church: A guide to the Tombstones, Monuments, and Mural Tablets.
    published by Bruton Parish Church, Williamsburg, Va.- page 81.

488) "The Virginians" - Thomas Powell and John Hardman and their Descendants by George T. Powell, Jr,(d.1995)
    College St, Apt 7A, Macon, Ga. 31201 (1987) (Florida Archives, Tallahassee)

Prepared by Robert E. Page, 87465 Old Hwy, Apt 107, Islamorada, Fla. 33036

Chart T 2 (5 pages)—16 Dec 2002—which is a "guessing chart" on where Abraham Page, b. 1704 (not 1716), England—the father of 5 sons and one daughter—that Y-DNA has revealed is somehow related to PAGE Line "C". The key factor in proposing this connection is the fact that Private Abraham Page served in Captain Thomas Williams Company and died in 1778, (chart NC 25) in North Carolina, while serving in the Army on an enlistment of 9 months during the Revolutionary War. Abraham Page fought at Battle of Moore's Creek, N.C along with Privates William and John Page and was awarded 640 acres of land (military Land Grant) and this land was awarded to William Page, Thomas Page and his son Henry Page—who owned land on Neuse River—in Bertie Co, N.C. where Abraham Page lived—next to Thomas Jernigan family that were long time friends in Virginia and County Suffolk, England. Henry Page, appears to have moved to Fairfield, S.C. in around 1790 (chart SC 36). And later moved to Alabama in 1830. (see ALA 22)

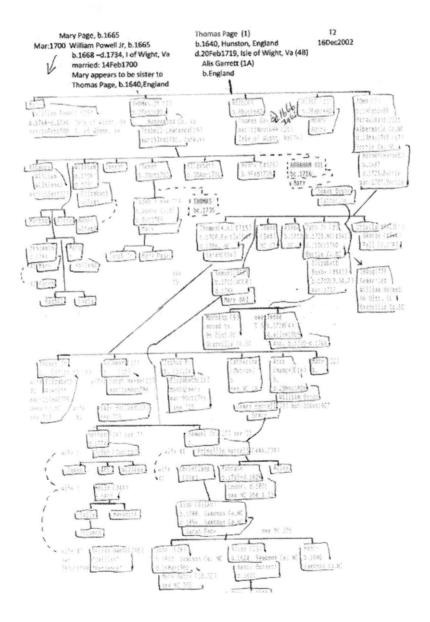

Chart VAS 4-2 ABRAHAM PAGE transported to Gloucester Co, Virginia in 1676/78

ABRAHAM PAGE   Gloucester Co., VA   VA 4-2

VR 4-1   created 1651 from York Co   24 Sep 97   GOUGESTER

11Jun1678 Mr. William Crimes (Grimes, Grymes-see VA 5)) received grant of 450 acres, Gloucester Co, Va on branch of Poropotank adjacent to Capt Richard Dudley, George Haynes and Spencer's land. (Patent book 6, p. 646) beginning at Capt Richard Dudley's in Dancing Valley to Curtis Path and branch to branch of Rich Land swamp - to Major Richard Lee and granted to Mr. Ja. Stubbins - granted to Major Stubbins on 23 Sep 1674 and deserted (land) and now due by order of court by the transport of nine persons:

ABRAHAM PAGE, John Spregg, Robert Hall, Ann Roberts, Nick Glasse, Mary Seayres, John Mill, Joane Nomes, and John Dyer. (info on page 185 of (483)

26Sep1678 John Collis awarded 620 acres in Gloster Co, Va - Kingstone Parish from head of the Beaver Dams to Math. Gayle for transporting twelve persons:

ABRAHAM PAGE, John Spregg, Robert Hall, Ann Roberts, Nick Glasse, Mary Seayres, Samuel Carriage, James Grenhill, John Smith, Edward Andrews, Adam Armstrong, & Eli Taylor. (info on page 190)

50 acres was given to each person that should adventure into the country...but the land usually went to established planters instead of the newcomers. It was common to report the same people in different courts and be awarded another 50 acres again.

Interesting Info:
8Oct1672 William Grimes was listed in very long list of immigrants, that Col Augustine Warner was awarded 10,100 acres in Rappa and New Kent Co. -see p. 110 of (483)

In 1741 Alice Grymes, b.1723 married Mann Page, b.1718. (see VA 4-1) She was daug of John Grymes, Middlesex Co, Va

Info from (483) Cavaliers & Pioneers - abstracts of Va Land Patents and Grants (Vol II) (Patent book 6) (1666-1695) - Va State Lib - Richmond, Va (1977) (Largo Library)

INTERESTING INFO:
ABRAHAM PAGE is the subject of interest here. The only one during this time period on the southeastern coast of America is:

see VA-4-1 ABraham Page, b. 1651 was married to Mary Devill. REPbR

see NC 35
1740 Abraham Page was witt. to land sale in Edgecombe Co, NC
1775 ABRAHAM PAGE is the one that fought at Battle of Moore's Creek, N.C. during the beginning of the Rev War.
1778 ABRAHAM PAGE died while serving in Rev Army
This Abraham Page might be the son of the Abraham Page that immigrated to Gloucester Co, Va in 1678.

Prepared by Robert Page, Box 1195, Indian Rocks Beach, Fla. 33785

Y-DNA Background

According to Y-DNA results there are at several different sets of Page's living in Co. Norfolk and Co. Suffolk, England. One set is Family "C" which has about ten very close DNA 67 matches.

Current research seems to indicate this large family "C" seems to have appeared around **Bury St. Edmunds, in early 1300 and Walsham le Willows, Co. Suffolk in early 1400's.**

There is another set of Page family **line "D"** that seem to be from the same general area and one of the sons, Thomas Page, d. 28Dec1630 married wife #1, Bridgitt, d.25Mar1607,—then married on 13Sep1607, wife #2, Johan Baker, d. 4Dec1609,—then wife #3, Cisley, d. 11Nov1617 from town **Rattlesden** in Co. Suffolk, which is only 10.8 miles from Walsham le Willows. Both wife #2 and #3 appear to be from Rattlesden. This Thomas Page, and wife #2, Johan, appears to be the parents of John Page, b. May 1614, **Worlingham**, Co. Suffolk (not Norfolk), England, who arrived about 1635, in Haverhill, Mass., BUT the date of death of Johan rules this out, which leaves wife #3 as a probable. (See MASS 1) Other names buried in **Rattlesden** are: James Page, d.8Nov1561—Malde Page (widow), d.18Jan1562,—Marmaduke Page, son of Edmunde and Anne, baptized 14May1592.—George Page, son of Thomas and Bridgitt, baptized 14Dec1600—Lidia Page, d. 25Jun1630—Thomas Page, d. 28Dec1630,—Laurence Page (old man) d.19Dec1632., Will reveals Lawrence Page's wife was Helen, named extrix, and children: Paul, Thomas, Anne, Dorothy and Elizabeth. All appear to be under 21, and appear to be from **Family Line "D"**, Thomas Page and wife Joann Baker, were married 14Sep1607, in **Rattlesden**, Co. Suffolk.
And last—John Page (Dumb man) d. 24May1642, & Mary Page, d. 15Nov1668.

Also connected to this (chart MASS 1) Page family line "D" is one Abraham Page, b.1683, who was son of Benjamin Page, b. 1644, that was son of the immigrant John Page, b. 1614, in **Hingham**, Co. Norfolk, England married to Mary Marsh, b. 1622, that immigrated to **Haverhill, Mass** in 1635, left from **Rattlesden** (Co. Suffolk). This Abraham Page, b. 1683, had son Abraham Page, b. 1716 (MASS 1-6). This family line "D" that uses Abraham, Isaac (see NC 1) and Jacob, often which seems to have originated in Co. Essex, just south of where, Family Line "C" seems to have originated in Co. Suffolk. Page **LINE L**, which is Robert Page, **Ormesby**, Co. Norfolk has ties to this **Rattlesden**.

The town of **Worlington** in Co. Norfolk, is only a few miles from another of the Walsham le Willows Page line, that moved to **North Walsham** in Co. Norfolk. The Page family **line**

"L", according to Y-DNA is the Robert Page family that immigrated in 1635 to the Colonies and settled in Hampton, NH. This line L comes from around **Ormesby**, St. Margaret, in Co. Norfolk, England.

The Page family line "A", "C", "D", "E", "F", "K", "H", "J" and "L" are very close to each other, in distance, and easy to mix them up. We need to try and identify the towns as the various Page names pop up—to try and keep separate—the various other Page families.

So far, we have over 150 Page males, that have been tested, and divided into the following 15 family lines. There are a number of non-Page names tested and are very close in their Y-DNA Scores, so probably are related, before last names come into play.

Family line "A" comes from Jeremiah Page, bc.1730/40, Co. Norfolk, England. His line showed up in New London, Ct, in 1750 (see CONN 6-1 & CONN 6-2), then moved over to Chenango Co, NY.

Family line "D" associated with immigrant John Page of Haverhill, MA who immigrated in 1635. (see MASS 1) He was the son of Thomas Page, b. Worlingham, (Co. Norfolk) & Johan (Joan) Baker who were mar 14Sep1607 in Rattlesden, Co. Suffolk, England. Contact June Page Saxton for line D info.

Family line "E"—John & Phebe (Payne) Page arrived in Boston in 1630 from **Boxted** (Co. Essex), England. Ruthanne Page and Ronald Page, Kit 74295 are from this line. (see MASS 5) Parents are Robert Page, Co. Essex, England married to Susan Syckerling. See ENG 10-1 (560-17) for a detailed genealogical summary of this Family Line "E" as researched by Ruthanne Page (2012)
This is George W. Page line.

Family line "F" is Col. John Page, b.1627, Gent, of Co. Middlesex, England (maybe **Sudbury**, Co. Suffolk) that arrived in Williamsburg, Va around 1650. He was married to Alice Luckin. This line produced the famous governor of Virginia John Page. (See VA 5)

Family line "G" is George & Sarah (Linsley) Page, in Branford (New Haven Co), Ct who arrived in 1662 from **Shorne**, (Co. Kent), England. Also line of Thomas & Elizabeth (Felkin) Page of Mark Lane, London, that arrived in Saco, Maine and died there in 1645. This is George W. Page line—our Page Administrator of Line "C". (see chart Maine 1 & CONN 3)

Family line "H" (Anthony Brian Treacher) traces his line back to William Page, b. 1778, **Fulmodeston**, Co. Norfolk, England. Another goes back to Edmund Page, (early 1600) **Alverstoke** (Co. Hampshire), England. Y-DNA matches has revealed many with last name

"Perry" that seem to be Scottish along the English border. There is a Perry family from Berwick on Tweed on the in English/Scotch border. The name Perry comes from the Scottish word "Pirie".

Family line "I" is Joshua Page, b. 1780, **Rotherhithe**, (S.E. London on the Thames), England. Robert Page, RobtPage@ntlworld.com—3 Darfield Rd, Burpham, Surrey, GU4 7YY, England, comes from this line "I", that appears to be from Edward Page, bc.1786, Maidstone, Co. Kent, England. Robert Page has offered his "limited" services for research in the London archives.

Family line "J" is George Page, b. 1795, in Wingfield, (Co. Suffolk), England.

Family Line "K" has a researcher, Philip Ian Page, who lives in Henley-on-Thames, England, who has a paper trail back to Richard Page, d. 1639, yeoman at **Walsham** le Willows (Co. Suffolk). (Conflict on that family connection) Philip did his Y-DNA 10 with Oxford Ancestors and his results, show that Robert E. Page III and his "family line C" are NOT related. This NEW grouping under our PAGE DNA project is "Family K" and his Y-DNA results are listed in my document ENG 10-2.

Research efforts by Charles William Paige,—kit 80186 Page **LINE "C"**—shows a solid paper trail back to Wayne Co, NY in 1829 when his ancestor William Henry Page, b.19Feb1797 left England in 1829. It appears he was born in Co. Essex, England. **SEE NY 56 (5Apr2012)** So much confusion now reigns and it appears an adoption or NPE occurred around 1829. There are many lines of this family that go back to County Norfolk, County Suffolk and County Essex. It will take a lot of Y-DNA testing to sort out this confusion.

Philip I. Page only had Y-DNA 10 by Oxford Ancestors and he needs to get more testing to sort out this issue. Oxford Ancestors only test for ten Y-DNA, where the rest of line "C" are mostly Y-DNA 67 results. This was really puzzling and maybe more testing needs to be done. This new line "K" is shown in my chart ENG 10-2, as Robert E. Page researched this line, but Philip Ian Page, has since provided his family research, which is now identified as Page Family "K". This version of Richard Page, d.1639, Walsham le Willows, can be found in ENG 10-3. This line shows, one John Page, b. 1799 as staying in England and his brother Thomas Page, b. 1796 as immigrating to Athens, Pa in 1832 (PA 50). RHP of Auckland, New Zealand, is descended from Robert Page, b. 1800, Great Yarmouth, Co. Norfolk, England.

We have a new possible DNA connection to this line that also backs up from Pennsylvania (PA 50) back to Co. Norfolk, and then back to Walsham le Willows. Christine (Page) Barnes, visited both Co. Suffolk and northern part of Co. Norfolk, England in May 2008, has ancestors that "paper research" has indicated her line backs up to this Thomas Page, b. 1796. (see PA

50) She is pursuing this connection with one of her brothers and it will be interesting to see the FTDNA results. Having looked at both lines and the paper research, "seems" to confirm, these two brothers and their connection to the original Richard Page, d. 1639, Family Line "K".

There are now four individuals in Family Y-DNA line "K"—Raymond Henry Page, Richard Gerald Walter Page, Philip Ian Page and Anthony Brian Page, plus Christine (Page) Barnes, which has not joined Y-DNA and her paper trail is not solid. All of these researchers paper trail line begins in Walsham le Willows, Co. Suffolk with one Richard Page, d. 1639 and is (21) on the Page families identified in this ENG 10-1. Further research now seems to find this Page family line is from Line "C" and not "K' based on WILL's and property transfers.

Family line "L" is Robert Page, b.1604, of **Ormsby**, (Co. Norfolk), England, immigrated to the colonies in 1637 and died 1679, Hampton, N.H. (See NH 1)(MASS 1)(VA 19-3)(ENG 9-1) Contact Warren Page for this line.

Family line "M" Raymond Page (Ramoun Pagez) b. 1604, **Quierzy**, Picardie, France who married Madeleine Bergeron about 1641, France and immigrated to Canada, c. 1642.

Family line "N" a Londoner emigrated to Brisbane, Australia in 1980 comes from **Stevenage** (Co. Hertfordshire), England in around 1704.

Family line "P" is the Axcel Heath Page line in Goochland Co, Va that "seems" to come from Nathaniel Page bc.1645 in (Co. Devon), England that immigrated to Hardwick, Mass, c. 1675 with wife Joanna. Lead researcher is Art Klinger.

Since the Oxford Ancestors only examined 10 DYS numbers, it would be most interesting, if all Oxford researchers contributed their Y-DNA to FTDNA 67 and see how many would remain connected. There is usually a big drop off between 25 and 37 and then some drop off from 37 to 67. For DYS scores with FTDNA see my "Anglo" document.

George W. Page, Administrator of the Page Family DNA Project has furnished the following information. Bury St. Edmunds was historically famous from before the time it was established by Edward the Confessor in 1044. It was a separate jurisdiction under the control of the abbot of Bury St. Edmunds until the dissolution of the monasteries in 1539. (see http://en.wikipedia.org/wiki/West_Suffolk)

Bury St. Edmunds was once among the richest Benedictine monasteries in England. Its ruins lie in Bury St. Edmunds, a town in the county of Suffolk, England.

In 869 AD, the martyred remains of Saint Edmund the Martyr were enshrined at the Saxon monastery; the site had already been in religious use for nearly three centuries. During the reign of Canute, monks were introduced from St. Benet's Abbey under the auspices of the Bishop of East Anglia. Two of them became Bury's first two abbots. Ufi (d. 1044) and Leofstan (1044-65). After Leofstan's death, the king appointed his physician Baldwin to the abbacy (1065-97). Baldwin rebuilt the church, and re-interred St. Edmund's body there with great ceremony in 1095. The cult made the abbey a popular destination for pilgrimages.

The abby of St. Edmund was built in the 1000s and 1100s, in cross shape, with its head (or apse) pointed east. The shrine of St. Edmund stood behind the high altar. At some 505 feet long, and spanning 246 feet across its westerly transept, Bury St. Edmunds abbey church was one of the largest in the country. St. James Church, now St. Edmunds Bury Cathedral, was finished around 1135. **St Mary's Church** was first built around 1125, and then **rebuilt in the** perpendicular style **between 1125-35**. The abbey was much enlarged and rebuilt during the 12th century.

Abbey Gate opened onto the Great Courtyard. It was the secular entrance which was used by the Abbey's servants. In 1327, it was destroyed by the local people, who were angry at the power of the monastery and it had to be rebuilt. Norman Gate dates from 1120-48 and was designed to be the gateway for the Abbey Church and it is still the belfry for the Church of St. James, the present cathedral of Bury St. Edmunds. This four-story gate-hall is virtually unchanged and is entered through a single archway which retains its portcullis. The Crankles was the name of the fishpond near the river Lark, and the vineyard was first laid out in the 1200s. There were three breweries in the Abbey a s each monk was entitled to eight pints a day.

The Abbey's charters granted extensive lands and rights in Suffolk. The Abbey held the gates of Bury St. Edmunds, they held wardships of all orphans, whose income went to the abbot until the orphan reached maturity, they pressed their rights of corvee. During the 13th century general prosperity blunted the resistance of burghers and peasants, in the 14the century, the monks encountered hostility from the local populace. Throughout the summer of **1327, the monastery suffered extensively**, as **several monks lost their lives in riots**, and many buildings were destroyed. The hated charters and debtors accounts were seized and triumphantly torn to shreds. Already faced with considerable financial strain, the abbey went further into decline during the first half of the 15th century. **In 1431, the west tower of the abbey church collapsed.** Please refer to the payment to **Thomas Page** (3A) in **1437** for the **repair cogs and staves, for mending the mill**, this year, and again the repair of the Wind Mill in Walsham in 1445 by Thomas Page (3A). Two years later Henry VI, which would be year 1433, moved into residence at the abbey for Christmas, and was still enjoying monastic hospitality four months later. More trouble arose in 1446, when the Duke of Gloucester died in suspicious circumstances after his arrest, and in 1465, the entire church was burnt out by an accidental fire. Largely rebuilt by 1506, the abbey of Bury St. Edmunds settled into a quieter existence until dissolution in 1539. Subsequently stripped of all valuable building materials and artifacts, the abbey ruins were left as a convenient quarry for local builders. The ruins are now owned by English Heritage and managed by St. Edmundsbury Borough Council.

It is clear to our small group of Page line "C" researchers that our Thomas Page/Alis Garrett line came from Walsham le Willows area. Circumstantial evidence, including many prominent allied families, closely associated in Walsham le Willows and very close surrounding towns, are also found in Isle of Wight, Va, and almost all were recorded in the newly founded Quaker church. We have finally narrowed down, which, of several individuals, was the parent of this Thomas Page, b. 1640, **Hunston**, (Co. Suffolk), England. (560-183)

Family Tree of 5 Page brothers and 1 sister

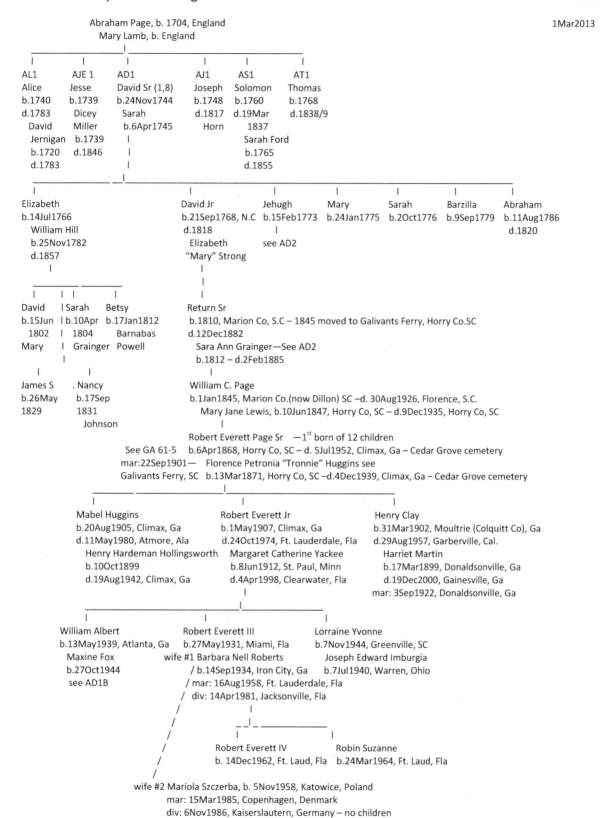

Abraham Page, b. 1704, England
Mary Lamb, b. England

AL1	AJE 1	AD1	AJ1	AS1	AT1
Alice	Jesse	David Sr (1,8)	Joseph	Solomon	Thomas
b.1740	b.1739	b.24Nov1744	b.1748	b.1760	b.1768
d.1783	Dicey	Sarah	d.1817	d.19Mar	d.1838/9
David	Miller	b.6Apr1745	Horn	1837	
Jernigan	b.1739			Sarah Ford	
b.1720	d.1846			b.1765	
d.1783				d.1855	

Elizabeth	David Jr	Jehugh	Mary	Sarah	Barzilla	Abraham
b.14Jul1766	b.21Sep1768, N.C	b.15Feb1773	b.24Jan1775	b.2Oct1776	b.9Sep1779	b.11Aug1786
William Hill	d.1818					d.1820
b.25Nov1782	Elizabeth	see AD2				
d.1857	"Mary" Strong					

David	Sarah	Betsy	Return Sr
b.15Jun	b.10Apr	b.17Jan1812	b.1810, Marion Co, S.C – 1845 moved to Galivants Ferry, Horry Co.SC
1802	1804	Barnabas	d.12Dec1882
Mary	Grainger	Powell	Sara Ann Grainger—See AD2
			b.1812 – d.2Feb1885

James S	. Nancy	William C. Page
b.26May	b.17Sep	b.1Jan1845, Marion Co.(now Dillon) SC –d. 30Aug1926, Florence, S.C.
1829	1831	Mary Jane Lewis, b.10Jun1847, Horry Co, SC – d.9Dec1935, Horry Co, SC
	Johnson	

Robert Everett Page Sr   —1st born of 12 children
See GA 61-5   b.6Apr1868, Horry Co, SC – d. 5Jul1952, Climax, Ga – Cedar Grove cemetery
mar:22Sep1901—   Florence Petronia "Tronnie" Huggins see
Galivants Ferry, SC   b.13Mar1871, Horry Co, SC –d.4Dec1939, Climax, Ga – Cedar Grove cemetery

Mabel Huggins	Robert Everett Jr	Henry Clay
b.20Aug1905, Climax, Ga	b.1May1907, Climax, Ga	b.31Mar1902, Moultrie (Colquitt Co), Ga
d.11May1980, Atmore, Ala	d.24Oct1974, Ft. Lauderdale, Fla	d.29Aug1957, Garberville, Cal.
Henry Hardeman Hollingsworth	Margaret Catherine Yackee	Harriet Martin
b.10Oct1899	b.8Jun1912, St. Paul, Minn	b.17Mar1899, Donaldsonville, Ga
d.19Aug1942, Climax, Ga	d.4Apr1998, Clearwater, Fla	d.19Dec2000, Gainesville, Ga
		mar: 3Sep1922, Donaldsonville, Ga

William Albert	Robert Everett III	Lorraine Yvonne
b.13May1939, Atlanta, Ga	b.27May1931, Miami, Fla	b.7Nov1944, Greenville, SC
Maxine Fox	wife #1 Barbara Nell Roberts	Joseph Edward Imburgia
b.27Oct1944	/ b.14Sep1934, Iron City, Ga	b.7Jul1940, Warren, Ohio
see AD1B	/ mar: 16Aug1958, Ft. Lauderdale, Fla	
	/ div: 14Apr1981, Jacksonville, Fla	

Robert Everett IV   Robin Suzanne
b. 14Dec1962, Ft. Laud, Fla   b.24Mar1964, Ft. Laud, Fla

wife #2 Mariola Szczerba, b. 5Nov1958, Katowice, Poland
mar: 15Mar1985, Copenhagen, Denmark
div: 6Nov1986, Kaiserslautern, Germany – no children

Prepared by Robert E. Page, 87465 Old Hwy, Apt 107, Islamorada, Fla, 33036 (305) 852-5337

In an attempt to bring Y-DNA into play again, Robert E. Page joined the East Anglia Y-DNA (England) project, which hopefully will provide a living PAGE relative, in England, that might know his family tree back to the time period of middle 1600's. If you would like to explore this web site, go to: www.geocities.com/thurlowons/eagdna/ David Weston westondm@qmail.com was the creator in 2006 but in 2012 Dr. John Pelan dna@pelan.org became the administrator and will respond to questions.

Other projects I recommend you consider joining (free) are:
East Anglia-DNA ENG-EAST-ANGLIA-DNA-admin@rootsweb.com David Weston
French Heritage DNA project at www.FrenchDNA.org—Doug Miller djmill@earthlink.net

Normandy DNA—Richard Stevens rmstevens2@gmail.com This project offers Y-DNA comparisons and the name PAGE is listed which convinces me that the name PAGE seems to come from this area in Normandy, France. Go to their Y-DNA charts (page 2) and you will see the matches.

Other English National Archives research is: http://www.nationalarchives.gov.uk/records%5Cdefault.htm which is in Kew, West London. Robert (UK) Page at robtpage@gmail.com might help if you find a document you want.

Our Family "C" has 15 Page's that have perfect or close 66 out of 67 Y-DNA. Four of the 15 (Robert E. Page, Harry L. Page, James C. Page and Fred A. Page) do not appear to be clearly in the Thomas Page/Alis line and their oldest known ancestor is **Abraham Page married to Mary ? (maybe Lamb) (see chart AD1B) (560-50C for marriage) Abraham Page a**ppears in Dobbs Co, N.C. (NC 25) area in 1740's with wife Mary and they have five sons & one daughter, the first one Jesse, born 1739. All five sons of Abraham Page resided on the NC/SC border, living on both sides of the border line. (see Robert Page CAROLINA PAGE's chart AD 1)

Allied Families Connected to the Page Family

An interesting way to track movement of ancestors as they grow in size and migrate to other locations is to also track "allied families" that sometimes intermarry but do travel together. There were many families in County Suffolk, England in the area near Bury St. Edmund—a little village of Walsham le Willows that emigrated to Virginia and settled in the Isle of Wight, area. Most of them joined the Quaker movement—that was just getting organized in the late 1600's. I will just mention one family named Runnels (sometimes spelled Reynolds) that joined the movement to Virginia. They are found in publication (173) under the name Reynolds and have 16 listed as marrying in Isle of Wight, Va and one was Dorcas Runnels, daughter of Henry Runnels that married John Bowen in 1725. **Henry Runnels** is mention on page 42, of this document. In publication (173A) over 40 individuals are listed including Henry Reynolds. Movement from Virginia to North Carolina and on (NC 202) Dredzel Runnels in **Sampson Co. N.C.** (see 60, p.160) for **Thomas Page**—1790 bought 300 acres and chain carriers were **Drezell Runnels** and **Buyas Boykin** and then on (SC 23-7) is Dreadzel Runnells, d.1809 in **Marion Co, S.C.** His property was next to **David Page** plantation in N.C. (AD1) on Buck Swamp, which is NE side of Drowning Creek near Gapway, SW on Poplar Branch. Then I find **William Runnels in Decatur Co, GA**—where my grandfather Robert E. Page Sr, b.1868, Horry Co, SC—(died 1952, GA) moved to Decatur Co, GA in early 1900.

Research has revealed the following Abraham Page's, and I have added Isaac Page (see NC 1) and Jacob Page because they seem to appear to be closely related to Abraham Page line "D or P", and are "maybe" brothers, with the father being Samuel Page. This was a weak, but a possible connection to line "C", that now appears to be Page Line "D". (see MASS 1)

1615 (born before)—Abraham Page, Great Baddow, Co. Essex, England—see (29)

1625   Isaac Page born England,—d. 5Jul1680, Pasquotank, N.C.—see Page chart NC 1— father of Isaac is Samuel Page. (MASS 1-6) Page Line "D"

1627, Jacob P. Page, born, Great Baddow, Essex, England. (29)

1628   Abraham Page, bricklayer, Great Baddow, Marriage at Curry Rivel #110 BW 49, file at Chelmsford, Essex, England (141, p. 262)

1628—1 Nov Abraham Page **will**—Great Baddow—bricklayer

1636   Abraham Page—tailor, had bond by **William Vincent** (1627-1697) for 20 E. pounds, when 21 years old—at Great Baddow, Essex, England (gave letter of atty—23Oct1645-wife Mary)(99)(100)

1645   Abraham Page, tailor from Baddow Magna, Essex, England emigrated to Boston, Mass with wife, Mary of Braintree (Co. Essex) church, had son, Abraham, b. 7Mar1646, Boston but son died same month. (39, p.397) (82, p.330)

1648   Abraham Page, b. 27Feb1649 or Dec, 1648, son of John Page and Elizabeth Gile, Haverfield, Essex, England. (29) I think this is in error. Should be John Page/Mary Marsh. (see MASS 1 and MASS 1-6) Page line "D"

1650   Abraham Page, born Kent, England (29)

1665   Abraham Paige, Boston, Mass (39, p. 215)

1674   Abram Page, Hearth Tax Return, Chattisham, (Chatsham), Samford, Co. Suffolk, England

1674   Abram Page, Hearth (2 fireplaces) Tax, **Lowestoft** (Lowstolfe), Mutford, Co. Suffolk, England

1674   Alice Garrett, Hearth (3 fireplaces) Tax Return, **Lowestoft**, Mutford, Co. Suffolk, England

5Jun1678 Abraham Page imported (someone else paid) to Gloucester Co, Va by William Grimes.—who got awarded 450 acres (129) see NC 25-1 Alice Grymes, b.1723 married Mann Page, b.1718 and was the mother of Va Gov John Page, b.1744—see. VA 4-2 and VA 23.

26Sep1678 Abraham Page, imported Gloucester Co, Va by John Colles—got 620 acres (two different individuals got credit for this transportation) see VA 25-1

1701   Abraham Page, a tailor, and a Baptist of **Hawstead**, in County of Essex, England made **WILL** (560-50) and names wife Ann, son Abraham, grandsons Jacob and Joseph, Charles, Benjamin and Gamaliel. He also names his daughter Deborah, married to a Choat, as sole Executrix of the **WILL**. Signed 22Sep1701. For another version of this information—see AD1B

    The below Abraham Page, tailor of **Halstead**, "appears" to be the son of the above Abraham.

1704   Abraham Page, tailor, **Halstead**, Co. Suffolk, England Marriage at Curry Rivel, 50 BR 15—Records at Chelmsford, Co. Essex, England (141, p. 262)

WHAT IS CONFUSING—THERE IS HALSTEAD in Suffolk and HAWSTEAD in Essex)

1716—6Jun—Abraham Page, born—St. Bride, Fleet St, London, England parents: Abraham Page/Ann (560-50D) NOT Line "C"—maybe "D"

3Oct1727 Abraham Page mar Mary Lamb—**Grundisburgh**, Co. Suffolk, England (29) (560-50C)

Another source says marriage at Withersdale Street (560-50C)

30May1730 Abraham Page—christened

—parents Abraham/Mary Page, Copdock, England (29)

30Jun1732 Abraham Page-christened parents Abraham/Mary Page, Chelmsford, Co, Suffolk, Eng. (29)

30Sep1734 Abraham Page had son, christen at Barton in the Clay, England, wife Mary Page (29)

13Oct1734 Abraham Page mar Mary Kirby, Bedford, Barton in the Clay, England (29)

1735   Abraham Page mar Mary Kirby, (72, p. 104)

1739   30Sep Abraham Page born, par: Abraham/Mary—Barton in the Clay, England (29)

1740   Abraham Page witness to land sale in Edgecombe Co, NC (NC 25)

1741   Abraham Page—Bonded passenger to America (560-50E)

1776   Pvt. Abraham Page fought at Battle of Moore's Creek Bridge, NC—along with William, Thomas and John Page. (440) Roster of the Patriots in the Battle of Moore's Creek Bridge by Bobby Moss.

1778   Abraham Page died while serving in Revolutionary War in North Carolina and was awarded 640 acres of land.

SEE APPENDIX "A" of this publication for more on ABRAHAM PAGE.

THE SEARCH IS STILL ON FOR MORE INFO ON ABRAHAM PAGE IN ENGLAND.

ORGINATION OF THE SURNAME PAGE

SOME mention of the Page name in France should be made. During the dark period of history known as the Middle Ages, the name Page was first used in France. While the patronymic and metronymic surnames, which are derived from the name of the father and mother respectively, are the most common form of hereditary surname in France. Occupational surnames also emerged during the late Middle Ages.

Many people, such as the Page family, adopted the name of their occupation as their surname. However, an occupational name did not become a hereditary surname until the office or type of employment became hereditary. The surname Page was an occupational name for a young servant to a nobleman who was in the first stage of training for knighthood. Such a servant was known in Old French as a page.

First found in La Dauphine near to the Rhone River, in the department of Isere, in the district of Vienne, which is 20 miles south of Lyon. Some of those, with the name PAGE moved from France to England into Wales, Ireland and Scotland. County Norfolk, a large county in Eastern England and just across the English Channel and was very near Northern France.

Normandy is a region in northwest France, which in the 155 years prior to the 1066 invasion, experienced extensive Viking settlement. In the year 911, French Carolingian ruler "Charles the Simple", had allowed a group of Vikings, under leader **ROLLO**, bc. 846, Denmark—dc.932 France (see 551D, page 2), to settle in northern France with the idea that they would provide protection along the coast against future Viking invaders. This was successful and the Vikings in the region became known as the "Northmen" from which Normandy is derived. They renounced Paganism and converted to Christianity and baptized **Robert I**. They also intermarried with the local populations and transformed it into the Norman language. Meanwhile in England, the Viking attacks continued and in 911, the Angle-Saxon King of England Aethelred II (978-1016), agreed to marry **EMMA**, the daughter of the Duke of Normandy, to cement a blood-tie alliance for help against the raiders. (See 551D page 3 for genealogy of this family.

The Viking attacks grew so bad, that in 1013, the Anglo-Saxon kings fled and spent the next 30 years in Normandy and did not return to England until 1042. In 1066, Anglo-Saxon King Edward (1042-1066) the Confessor died, with no child, a power vacuum was created with three competing interest fighting for the throne of England. For more history of early England, mainly Norfolk and Suffolk, from 865 to the 1066 conflict go to www.stedmundsbury.gov. uk/sebc/visit/865-1066.cfm.

King Harald of Norway invaded northern England in September 1066, which left Harold of England little time to gather an army. Harold marched north from London and surprised the Vikings at the Battle of Stamford Bridge, killed King Harald and the Norwegians were driven out. The English army was left in a battered and weakened state.

Meanwhile **William "the bastard" of Normandy**, (1027-1087) (**a descendant of ROLLO**, dc. 932) (551D, p.2) assembled an invasion fleet of 600 ships and an army of 7000 men. He finally landed at Pevensey, England on September 29, 1066 and began to lay waste to the area. The final battle took place on October 24, 1066, seven miles outside of **Hastings** and in the final hours, Harold was killed and the Saxon army fled. This became known as the **Norman Conquest**. The invention of the "stirrup" was first used by William in the battle at Hastings and later in the Crusades.

On Christmas day 1066 William was crowned King in Westminister Abbey. (519C, p. 29) Between 1066 and 1086, the invaders were a small portion of the population in England (about ½ %) but they had acquired almost all of the land, etc.

There was a Ralph Page listed in the 1230 Pipe Rolls (Devonshire) and a William le Page in the 1240 Feet of Fines in Essex, England. (560-19 & 19A) All evidence points to the origin of the surname "Page" being **Norman**. David Weston gives the following warning. Do not confuse the surname origin with patrilineal genetic origin. They are not necessarily nor likely to be the same thing. Historically, England experienced a 3-5% illegitimacy rate per year between 1500 and 1900 (ref. Laslett & Oosterveen pop stud. Vol 27 No. 2 (July 1973) pp. 155-186) This gives a cumulative probability of 50 to 70 % that an illegitimate birth will occur on any given line over a 700-800 year time frame, or since surnames have been used. Nor does this include other causes for name changes such as adoption, clerical errors (most people were illiterate before the 20th century).

Thus, although while there will likely be a direct link for a surname line to the founder, that line is unlikely to follow a direct patrilineal line. What is interesting—Y-DNA Haplogroup **I1**—is our group—and our Y-DNA is jumping back to Normandy, which "might" be the **haplogroup** of **ROLLO**—down to "William the Bastard" that conquered England in 1066. They are digging up the bones of relatives of ROLLO to confirm his DNA. William "the Bastard" or Conqueror who died 1087 is buried in Caen, Normandy, France. Will they did up his bones for comparison? (see 519C, page 28) THAT IS A GIANT REASON TO REPORT THE y-DNA RESULTS—good or bad!

In the latest issue of Genealogy-DNA Digest, Vol 8, Issue 137, February 5, 2013, Brian Swann commented "(f) I am looking into the Norman Y-DNA signature, and there is a proposal to break into the tomb of ROLLO the Viking, ancestor of the Norman household, in Normandy this year, and King Henry I left 20 illegitimate children. I believe it is possible, in theory, to get at the Y-DNA of the Saxon King royal bloodline." (See 560-186)

In closing—of this latest "update" of my "search for truth" of the origin of Page Family "C" has brought to surface (that needs to be discussed) is the contested issue "only" by Chris Page, (who believes he is of the Thomas Page, Isle of Wight, Va line) and NOT the ABRAHAM PAGE line—and "how" it "might" be connected to the Thomas Page/Alis Page line. It is CLEAR Thomas Page and his wife Alis Page were in Virginia and North Carolina area in 1659 or before. (560-181) Abraham Page (father of 5 sons and daughter Alice. b.1740)—(I always wondered—if—Alice was named after Alis Page) which does not appear until around 1740 when Alice was born, as the daughter of Abraham Page.—in the middle of N.C. So we have at least one or two generations missing to understand. Almost nobody has devoted research time to the ABRAHAM PAGE issue.

I prepared a chart "ABE 1" in 1990 that had every Abraham Page I could find—with no intent to show which one—was the one—I was searching for but now after over 30 years of searching, many on that chart appear valid.

APPENDIX A

I have added "Appendix A" to this document which after 30 years of research offers a possible link to the Thomas Page, b. 1640, Hunston, England line that arrived in Virginia area in 1659. See VA 50 which is a chart developed from several sources, including Author Jesse Page. Chart T 2 is the "educated guessing" chart that reflects the most likely connection.

There was a Page family in Massachusetts (see MASS 1)—that had an Abraham Page, b. 1716, (Page line "D") (see MASS 1-6 & 1-9) that others have often reported our Carolina Abraham's birth date, as 1716, which is false. I believe it to be a different Abraham Page, b.1704.

My religious history is pretty faulty, but I do remember that ABRAHAM was a big word in the Muslim religion (at Mecca) and if one looks at the five sons of ABRAHAM PAGE—you will see much religious influence—in the naming pattern—but "missing" is Issac. If my research is of the right ABRAHAM PAGE—in England—is on target—then he served time (1695) in an English goal (jail) at Chelmsford, until he renounced his religious beliefs—against the "official" Church of England. See AD1A-1 and 560-50 series for this ABRAHAM PAGE.

Sources of Information.

29	LDS, IGI, Kaiserlautern, West Germany
36	Royal Descents of 500 Immigrants to the American Colonies or the United States by Gary Boyd Roberts—Genealogical Publishing company, Baltimore, Md.
39	Genealogical Guide to Early Settlers of America by Mary Witmore. (1967).
60	Page Family in North Carolina by Jesse M. Page Jr (1685-1850) (1987)
72	History of Marion County, South Carolina by W. W. Sellers
99	Letter from Dorothy Jewell Page
100	Genealogical Guide to the Early Settlers of America by Mary Witmore, (1967)
129	Letter from Sheridan C. Randolph
137	Early Page Families by John Buford Page, (1989)
141	**WILLs** at Chelmsford, Co. Essex, England
173	Marriages of Isle of Wight County, Virginia (1628-1800) by Blanche Adams Chapman (1982)
173A —	**WILLs** and Administrations of Isle of Wight, Va (1647-1800) by Blanche Adams Chapman

221   Descendants of Thomas Gleason of Watertown, Mass (1607-1909) by John Barber White, Haverhill, Mass, (1909)

279   The Record of the Nathaniel Paige Family by Elijah Ransom Page, Canadaigua, N.Y.1904

281   Page Descendants—Line of Descent from Nicholas Page of England, Salem Press Co, Salem, Mass (1915)

281-1   Name and Family of Page/Paige, Manscript #2001, (1984) Roots Research Bureau,

282   History and Description of the Great Page Estate, by Charles N. Page, Point Loma, Calif

314   The Powell Families of Virginia and the South by Rev. Silas Emmett Lucas, Jr.

399   Descendants of Robart Page of the King's House, Probable English Origins, Ancestors, and Relatives of George Page of Branford, Connecticut and Thomas Page of Saco in the Province of Maine. By Col. George W. Page (1992)

440   Roster of the Partiots in Battle of Moores Creek Bridge, NC by Bobby Moss.

472-1   Genealogy of Pages in England (Va Gov John Page line) by Haywood Page.

483   Virginia Cavaliers and Pioneers, Vol 2—by Nell Nugent and Grundman, Va. State Library, Richmond, Va (1977)

519C   Kings and Queens of England and Great Britian by Eric R. Delderfield—David & Charles, London. (1981)

551D   Queen Emma and the Vikings by Harriet O'Brien—Bloomsbury—New York and London.

551E   Scotland—A History—edited by Jenny Wormald—Oxford University Press, (2005)

551I   The Vikings by Robert Wernick, Time Life Books, Alexandria, Virginia. (1979)

551F   The Vikings—A History—by Robert Ferguson—Penguin Books, New York (2009)

551G   Britain B.C.—Life in Britain and Ireland Before the Romans. By Francis Pryor. (2003)

THE FOLLOWING SERIES OF DOCUMENTS ARE THE SOURCE DOCUMENTS THAT FOLLOWS THE PAGE FAMILY AROUND COUNTY OF SUFFOLK, ENGLAND

560   "Who Lived in Your House?—People at Home in Early Walsham le Willows", by Audrey McLaughlin, 159 pages—10 English pounds—Phone: **0**1359-258535 The country code for England from the United States is 011-44—and you drop the **0**, and then dial 1359-258535.

Mailing address: Mrs. D. Daniels, Bridge House, The Street, Walsham le Willows, Bury St. Edmunds, Suffolk, IP33AZ. Plenty of pictures, Wills, property transfers, and local historical info. Thanks to my daughter Robin Page for getting this valuable book. See 560-184 for more on houses in Walsham le Willows.

560-1   Anglo-Saxon England, by F.M. Stenton, Oxford Univ Press, England (1971)

560-2 Knight-Noble Warrior of England 1200-1600 by Christopher Gravett,—(2008) Oxford, England

560-3 National Gazetter—Great Britian and Ireland—Vol 1, London, 1868

560-4 National Gazetter—Great Britian and Irleand—Vol 3, London, 1868

560-5 History of Pakenham, St. Mary Church by Martin Harrison (July 2003) www.crsbi.ac.uk/ed/sf/paken/index/htm

560-6 St.Mary Church, **Walsham le Willows** by Brian Turner (2004)

560-7 Gravestones in Walsham le Willows, Co. Suffolk, England by Walsham History Group (Sep 1999)

7A Pages Christened at **Walsham le Willows**

7B LDS IGI for Walsham le Willows

7C Ancient Walsham le willows (1086-1348)

7D 1639 Ship money returns—Walsham le Willows—John, Raynald, Thomas, & Joseph Page

7E The Vincent Family—Walsham le Willows

560-8 Hundreds of **Shropham**: An Essay towards a Topographical History of the County of Norfolk, Vol 1 (1805) (about Henry Page Manor in 1338)

560-9 **Pakenham** Cartulary for Manor of Ixworth Thorpe, Co. Suffolk (1250-1320)

9A Pakenham—Suffolk—Wills from 1583 to 1679—probably LINE "D"(see ENG 10-1A (96)

560-10 The Knights of Saint Edmund—www.knightsofstedmund.com

560-11 Church of England, **Walsham le Willows** Parish, Co. Suffolk.

560-12 County Suffolk in 1674—Hearth Tax Returns-Suffolk Green Books), #XI, Vol 13, Woodbridge: George Booth, Church Street (1905)

12A Hearth Tax history—Thomas Page had 3rd most hearths of all the Page families.

12B Taxation in England Lay Subsidies (Subsidy Returns)

12C Burials in County Suffolk in Riot of 1327 of 20 individual Page people.

12D **Co. Suffolk**—IGI of all Thomas Page's born in County Suffolk, England

12E County Suffolk—Ship Money—List of Pages 1639-1640.

12F County Suffolk—Surnames list—Page—

12G Co. Suffolk—Local and Family History

12H Co. Suffolk Family History Society.

560-13 The Norman People and their existing descendants in the British Dominions and the United States of America. London (1874) Genealogical Pub Co., Baltimore, Md.

560-14 **Somerleyton**, Co. Suffolk—Seized by William the Conquerer 1066 and given to Roger Bigod, as stewart, then later to the Jernigan family. (Is Roger Bigod—aka—Roger Page?)

14A William the Conqueror and the Battle of Hastings, (1982) Pitkin Pictorials.

560-15 7May1400 Land transaction mentioned several parcels of land near **Pagefield (then Lowestoft)** and Somerleyton owned by the Jernigan family and Thomas

Page, who appears to be the Rector of **Hinderclay** Church (4 miles from Walsham le Willows) from 1391-1399

560-15A Samuel Robert Page, born **Lowestoff**, circa 1870 joined British Army Battalion Suffolk Regiment in 1914 at age 44. His regimental was ??0277. source ancestry. com.

560-16 28Jan1783 **WILL** of David Jernigan Sr, Wayne Co, N.C. archives, who was married to Alice Page, bc. 1740, daughter of Abraham Page, bc. early 1700.

560-17 **Pakenham**—Village of Two Mills by N.R. Whitwell

17A Pakenham—Birth, **WILL** records (1567-1670)

560-18 Norfolk Hearth Tax Assessment in 1664 by M.S. Frankel, P.J. Seaman.

560-19 Castle of Pirou (**Normandy**), **France**—Baron of Pirou, his son was William le Page

19A Page Coat of Arms and Family Crests—mentions William le Page.

560-20 Dictionary of English Surnames, Reaney & Wilson, Rev Ed, Oxford University Press, 1997.

560-21 **Thornham Magna**, Co. Suffolk, England—Baptisms (1581-1616)

560-21A Thornham Magna baptisms, marriages, burials

560-21B ″ ″ ″ ″ ″

560-22 **Ingham**, Co. Suffolk, England—Baptisms marriages, burials (1592-1635)

560-22A Ingham and **Finningham** (William Page (60)

560-22B Ingham and **Risby** (Roger Page) (91-2)

560-22C Ingham—1323 Bruce Page sued by Parson Robert de Askeby and fined.

22D Ingham—Hammond family Ingham to Boston, Mass

22E Ingham—(Henry Page, b.1610 Co.Norfolk—Bacon rebellion

22F Ingham Register (1665-1693) Henry Hearne mar Elizabeth Peak, on 24Oct1665 Further research casts doubt on above Herne/Peak marriage—see 560—Rebeckah Page mar Henry Turner May 1670 (see ENG 10-1B)

22G Ingham Parish Registers (59, 61) Page and Hawes families

560-23 Parish register—**Woolpit** (Co. Suffolk) Baptisms, marriage, deaths (1628-1811)

560-24 Rectors of **Hinderclay** Church—(Co. Suffolk)—Thomas Page (1391-1399).

560-25 Reynolds Historical Genealogy Collection. 1593 Thomas Page (59-1) baptized, son of John

560-26 A list of Persons—John Page (20), John Page (20-1), Phillip Page (20B), who were disclaimed as Gentlemen of Coat—Armour by John Paul Kylands, F.S.A. Guildford, printed by Billing and Sons, 1888.

560-27 John Page (20-1) and Phillip Page (20B) Obituary prior to 1800 by Sir William Musgrave, 6th Bart, of Hayton Castle, Co. Cumberland., England

560-28 1577 **Walsham le Willows** Field Survey Book

28A Thomas Page (12) family

28B Thomas Page (12) family history with Andrew Hawes(17A) **WILL** of 1610

28C Walsham Quarterly Review #4 (Jan 1998) **Blue Boar Inn** home of Richard Page (21A).

28D Page homes in Walsham le Willows.

28E Society of Genealogist for Walsham le Willows.

28F Walsham Quartrly Review #8 (Jan 1999) Anne Page mar Thomas Hawes

28G   ”   ”   ”   #12 (Jan 2001) Thomas Page fix ditch

28H   ”   ”   ”   #16 (Jan 2001 Richard Page mar Dorothy Robwood (Cook)

28I   ”   ”   ”   #18 (Jul 2001) Thomas Page/Peter Umfrey—cut planks

28J   ”   ”   ”   **#29 (Apr 2004) Reginald Page—Blue boar Inn 1630**

28K   ”   ”   ”   # 3 (Oct 1997 House "Dages"—cottage "Cocksalls"

28L   ”   ”   ”   # 9 (Apr 1999) Thomas Lacy—Name—Walsham

28M Walsham le Willows News Update July 22, 2010—Author Audrey McLaughlin

560-29 **Timworth** and **Culford** Parish Register

29A Timworth (next to Ingham) Thomas Page (94) family

560-30 Finningham (Mill Field)

30A **Finningham** parish records (see 560-22A also)

560-31 Yeoman—what is a yeoman?

31A yeoman by George W. Page

560-32 **Hawstead** (Co. Suffolk) data

32A Hawstead Parish records

32B Thomas Page (30)

32C **Halstead** (Co. Essex) near Chelmsford—see 560-50B

32D Hawstead—Thomas Page (30) first wife was Susan. Son Joseph, b/d.1620 Joseph, b. 11Sep1622, Hawstead mar Mary Clayden, in 1651

32E Much info on Thomas Page(30A) and wife Susan.

32F More info on this Thomas Page line

32G More info on this Thomas Page line.

32H Hawstead—2Dec1669 Baptised Isaac Page, son of Joseph Page and Mary Hawstead—John Page buried 18Jun1669.

32I Hawstead—Sparkes family tied to Thomas Page family(15B)

32J Hawstead—Rebecca Page connected to Robert Wiffen (tailor) of Hawstead who seems to have married Rebecca Page (24Aug1637) (see 560-32 and 32J)

560-32K Hasted—Thomas Page, b.1638 (son of Thomas Page, d.18Feb1655 (20A), Hasted) was admitted to Magdalene College in 1657—graduated B.A. 1661 Thomas Page, b. 1666, Preston, Suffolk, (son of Thomas Page, b. 1638, Gent Of Kersey) had 2 years at Bury, then four years at Ipswich, and admitted to Caius College, in June 1683, age 17.and graduated B.A. 1687. He was admitted to pensioner's scholars table on 20Jun1683. (560-32K)

There is another PAGE (no first name) in Bury school list for 1713, and listed as Royalist. (560-32K)

560-33   **Bury St. Edmunds** data

560-33A list of **WILLS** at Bury St. Edmunds

   33B 1618 **WILL** of William Cooke, Gent of Bury and wit by Edward Page

   33C Bury st. Edmunds—Contracts and Marriages

   33D Bury marriages William Page/Ann Felgate 1605—William Page/Ann Mayr 1652

   33E Bury—St. Mary parish register. 1562-1680

   33F St. Edmundsbury Borough Council—Reformation and Civil War 1539-1699.

560-34   **Framingham** Page Family

560-34A   ”   ”   ”

   34B Framlingham and Ingham and Rattlesden records

   34C Framlingham Edward Page had son Philip Page transported to Va. John Sparkes, Grace and Mary Sparkes. Transported to to Va.

   34D 1638 Nathaniel Page and Francis Sparkes, James City Co, Va

   34E 1600's Philip Page, Robert Page, Henry Page, Frances Page

560-35   Possible Page Line D

   36   **Badwell** Ash parish records

   37   **Bacton** parish records

   38   **Hasketon** parish records

   39   **Thorndon** parish records

560-40   **Thornham Magna** parish records—1638 Thomas Page, yeoman deceased (12) that is somehow connected to Buckenham Castle

   40A Thornham Magna records

   40B Thornham Magna—1609 **WILL** of Andrew Hawes-yeoman-Walsham

      1616 Will of Julian Vincent (Thomas Page (15) line)

      1617 WILL of Thomas Page (12) Walsham

   40C 1638 Thornham Magna Deed Info that was owned by Thomas Page

560-41   **Westley Manor** in 1548 owned by John Page, then son Edward Page, d. no heirs and land went to sister Mary that married John Cropley.

560-42   **Walsham** le Willows civil suit by Christopher Smear vs. John Page,(8D) W le W, Alice Page (8F) daug of John Page, Gent (8) married a Smear.

560-42A more on civil suit

   42B Thomas Page (6) b.1535-d.1617, Walsham

   42C Edmund Page 1503 **WILL** wife: Isabel—son John, **HALL HOUSE** (Pages) on Church street

560-43   **Chevington** (part of Bury) near Ingham—(also see 560-84 for John & Joseph Page)

      1292 John Page served on a jury in City of London

      1399 John Page in **Culford** pays rent of 2 shillings per year for the tenement in which he lives.

1407   Thomas Page (91-3) of **Lackford** near Ingham—grant of garden close and 3 acres of land wit: John Page Gent of **Westley** (91-4) 1547 **WILL** of John Page, Gent (of Hessett)

     1452   John Page (2) (91-4) **WILL** in **Ixworth** (wife Agnes)(2A)

     1489   John Page land grant. John Page died circa 1510

     1532   Page's field in Chevington

     1535   John Page (son of Roger Page) leased manor le Sexteyns in Westley for 40 years. (1509-1547)

     1558   John Page rated Bury Monastery.

     1653   Thomas Page christened—parents: Joseph/Mary Page (see 560-84)

     1654   Joseph Page born, parents Joseph/Mary Page (see 560-84)

560-44   **Walsham** Village History Group Quarterly Review #27 Oct 2002—"the Lawn" owned by John Page, d. 1669 (20)

560-45   William Page of **Hessett**,(maybe (10) unnamed daug married George Nun, of **Tostocke**, Co. Suffolk.

560-46   **Rotherhithe**, Thames River Port, **London** where Joshua Page, b.1780?—sailmaker works.

     Also Capt Robert Caulfield, in 1674 transported some Page's to Stafford Co, Va (VA 8)

     Thomas Page, b.1666, Preston (30A-1) graduated from Magdalene College, in England in 1661 (see 560-46, 46A,47)

560-46A   Joshua Page, Sailmaker at Rotherhithe, London—Thames river. Robert (UK) Page

560-47   Thomas Page, b. 1638 and his son Thomas, b. 1666, **PRESTON**, Co. Suffolk, England

   47A   **PRESTON**—16Jun1667—**WILL** of Thomas Locke, Yeoman,

560-48   1477 Thomas Page, Knight of the Shire, Ipswich mentioned in a poll taken

560-49   William Page, **Bury** St. Edmunds in 1539 married Margery, Widow of John Bacon

   49A   William Page wit to **WILL** of Robert Bacon, son of John Bacon—Drinkstone.

   49B   Philip Page (father of Robert Page) married Alice Hoo,—of Hessett in 1543.

     Elizabeth Page, (daug of John Page (91-4), of Westley), married John Bacon, of Hessett.

   49C   Christopher Smeare vs. John Page (8D) of Walsham le Willows. (560-42)

560-50   Abraham Page, b.bef 1615, **Great Baddow** (Co. Essex) **WILL** of 1701—**Hawstead** (Co. Essex) Wife was Ann Page.

   50A   Abraham Page, bap 8Jun1716, **London** (St. Bride-Fleet St) and Thomas, b.25Dec1717—sons of Abraham and Ann Page that were married Mar 1628, (see 560-32Cs & MASS 1)

   50B   Mary Page bap 29Sep1734, Gl**emsford** (Co Essex) daug of Abraham/Mary(Lamb) Page that were married in **Halstead** (Co. Essex) in 1704.

   50C   Abraham Page, of Cobdack married Mary Lamb, of Capel on 3Oct1727.

50D List of ABRAHAM PAGE's in England.

50E more ABRAHAM PAGE'S in U.S.

560-51 William Vincent (1627-1697) yeoman of Bromfield (Co. Essex), and the Abraham Page family were close in England and later in Va.

560-52 see my chart PA 50 which is about the Richard Page (line K) and the town **Attleborough** (Co. Norfolk).

560-53 William Page, b. 1778, (98) **Fulmodeston**, Co, Norfolk, England—Anthony Treacher line H.

53A Ian Page, Anthony Treacher email

560-54 Thirteen towns in Co. Suffolk, England with various family data. The info will be listed on ENG 10-1A, under each town.

560-55 Henry Page, b.1760,-d,1840, **Haverhill**, Co. Suffolk, England (Helen Griffiths line)

560-56 George Page, b. 1781, **West Wickham**, Co. Cambridgeshire, d.1852, West Wickham (Helen Griffiths line)

560-57 **Horringer** parish register (1558-1850)

Horringer birth—25May1608 Ann, daug of William Page (see 560-33D)

17Dec1615 Marie,(24E), daug of William Page

14Sep1606 William, (24G), son of William Page

28May1618 Thomas,(24D), son of William Page

Horringer death—6Jul1624, William Page (23C)-

560-58 **Worlingworth** (Co. Suffolk) Henry Page (18A), Richard Page (21), John Page (31) Edmund Page (33), 1497 Richard Page—1601 Richard Page—

560-59 **Rattlesden**—Co. Suffolk—Burials—probably Page Line "D"

59A Thomas Page/Cisley Page, d. 11Nov1617

59B Thomas Page mar Cisley on 4Oct1607

59C Edmund/Anne Page had Marmaduke b/d.1592—Thomas/Bridget Page had Elizabeth1596, Laurence1599, George1600—John1603, Mary1620, Susan1623, Robert1627,— Sara, mother Mary Page,—Phillip/Anne Page, had Phillip (97-1)

59D Thomas Page had Susannah Page b.1Jan1622 (Eng 10-1, p.46)

560-60 **Ipswich**—Co. Suffolk—John, Thomas (12), and Robert/Alice Page (34)

60A Thomas Page, Yeoman—Robert Page, son of Thomas Page

560-61 **Whepstead** (next to Hawstead) Mary Page, daughter of William & Mary Page, bap 18Aug1677—William Page, son of William/Mary Page, bap 16Jan1679.

61A Mary Page, William Page, Elizabeth Page

61B John Page mar a Sparkes in Whepstead.

560-62 **Wickhambrook,** Co. Suffolk—

560-63 **Fornam St. Martin**—Co. Suffolk—Boldero family

560-64 **Framsden**—Co. Suffolk—1560 Robert Page mar Jane Blomefield

560-65 **Little Whelenetham**—Co. Suffolk—Scarpe family

560-66 **Aldringham—Co.** Norfolk—George Page's (MICH11) father died in Aldringham. This is a Charles William Paige connection. Oldest ancestor is William Henry Page. England to America in 1829

   66A John/Cicely Page

560-67 **Swaffham** Co. Norfolk—William Page, b.19Feb1797—par: James/Mary Page

560-68 **Lavenham—Co.** Suffolk—Parish Register—1621 John Page/Phebe Paine mar— Page line E.

   68A John Page/Phoebe Paine—Watertown, Mass.

560-69 missing

560-70 **Wells—Next-to-the-Sea,** Co Norfolk-Thomas Page, bap15Jun1650—son of James/Ann Page.

560-71 **London**—Thomas Page (112) bap 4Aug1650, St.Margaret, Westminister son of John/Jane Page.

   71A Thomas Page, of Romford (**LONDON**) Will of 1535,

   71B 1258 One-third of Londoners died from volcano caused global catastrophe.

560-72 **Dickleburgh**—Co. Norfolk—22Oct1562 Nicholas Page mar Elizabeth Wright,

560-73 **Scole**—Co. Norfolk—William/Anne Page had son Miles Page bap 13Apr1567 12Jan1698 Elizabeth Page mar Robert Read

560-74 **Garboldisham**—Co. Norfolk—24Aug1634 John Page buried. William/Marie Page had Alice Page 19Oct1697

560-75 **Old Buckenham**—Co. Norfolk—Thomas Page had son Thomas Page 16Dec1629

560-76 **Attleborough**—Co. Norfolk—see ENG 10-2 & 10-3 for Thomas Page line D

560-77 **Assington,** Co. Suffolk—Jefferie/Mary Page

560-78 **Ashfield**—Co. Suffolk—William/Mary Page-William/Sarah Cross Page (see 560-54)

560-79 **Bardwell**—Co. Suffolk—Phillip Page—Christian b.1549 and Robert b.1550

560-80 **BRADFIELD St. George**—Co. Suffolk—John/Rachel Page 1705

560-81 **Brantham—Co. Suffolk**—Elizabeth Page mar Richard Garwood 1710

560-82 **Brundish**—Co. Suffolk—Edmund/Ann Page children 1566-1572

560-83 **Burgh**—Co. Suffolk—many Page names 1671-1712—

560-84 **Chevington**—Co. Suffolk—Thomas Page christened 18Apr1653 par: Joseph/ Mary Page
   Joseph Page.13Nov1654—parents: Joseph/Mary Page

560-85 **Culford**—Co. Suffolk—John Page has son William christened 21Jul1602 (see 560-43)

560-86 **Covehithe**—Co. Suffolk—Francis bap 1618 & Henry bap 1622 par: Francis/ Tomazine Page

560-87 **Chelsworth**—Co. Suffolk—Anne, b. 1633 & Gyles Page b. 1635 par: John/Ann Page (next to Semer)

560-88 **Dallinghoo**—Co. Suffolk—Benjamin/Elisabeth Page had Mary 1682 (560-88)

560-89 **Cratfield**—Co. Suffolk—Richard Page mar Mary Frie 1639

560-90 **Drinkstone**—Co. Suffolok—Edward Page had Robert, b.1588 and Jonathan Page b.1592

560-91 **Euston**—Co. Suffolk—Margaret Page mar Robert Gent,1601

560-92 **Felixstowe**—Co. Suffolk—Michael Page mar Margaret Marsh 1681 (see 560-12C)

560-93 **Felsham**—Co. Suffolk—Phillip Page had son John Page b. 1659 & Joseph Page mar Ann Lovell 1659 (next to Gaedding & Rattlesden)

560-94 **Fressingfield**—Co. Suffolk—Thomas/Ester Page had Mary 1675 & Elizabeth b.1690 == Thomas/Mary Page had Mary, b.1679 == Thomas Page had John b.1683 == Francis/Ann Page had John b.1689,

560-95 **Gedding**—Co. Suffolk—Phillip Page had Robert Page/Margry Page info— probably Page line D. (see 560-49B)

560-96 **Glemsford**—Co. Suffolk—very large list of names including Abraham Page line. Not sure if this is Page Line C or D. also see 560-50B and 560-72.

560-97 **Great Bealings**—Co. Suffolk,—Samuel/Ann Page had Samuel, b.1690—Sarah b.1696—John b. 1699 and Thomas b. 1705. Must be linked to Grundisburg and Woodbridge families.

560-98 **Grundisburgh**-C. Suffolk—William Page mar Agnes Serson 1554 & Elizabeth Page mar: John Marten 1602.

560-99 **Groton**—Co. Suffolk—Edward Page had many children 1562-1581-1637

560-100 **Great Waldingfield**—Susan b.1551 and John b.1552 father was William Page

560-101 **Great Wenham**—Co. Suffolk Anne Page mar Simon Winns

560-102 **Hadleigh**—Co. Suffolk—marriages—Dyna Page1579—Elizabeth Page1602 & Ann Page1649.

560-103 **Hasketon**—Co. Suffolk—1562 John Page(15A) had son John (59)

560-104 **Heveningham 1541** John Page **WILL**—Robert/Joan Page had Anne 1579 & Edward 1581

560-105 **Icklingham**—Suffolk—William/Mary Page had William 1659 & Nathaniel/Mary Page had Mary 1725

560-106 **Ixworth**—Suffolk—John/Elizabeth Page had Elizabeth1664—John1666— Susan1670—George1676—Mary1678

560-107 **Kersey**—Suffolk—James/Elizabeth Page had Mary1693—James1696— Elizabeth1700—John1704—Thomas1707. 22Sep1605 Edward Page mar Rebecca Gosnold.

560-108 **Levington**—Suffolk—(next to Nacton) Robert Page & Nathaniel/Jane Page line 1599-1781

560-109 **Lowestoft**—Suffolk—Large Page family beginning with Symon Page mar Alice Wilde on 23Sep1583 and ending in late 1700's. Formerly Pagefield near Somerleyton (see 560-12 & 14 & 15).

560-110 **Martlesham**—Suffolk—Robert/Barbara Page had Robert 1717-John 1719—John 1722—Martha 1725 then Joseph/Mary Page had Mary 1791—Sarah 1793

560-111 **Melton**—Suffolk—Joan Page1569—Mary Page1716 & Anne Page1744 marriages

560-112 **Monk Soham**—Suffolk—Susan Page b.1792 mother was Elizabeth Page

560-113 **Monks Eliegh**—Suffolk—Jacob Page had Richard 1661

560-114 **Mutford**—Suffolk—Robert/Alice Page had Thomas, Margaret, Edward, Alce1636-1642

560-115 **Nacton**—Suffolk—Robert/Martha Page & Richard/Rebecca Page children

560-116 **Naughton**—Suffolk—William Page had Elizabeth 1582

560-117 **Nedging**—Suffolk—John/Alice Page had Thomas 1602

560-118 **Newmarket** Suffolk—Elizabeth, Gresham, Robert Page marriages

560-119 **Norton**—Suffolk—Robert/Grace Page had Elisabeth 1558—Andrew Page mar Margaret Gyllye 1584 and had Anna 1585.—Edmund Page had Anne 1698

560-120 **Parham**—Suffolk

560-121 **Polstead**—Suffolk—1494 WILL of John Page, John/Grace Page had Elizabeth 1543, Margery1558,—Thomas Page had Sara 1604, Elizabeth1606

560-122 **South Cove**—Suffolk—Robert/Margaret Page had Robert1607, Faith1609, Francis1610, Francis, 1620,—Francis/Anne Page had Thomas1646

560-123 **Shotley**—John/Susan Page had Phillip1706

560-124 **Redisham**—Suffolk—Thomas/Sarah Page had Martha1739—Mary Page had Hannah1739 and she mar Robert Ford1760

560-125 **Rendham**—Suffolk—Thomas/Margaret Page had Mary1736, Margaret1737, John1739, —John/Elizabeth Page had John1755

560-126 **Pettistree**—Suffolk—Daniel/Anne Page had Anne1702, Susanna1704, Mary1706, & Susanna1712—Edmund Page mar Katherina Turvye1596

560-127 **Spexhall**—Suffolk—John Page b.1691

560-128 **Stoke by Nayland**—Suffolk—William/Hannah Page, Francis Page,

560-129 **Stratford St. Mary**—Suffolk—Robert/Eleanor Page 1574—Abakuk/Bridget Page 1590

560-130 **Sudbury (all saints)** Suffolk—Too many to list (1570-1730)

560-131 **Swefling**—Suffolk—John/Ann Page had Ann1702 and John1704

560-132 **Tannington**—Suffolk—John Page (cooper) & Audrie Page had Henry 1574—Benjamin/Ann Page had Richard 1634

560-133 **Timworth**—Suffolk—Thomas Page had Susan1570, Thomas1576

560-134 **Tuddenham St. Mary**—Suffolk—Thomas Page1570—

560-135 **Wilby**—Suffolk—Henry Page-Yeoman (18A)—**WILL** 1653

560-136 **Woodbridge**—Suffolk—large Page family

560-137 **Ufford**—Suffolk—Robert/Margaret Page had William1575, Jacob1580, John1581

560-138 **West Stow**—Suffolk—Thomas Page b. 1696

560-139 **Westhall**—Suffolk—Margaret Page mar Daniel Salter 1654

560-140 **Whatfield**—Suffolk—Edmund Page mar AlicePegg1644 had Edmund1645, William1647,

560-141 **Wherstead** Suffolk—William/Mary Page had Mary1677, William1679

560-142 **Wingfield**—Suffolk—Edward Page had John 1589, William1590, Edmund1592

560-143 **Withersfield**—Suffolk—Amy Page mar James Cornill 1586

560-144 **Woolverstone**—Suffolk—Thomas Page mar Marie Paris 1620

560-145 **Worlingham**—Suffolk—Thomas/Joan Page had John1614, Rose1617, Jane1622

560-146 **Walcott—Co. Norfork**—(near North Walsham) Thomas/Margaret Page had Margaret1563, thomas1565, edmund1566, William,1568, Nicholas1572, Cicely1571, Myles1578,—Edmund/Margaret Page had Margaret1603, Katheryne1600, Edmund1609, Elizabeth1613, Edmund1631, Ann1633, richard1634, John1635, Dorothy1638,

560-147 **Wrentham**—Suffolk (by Covehithe)—Francis/Frances Page had Thomas 1637

560-148 **North Walsham** Co. Norfolk—Too many to list

560-149 **Framlingham Castle**—Suffolk—1596 William Page, Esq.—1603 Mary Page,

560-150 **Wenhaston**—Suffolk—1653 John Page yeoman

560-151 **Debenham**—Suffolk—Thomas Page—3 hearths

560-152 **Dennington**—Suffolk—Mr. Page 5 hearths (also is William Vincent & widow Vincent)

560-153 **Norwich WILLs**—Filed under each town—

1497 Richard Page (21) Worlingworth (560-58)

1601 Richard Page—Worlingworth 560-58)

1596 William Page Framlingham **(560-149)**

1603 Mary Page, widow of Edward Page—Framlingham Castle (560-28)

1653 Henry Page (18A) yeoman—Wilby—(560-135)

1653 John Page, yeoman—Wenhaston (560-150)

1541 John Page—Heveningham (560-104)

560-154 WILLS at **Chelmsford**—Co. Essex—Long list of names of Page's that are filed at Chelmsford archives. Too many to list but they are listed under each town but this is master list of all the Wills. This list was originally provided by Sheriden Randolph and assigned (141).

560-155 Documents from **Virginia** (from George W. Page) relating to William Garrett (Yarrett) land ownership and possible birthplace of Thomas Page, bc. 1650, in Rappahanock Co, (now Richmond Co), Virginia.

155A **Cavaliers and Pioneers,**—Abstract of Va Land Patents & Grants, Vol II, (1666-1695) by Nugent and Grundman, Va State Library, Richmond, Va (1977). This book is (483)list of research documents in my personal library, but Bobby W. Page has a copy also.

560-156 **Long Melford**—Suffolk—(next to Glemsford) Philippa Page, 1592 Widow and Thomas Page, Gent 1686.

560-157 **HUNSTON** (Suffolk)—WILLs—years 1568-1676.

560-158 **COCKFIELD**—Co. Suffolk—Thomas Gleason (1607-1696) married Susanna Page, (1Jan1622-1690)(30C) (daughter of Thomas Page,.(30) **Hawstead**, Co. Suffolk, England). (See ENG 10-1, p.33) **Cockfield** is next to **Alpheton** where John Locke married Mary Newton (VA 54) and near **Preston**—where Mary Page, b.1620 (30F) married Thomas Locke (30F-1) in 1635. (see 560-32) Info from 1638 Able Men of Suffolk County.

560-159 1638 County Suffolk—**Able-bodied Men of Suffolk**—register. Broken down by last names. This summary is on the "William Page" name, which will be revealed under towns of Downham, Deback, Hunston, Walsham le Willows, Burstall, and Flowton.

    159A Thomas Gleason Family as they moved from County Suffolk, England to Massachusetts with Susanna (Page) Gleason and her brother William Page from line of the father Thomas Page (30)—(Yeoman from **Hawstead**). See ENG 10-1, p. 33

    159B The Gleason Family of Watertown, Mass.—Genealogy information.

    159C Year 1638 Spreadsheet with Page names and towns where they lived.

560-160 **SAPISTON**—Suffolk—(NOW called **NORTH COVE**)—**1627**—WILL of John Aldham mentions John and Thomas Page—sons of Thomas Page that might go back to Robert Page (0-1) in years 1341-1344. Robert Page married Olivia Pagtel (of Walsham le Willows) in 1341 "without leave". 1344 Olivia paid fine for this marriage. Somehow one William Page (0-2) in 1391 might have been involved in this issue.

560-161 **NORTH COVE—Suffolk—**(formerly Sapiston)—see 560-160.

560-162 History of Britian Vol 1 (3000 BCV—1603 AD—by Simon Schama—BBC Books

560-163 History of Britian Vol 2—1603-1776 by Simon Schama—BBC Books, London

560-164 History & Genealogy of **HEARN** FAMILY by William T. Hearne, Independence, Missouri.—Examiner Printing Co, Independence, Mo. (1907) Does NOT reveal any Hearne connection to the Page family of County Suffolk, England or Isle of Wight, Va.

560-165 Battle Abbey Rolls—listing of those that supported William "the Bastard" 7th Duke of Normandy in his 1066 invasion of England and winning the battle to become King of England Go to internet and enter the above info.

560-166 Name Dropping—Clues to ancestors given names help identify earlier generations.

560-167 Great Britain Road Atlas, Geographers A-Z Map Company, Kent TN 15 8 PP.

560-168 Grand Priory of Knights Templar in Scotland

560-169 1309 Knights Templar established in Scotland

    169A The Crusades by Michael Paine—(2005)

    169B Crusades and the Crusader Knights by Charles Phillips

    169C Holy Warriors by Jonathan Phillips—Random House, NY (2009)

560-170 Templar Ships left at midnight from La Rochelle, France heading to Scotland,.

560-171 Bannockburn—Battle for Scotland's Freedom

560-172 1320 Declaration of Arbroath

560-173 1329 Bruce lay dying and asked Sir James Douglas to take his heart into battle in Spain.

560-174 Taxation in the 14th Century in England.

560-175 PAGE family "E" line research (11 pages) by Ruthanne Page (15Jan2012)—as it deals with Charles Nash Page—famous book on the PAGE family genealogy—that has been criticized as "somewhat inaccurate". Ruthanne remarks that it "is amazing that C.N. Nash—got as much right—as he actually did. The Benedict Arnold issue is mentioned and gives further insight on why he changed sides and his "maybe" connection to one THOMAS PAGE.

560-176 Time Lines of History by Smithsonian Library,—DK Publishing, NY, NY 10014

560-177 Scotland's DNA: Descended from lost tribes and related to Napoleon.

560-178 Marriage of Thomas Page and Alice Garrett in mid-Atlantic by Ship Captain.

560-179 **CAROLINA PAGE's** by Robert E. Page (1990) Page Line "C"

560-180 Religious Society of Friends/Quakers—Virginia—1650 until present.

180A **CHUCKATUCK** (Virginia) Monthly Meeting beginning 1672—discontinued 1737

180B Chuckatuck (VA) Comprehensive Quaker report on the many marriages and births of the Thomas Page/Alis family and Yarrett family—(1680-1723) ties the English/ Va line.

180C Richard Ratcliff marriage in Chuckatuck

560-181 Thomas Page and wife Alis—recorded as being in Perquimans Distict, N.C. in year 1659, 1663 and1684—source: LDS IGI for N.C.

181A Family Tree of Thomas Page/Alis—by Jesse M. Page Jr.

181B Bio on Jesse M. Page Jr (1914-1991)—which gives his educational background, which seems to indicate his parents were USMC while he was attending high school, Camp LeJeune, N.C. and college at N.C. State University and graduated as an architect and opened a firm in Raleigh, N.C.

181C Did Thomas Page, that appeared in Perquimans District, NC in 1659, with wife Alis—really be Alice "Garrett". Bobby W. Page (Okla)—father of Chris (Ark) Page—says YES but his son Chris says NO.

560-182 William Hollowell, b. 27Jan1592, Ashby St. Ledger, Northamptonshire, England —died 1645, Flore, Northhamptonshire, England does not seem to be the father of Alice Hollowell, the wife of Thomas Page, b.c 1640 as proposed by Chris Page. See research by George W. Page in this document.

560-183 **HUNSTON** (Co. Suffolk) Parish Registers,—Baptisms—Burials—Marriages 11 Wills from 1568 to 1676—Many John, Joan, Robert, Thomas, Prudence Pages. Many of these can be found on (560-60).

183A 24May1683 Hunston—Gentleman Thomas Page, d. 1664 (15) and Mary Page, d. 1694 (15-1) left daughters Ann, 1703 and Mary Page, d. 1731—a charity to provide funds for a school for Education and Instruction of Daughters of Gentlemen. The charity is still operating in Hunston and owns 10 acres of land providing rental income to support the charity. Parents Thomas and Mary Page, and daughters Ann and Mary are buried in a great chest-tomb just east of the Church.

183B Hunston—18 names from St. Leonard Shoreditch Baptisms (1558-1640)

560-184A Trail Around Historic Walsham le Willows. Short description of Houses and their owners in Walsham le Willows. (26 pages) This is another version of 560 Who lived in your House.

560-185 Richard Martineau (**THE LAWN**) is giving away 12 of his cottages to charity.(8 pages)

560-186 Genealogy-DNA Digest, Vol 8, Issue 137, 5Feb2013 mentions "breaking" into the tomb of ROLLO the Viking and get at the Y-DNA of the Saxon King Royal bloodline.

WILLS—English

561-1   John Page (the elder) yeoman of walsham 1605

561-2   John Page (20)

561-3   William Page (5)

561-4   Marion Page (5A)

561-5   William Page (8B)(23)

561-6   William Page (16)

561-7   William Page (60)

561-8   Thomas Page Hawstead

561-9   Thomas Page (6) Walsham

561-10   Thomas Page (20A)

561-11   John Sparke (41-1)

561-12   Richard Page (3)

561-13   Richard Page (21)

561-14   Marie Page (23C-1)

561-15   George Page (28)

561-16   Edmund Page (4C)

561-17   Edmund Page (33) 1633

561-18   Edmund Page (57) 1659

561-19   Henry Page (18A) 1670

561-20   Listing of PAGE **WILLs PRESERVED in Chelmsford, Co. Essex, England**
Also this list is under 560-154—which I picked out those of interest and noted them in the Town reported.

561-21   Andrew Hawes of Walsham le Willows WILL 1610

561-22 List of Wills at Walsham le willows (1396-1798) (9 pages long)

561-23 Thomas Cook Walsham le Willows Will 1616

561-24 Silvester Howlett—WILL 1668—Walsham—his daug Ann married Samuel Page

561-24 A Silverter Howlett—WILL 1676—mentions nephew Robert Page

561-25 Stephen Vincent—Walsham—Will 1665—mentions William Rainbird

561-26 Thomas Cook—Walsham—WILL 1663—wit: Thomas Rampley

561-27 Richard Turner—Walsham—WILL 1661—Wit: Stephen Vincent and Reynold Page

561-28 Richard Rampley—Walsham—WILL 1584—wit: Thomas Lacye and Thomas Page.

561-29 John Rampley—Walsham—WILL 1613—wit: Steven Vincent

561-30 Dorothy (Page) Curtis—Walsham—WILL 1662—Was 1st married to John Rainberd (Woolpit)

561-31 William Complyn (Gent)—Walsham—WILL 1667—was High constable.

561-32 John Robwood (Gent) Walsham—WILL 1595—Wit: John Page, the elder and Thomas Page, "the elder".

561-33 William Baker—Walsham—WILL 1556—Wit: John Page, Thomas Lacy

CHAPTER THREE

INDEX TO TOWNS LISTED IN ENG 10-1 AS OF 1 FEBRUARY 2013

This index is focused on PAGE Line "C" but occasionally other lines appear in same town—so they are also listed—to help avoid any mixing of different DNA lines. I have tried to show (p2) as the page number where it appears in ENG 10-1.

Acle—Co. Norfolk—Robert Page, bc.1550 = Henry Page, bc.1535 NH 1—VA 19-3
      Henry Page, b.1610 (NH 1-1) (Bacon rebellion)—**LINE L**

Acton (Ipswich) Philip Page, Market Weston & son of John Page, Acton, married

Anne Cheeswright on 23Sep1657 (560-33C)

Acton, Suffolk—Brasss of Sir Robert de Bures, Church of all Saints, (560-2, p.99)

Aldeburgh—Suffolk—1625 John Page—daug Elizabeth—WILL of Joan Edwards mentions
      brother in law John Page.

Aldringham, Co. Suffolk—Philip I. Page line—**LINE K**—see MICH 11 and
      ENG 10-3. William Henry Page—b. 1797 to America in 1829.
      (560-66) (see MICH 11) which is Charles William Paige line C. so it appears this
      LINE IS "C"—NOT "K".

Alpheton—Co. Suffolk—John Locke (30F-1) married Mary Page see (VA 54)
      (ENG 10-1, p.46)(560-183)

Alverstoke (Co. Hampshire) Line H—Edmund Page in 1600's.

Ashby St. Ledger, Northamptonshire, England—William Hollowell family—see 560-182.

Ashbocking—Co. Suffolk—see 560-54. John Page family (see Easton-John Page)

Ashfield,—Co. Suffolk—see 560-54—William(5), Robert, John Page(15) 1677—
      Four Ashes House (see 560-p.104 & 166)
      John Page, 1517 bought Grove Cottage (old name Vauncys) from
      John Withers (560p107) then in 1536, son Thomas Page, d.1560—wife Katherine,
      sons Andrew, William, Thomas and Nicholas, who assumed possession in 1567 to
      1570.(560p.107) see 560-78 for William/Mary Page,1768—William/Sarah Cross
      Page,1789

Ashfield Magna—Co. Suffolk—Richard Page—
      1639 Thomas Page—Ship Money Returns (560-12E, 54 & 107)

Assington—Co. Suffolk—Jefferie Page

Attlebridge—Co. Norfolk—Richard Page LINE—PA 50—see ENG 10-2 & 10-3—Family
LINE K (560-52) NO—
It looks like Line "K" but is REALLY LINE "C"—see revision to ENG 10-2

Attleborough—Co. Norfolk—Thomas Page LINE D see Eng 10-4 and ENG 10-5

Ayr, Scotland—10 graves of KNIGHT TEMPLARS (p.11)

Ayrshire, Scotland—1068—Hunger family (Page LINE "C") leaves France for Scotland
then moves to Crichton Dean, Scotland (p.11)

Bacton—Co. Suffolk Robert Page, d.1570—John Page, d.1601/Ann(100) see ENG 10-1A
—Robert Page, d.1639 see 560-54

Badingham—Co. Suffolk—Robert Page mar 1666 Ann Danbrooke

Badwell Ash, Co. Suffolk—William Page, b.1599, son of William Page (10) (p29)
John & Robert Page born (see 560-54) see ENG 10-1A

Balantrodoch, Scotland—Knight Templars created.

Bann or Bannockburn, Scotland 1314—Robert de Bruce won battle (p.11)

Bardwell, Co. Suffolk,—Phillip Page 1550 (10) (p29)

Barton Mills—Co. Suffolk—Juliana Page—burial 1327—(560-12C) (next to Worlington)

Belsted—Edmund Page 4 fireplaces

Besthorp, (Co. Norfolk) next to Attleborough—Line "D"
Page's Manor—Henry & John/Margaret Page (year 1345)

Billericay (Co. Essex) Philip I. Page—LINE K—NO line "C"

Blakeney—Co. Norfolk—Philip I. Page LINE K—NO—line "C"

Boxted—(Co. Suffolk) Robert Page, b. 1558 the father of John Page, b. 1585, London
LINE E—(560-68) (see MASS 5 chart). Also John Page/Phoebe Paine that arrived
in Mass in 1630—appear to be from County Essex, England.
George W. Page and Ruthanne Page line.

Brampton—Co. Suffolk—Alexandro Page—buried 1327—(560-12C) (near Spexhall)

Bradfield St. Clair—Co. Suffolk—Georgio Page—buried 1327 (560-12C)(near Gedding)

Breston—Co. Norfolk—Edmund Page, Gent, d.1659—WILL 1633
—son of Christopher Page (57)

Brightingsea (Co. Essex) Thomas Hawes (17A) /Ann Page, b.1594 (17) moved from
Walsham le Willows to Co. Essex.

Brinton—Co. Norfolk—Sarah Fountain mar John Page, b.1799—Philip I. Page LINE K—
see PA 50

Breston—Co. Norfolk—Edmund, Gent d.1659—WILL 1633-son of Christopher Page (57)

Brix, (Normandy), France—Robert de Bruce, b. 1274. (p. 3)

Bromeswell—Co. Suffolk—Phillip Page (95) (105)

Burgh (Suffolk)—near Grundisburg

Burstall—Co. Suffolk—William/Ann Page(105) family—George/Susanna Page
Robert Page mar Sarah Bacon—1695 Robert Page burial (560-12)

Edmund Page/Ann Bagley mar see 560-54

1638—William/Ann Page (105) Suffolk Able men—(560-159)

1639—William Page—Ship Money Returns—(560-12E)

Bury St. Edmunds—Margaret Oversath (4), Henry Page (18A)

(560-33) Robert Page (well street) 2 fireplaces—Edward Sparke—3 fireplaces

James Page/John Page—each had 5 fireplaces (91-1)

Bury—John Page (year 1558) had part of the monastery of Bury.

Bury St. Edmunds—1539 William Page mar Margery Bacon

21Oct1652 William Page mar Anne Mayr. (560-33C & 33D)

Paul Page (88)/Mary

Bury—St.Mary Parish marriage register—1561-1696 many names (560-33)

Bury—John Page of Hopton—mentioned (560-33)

Buxted—Co, Sussex—John Page (95) Parnell Page (95-2)

Caulfield—Co. Suffolk—John Page was wit to **WILL** about Samuel Newton

Carlton—Co. Cambridgeshire—George Page, b. 1781, Carlton-d.1854—Helen Griffiths line

Cavenham—Co. Suffolk—next to Icklingham—Henry Hearne family moved to Cavenham and the widow died/buried there.

Champaign, France—**KNIGHT TEMPLARS** headquarters in France. (p.8)

Chattisham—Suffolk—1674 Hearth tax—**ABRAM PAGE** next to **THOMAS NEWTON** **(**560-12)

Chediston—Suffolk—Henrico Page—buried 1327 (560-12C) (near Spexhall)

Chelsworth—Co. Suffolk—Anne, b.1633 & Gyles b.1635 par: John/Anne Page (next to Semer) see 560-87

Chillesford—Co. Suffolk—Johanne Page—burial 1327 (560-12C)(near Ufford)

Chelmsford—Essex-Abraham Page placed in Gaol for what appears religious reasons. (p.49) (see 560-156) Abraham Page/Ann Page had son **ABRAHAM, b.8Jun1716—Is this the MASS Page line.** (560-50A)—chart AD1A

Chevington (SW of Bury)—Co. Suffolk—John Page, d.1452 (2) (560-43) (p.17)

Joseph /Mary Page—son Thomas b.18Apr1653 & Joseph b. 13Nov1654 (560-12D, 43 & 84)

Chichester—(Sussex) John de Pagham, son of William—got his father's lands. (p.8)

Chrichton Dean, Scotland—Oliver Hunter family.

Chuckattuck, Va—Quakers church (p.5) Many from County Suffolk, England joined the Quaker church in Isle of Wight, Virginia. Richard Ratcliff family (560-180C) Thomas Page/Alis Garrett Family records (560-180B)

Cockfield—Suffolk—Thomas Gleason (1607-1696) (30C-1) mar Susanna Page (30C)(1616-1690) (560-32 & 158) (see ENG 10-1, p.33)

Copdock—Suffolk—1730 Abraham Page born—parents: **ABRAHAM PAGE**, b.1704/ MARY (Lamb) Page (see AD1A)

Co. Ayr, Scotland—Hunter family (p.6)

Co. Middlesex—**LINE F**—Col. John Page—Williamsburg, Virginia.

Coutances—see castle of Pirou. (p.2)

Covehithe—Suffolk—Francis, b.1618 & Henry b.1622—par: Francis/Thomazine Page not
    far from Worlingworth. (560-86)

Cratfield—Suffolk—Richard Page mar Mary Frie 1639 (560-89)

Creeting St.Mary—Suffolk—1638 Thomas Page-Able Bodied Men of Suffolk (560-159)

Culford (Co. Suffolk) home of James, Duke of York, that shows up in **1674**.

    Near Ingham—just outside of Bury—on the road to Icklingham. (560-43)

    Year 1292—John Page? (2) seems to serve on a jury in London.

    Year 1399 John Page (2) paid 2 shillings per annum for the tenement in which he
    lives. Not clear who this John Page is? Maybe John Page (91-4)

    Year1602 John Page (95) had son William Page, bap 21Jul1602 (see 560-85 & 43)

Curry Rivel—Co. Someset—1704 **ABRAHAM PAGE** married (near Port of Bristol)

Documents at Chelmsford—Co. Essex—**WILL** 50 BR 15-info from Sheridan Randolph

Dallinghoo—Co. Suffolk—Benjamin/Elizabeth Page had Mary b.1682 (560-88)

Deback—Suffolk—1638 William Page—Able Men (560-159) (near Ufford)
    —see William Page, b. 1575 (560-137)

Debenham—Suffolk—1638 Thomas Page (560-159)

    1674 Thomas Page 3 hearths (560-151)

Dennington—Suffolk—1674 Mr. Page—5 hearths (William Vincent nearby) (560-152)

Devon, England—Nathaniel Page/Paige arrived colonies in 1675.

Dickleburgh—Co. Norfolk—1562 Nickolas Page mar Elizabeth Wright—see ENG 10-4

Drinkstone—two Philip Page's—1 & 5 fireplaces—Rector John Page, d. 1582

    Edward Page had Robert, b.1588 & Jonathan b.1592 (560-90)

Dumfries, Scotland,—1306—Robert de Bruce killed John Comyn. (p. 10)

    Easton—Co. Suffolk—1690 John Page buried (near Ufford John Page)

    1601 Margaret Page mar Robert Gent (560-91)

Felthorpe—Norfolk—Anne West mar Thomas Page, b.1796-next to Attlebridge-see PA50

Felixstowe—Co. Suffolk—1327 Willmo Page burial (560-12C) (next to Trimley St. Mary)

    1681 Michael Page mar Margaret Marsh (560-92)

Felsham—Co. Suffolk—Phillip Page had John b. 1659 &

    Joseph Page mar Ann Lovell 1659. (560-93) (next to Gedding & Rattlesden)

Finningham—Thomas Page, b.1637 (30A)—Elizabeth Page (41) mar in Finningham (p42)

    Thomas Page is "probably" the father of Thomas Page, bc.1640's married to Alice
    Garrett.

    Thomas Page (30A-1) & (40) married wife #3 Elizabeth Frere on 7Mar1670 in

Finningham (30-1) who died 23Feb1680, in Rickinghall but buried 2May1680 in

Finningham. (p.49) (551G, p. 17) (560-30A)

> The Rebekka Page,(30)(d.16Oct1653, Boston) married Thomas Leader on 25Mar1616, in Finningham (560-30A). Mr. Leader d.286Oct1663, Boston, MA (doubt this is Line C probably **LINE D OR L** See chart NH 1 for Henry Page, executed in Bacon Rebellion—which is **LINE L,**—Our line C is the Rebecca Page (30), that was wit: to will of Thomas Page (30) on 11Jul1637, at Ixworth—Co. Suffolk. Other wit: were George Scarpe and Thomas Page.

Flempton—Suffolk—Roger Page of Risby (1448-1505) (91-2) wit to many deeds.

Flowton—Suffolk—1638 William Page (105)—Suffolk—Able men—maybe father/son
> with William Page in town of Burstall (560-159)

Fornham St. Martin—Co. Suffolk—Roger Page (91-2)(of Risby)—
> 6Aug1579 Elizabeth Page (110) of Framlingham mar Edmund Boldero, (560-61 & 63)

Framsden—Co. Suffolk—1560 Robert Page mar Jane Bloomefield (560-64)

Framlingham—Co. Suffolk—Edmund Page, b.1535 (97) Edward Page, Gent (wife Mary)
> was father of Edward Page, probate 1609. William Page (60) (560-28)
> Philip Page, Robert Page, Frances and Henry Page (560-34E)

Fressingfield—Suffolk—many Thomas Page births (560-94)—might be Page line J.

Fulmodeston,—Norfolk—**LINE "H"**—William Page, b. 1778, (98) died 31May1865,
> **Shipdham, Co. Norfolk—which is Anthony Brian Treacher line—next town to Brinton—LINE K** (see 560-53B)

Garboldisham—Norfolk—William/Marie Page(560-74) had Alice Page 1697.-ENG 10-4

Gedding—Suffolk—Philip Page (father of Robert Page)—next to Rattlesden (**LINE D**)
> (See 560-49B)

Gipping—Suffolk—William Page mar Mary Hall 16Oct1677 (near Bacton)(560-33D)

Glemsford—Suffolk—Thomas Page, b.Apr1563 AND b. Jun 1628 (560-12D)
> Mary Page, b.1734—Parents: **ABRAHAM PAGE** (tailor) /MARY PAGE (p.55) mar: 1704—Halstead (Co. Essex) (560-50B & 560-96)

Great Baddow—Co. Essex—1628 marriage Abraham Page—bricklayer
> 1636 Abraham Page—bond from William Vincent
> 1645 Abraham Page emigrated to Boston, Mass

Great Waldingfield—Suffolk—William Page had Susan, b.1551 & John b.1552.(560-100)

Great Yarmouth (Co. Norfolk) Robert Page, b. 1800

Great Wenham—Co. Suffolk—1700 Anne Page mar Simon Winns (560-101)

Groton—Co. Suffolk—Edward Page line with many children (560-99)

Gloucester Co, Va—1678 **ABRAHAM PAGE** imported by William Grimes (NC 25-1)

Grundisburgh—Co. Suffolk—1727—**ABRAHAM PAGE**, b.1704 mar Mary Lamb (p59)
> Info: Dan Page, b. 1865—send to Dan/Moria Page—see my Canada book
> 1554 William Page mar Agnes Serson

1634 Katherine Page mar James Ellye (560-98)

Gunthorpe (next to Brinton) Philip I. Page **LINE K**—see PA 50—maybe Line **C**

Hadleigh—Co. Suffolk—Anne Page 1649 & Dyna Page 1579 & Elizabeth Page 1602 (560-102)

Halesworth—Co.Suffolk—author Audrey McLaughlin "Your House book" died July 2010 (560).

Hasketon—Co. Suffolk—John Page, b.1562 (59)—son of John Page (15A) (560-103)

Haverhill, Co. Suffolk—Helen Griffiths Helen_griffiths58@yahoo.ca 3 miles from West Wickham, Co. Cambridgeshire.—Henry Page, b. 1760, Haverhill

Halstead (Co. Essex) near Chelmsford—**ABRAHAM PAGE**—tailor—married 1704

Hawstead—(Co. Suffolk) Thomas Page (30) appeared in 1620, Thomas/Susan Page had son Joseph Page born, but soon died and 2nd son Joseph was born and appears in 1674 hearth tax. Thomas Page, (30) d.1639, Hawstead (see will—p.27) wit: Rebecca Page, Thomas Page (15C) & George Scarpe. (ENG 10-1, p.33)

1639 Thomas Page (paid high taxes) & George Scarpe—see Ship Money Returns (560-12E, 32D & 50)

Hasted (near Bury) "seems" to be a "shorten" version of Hawsted "MAYBE"

1564 Mary Vincent mar John Tillot of Hasted—Mary was servant to Thomas Page (20A) of Hasted.(560-33C)

Heveningham—Suffolk—1540 John Page mar Anne Warner—John Page **WILL** 1541 —Robert/Joan Page had Anne 1579 & Edward Page 1581 (560-104)

Hessett—Co. Suffolk—William Page's daug mar George Nun (560-45) (560-49A)

1543 Philip Page mar Alice Hoo

William Page, Gent—had **WILL** 6Nov1562. (560-45 & 49A)

Hinderclay (Co. Suffolk)—Church Rector Thomas Page (1) (1391-1399)(p.9/17)

Hingham—Co. Norfolk—John Page, b.6Feb1613, mar Mary Marsh, b. 1618, **LINE D** (**see** MASS 1)

Hintlesham—Co. Norfolk—1327 Rogero Page—buried—(560-12C)

Hollesley—Co. Suffolk—7May1684 William Page burial—near Woodbridge (560-33D) (next to Burstall and Chattisham)

Hopton—Thomas Page (26), and John Page (26A)—2 fireplaces and is related to **JOHN PAGE, who d.1668** (15A) (p35)

Horham—Co. Suffolk—7May1400 Thomas Page (1) owned land here.—near Pagefield. along with Jernigan family. (560-15)

Horringer—Co. Suffolk—(borders Hawstead & Ickworth)—Epinetus Page, b.11Jul1585 (62) (who's father is William Page—later shows up in Ingham—as father of Judith Page, b. 24Jun1617. (560-57)-William Page (8B) ("maybe" son of Thomas Page (8) is father to several children in Horringer, one being Rose Page. (560-33B)

The following parent William Page (Culford Estate)—had the following: (560-33D)

William Page,(24G) b.14Sep1606, Ann, (23C) b. 25May1608,
Margaret, b.13Apr1612,—Marie,(24E) b.17Dec1615—
Thomas,(24D), b.28May1618, Richard, b.21Dec1620, and then
Robert, b. 19Sep1613—who was son of William Page, the Younger.
See 560-33D for many more births of this William Page line.

Hunston—Thomas Page(12), Robert Page(13), Thomas Page (34), Robert **Page(34A)(p50)**
William Page (36), Thomas Page (37), Salomon Page (38), Edward Page (39)
Samuel Page 1 fireplace—Mr. Page had 8 fireplaces (560-12)
Thomas Page, b.1642 15B/20A) (560-12D)(560-157) (560-183)
1552 Thomas Page (6) of Hunston, (next to Woolpit) bought 5 acres of land, and
Parcel of Hardings from Edward Brooke, Gent. 1553 Widow Mary Brook signed
quit claim to Robert Page (34), son of Thomas Page. (560-60A)

Hunston—1636Thomas Page(30)mar Mary Newton—had **Thomas, b.6Dec1640** (30A)
Thomas/Mary Page had Mary, b.19Feb1642 (560-159D)
This Thomas (30A) & Mary (Newton) Page emigrate to Stafford Co, Va in 1674.

Hunston—1638 Thomas Page (15) is constable & living near William Page (16B)(p31)
(see 560-159) and Samuel Page (15A) (560-159)

Hunston—Baptisms (1557-1666—Burials 1559-1731—Marriages1563-1658—see 560-159D.

Hunston—WILLS—11 Wills listed (YEARS 1658-1676 see (560-157)

Hunston (Suffolk) is a very important town in this search for THOMAS PAGE who arrived
in Isle of
Wight, Va area in 1659 and important and supporting documents are:
560-12C & 12D—560-60 & 60A—560-157-560-159D—560-183

Hunterston, Scotland—Oliver Hunter Family—Page Line "C"

Ickingham—Co. Suffolk—Thomas Page d.1656 (20A)—Page **LINE D** has tenement here
and mar Dorothy Gosling (p35)

Ingham—Suffolk—1587 Thomas Page born (560-12D)
1591 Mrs. Thomas Page has female born
1593 Thomas Page born
June 1612 Thomas Page born

Ingham—John Page (5 homes from Lady Bacon) Ship Money Returns (560-12D & E)

Ingham, Suffolk (560-25) Parish register (1538-1811) then (see 560-22)(ENG 10-1B)
Parish register (1593-1635) John Page (63) and ENG 10-1B
Thomas Page, had daug Susanna, b.1614, and son, John Page, b. 1617. (p32)
Thomas Page then moved to Hawstead. Thomas Page had previously lived in
Rickinghall, then Ingham, then Hawstead.
Thomas Page, only child, in the 1610 **WILL** got all the property.
1323 Bruce Page named in suit "Parson of Ingram church vs. Bruce Page"(p9)
(560-22C)

Ingham—May 1670 Rebecca Page (74) and Henry Turner married

Ingham—1636 William Page (60) died—wife Susan Holte and many children listed
    (ENG 10-1, p. 22)

Ipswich—Suffolk—1552 Thomas Page (6)

Ipswich—Suffolk—Nicholas/Joan Page had Margaret1559, John1562

    John/Mary Page had Margaret1592, Wiliam1636, Ann1639,

    John/Mary Page had Thomas1662, Sara1665, Jonathan1667,(560-60A)

    James/Elizabeth Page had John1585, Phillip 1687 (560-60A)

    Thomas Page had Robert1599, Elizabeth1602

    30Aug1727 Thomas Page, Knight of the Shire at Ipswich (560-48)

Isle of Man—30 Knight Templars graves found. (p.11)

Isle of Wight, Va—Page Line "C" appears (p.14)

Ixworth—year 1452 John Page (1) John Page (8), William Page (5) (560-43)(p7)

    John Page had 1 fireplace—Thomas Page (20A)

    John Page (15A/20) d.1669 gives to Thomas Page (20A) land.

    John/Elizabeth Page had Elizabeth1664, John1666, Susan1670, George1676
    (560-106)

    1597 Andrew Page-clothier in Ixworth—married Margarite Gyllye 1584 in
    Norton (560-119) Andrew Page had daug Helen 23Feb1602.

    Andrew Page moved to Ixworth from Bury St. Edmunds because he had
    Sons Andrew1587, Samuel,1589 & John1592 all born in Bury (560-106)

Ixworth Thorpe—Suffolk—1304 Thomas Page got manor (560-9 & 60 & 60A) (p8)

    1315 Thomas Page (399p.30)

    1632 Paul Page, died (89)

    Kersey (near Alpheton)—Co. Suffolk—Thomas Page, b.1666, Preston (30A-1)
    attended school in Bury (560-47)

    James/Elizabeth Page had Mary1693, James1696, Eliz1700, John1704,
    Thomas1707

    See (560-107)

Kingston—Upon The Hull (Co. East Yorkshire) Alan Alls birthplace. **LINE C**

Kirton—(near Trimley St. Mary) 1638 Thomas Page—(560-159)

    1327 Willmo Page buried (560-12C)

Knettshall—Co. Suffolk—Isaac Page (98)

Kelsale—Co. Suffolk—Alse Page (31-1) Thomas Page, John Page (31)(560-30A)

    1639 John Page, Ship Money Returns (560-12E)

La Rochelle, France—Knight Templars ships left France 10Feb1307 (p.13) (560-170)

Lackford—Co. Suffolk—year 1407 Thomas Page (1)(91-3) and John Page (2)(91-4),

Agnes Page (2A) 3Aug1407 Deed lease to John Ingham in Lackford and land was next to Thomas Page (1) (91-3) property (560-43)

Thomas Page (560-15) Thomas Page, b.1550, (560-12D)

1327 Willmo Page—buried—(560-12C)(near Icklingham)-**LINE D** maybe

Langham,—Co. Suffolk—Robert Page (90)

Lavenham Co. Suffolk—1540 William Page, yeoman—bond to Edmund Kneyett of Buckenham Castle. Parish records—1621 John Page/Phebe Paine married—**Line E**—(560-68) (see chart MASS 5) George W. Page and Ruthanne Page line.

Levington—Co. Suffolk—Robert/Martha Page 1604—Nathaniel/Jane Page 1700s— Robert Page 1599 (next to Nacton) (560-108)

Little Whelenetham—Co. Suffolk—Scarpe family (560-65)

London—Thomas Page, b.1650 (112)—St. Margaret—Westminister
—parents: John/Ann Page (560-71)
ABRAHAM PAGE/Ann had son Abraham Page b.8Jun1716, St. Bride-Fleet street and son Thomas Page, b. 25Dec1717. (560-50A) This is NOT line "C"
1535 Thomas Page WILL—of Romford (London) (560-71A).

Long Melford—(next to Glemsford)—where 1704 **ABRAHAM PAGE**/Mary got married
1592 Philippa Page, Widow and Thomas Page, Gent 1686. (560-156)
Might be Thomas Page b.Jun1628 (560-12D)

Lowestoft—Co. Suffolk—formerly called "Pagefield"—see below Somerleyton (560-14)
1300's Fishing village
13Jun1665 Naval battle of Lowestoft—109 English ships won against 103 Dutch ships
1583 Large Page family began with Symon Page mar Alice Wilde (560-109)
1674 Abram Page (2 fireplaces) and Alice Garrett (3 fireplaces) (560-12) (p48)
1674 Araham Page & Alice Garrett—both living in Lowestoft (p.48)
Apr 1756 Thomas Page born (see 560-12D) (p.16)
1914 Samuel Robert Page, b.Lowestoft—(age 44), joined British Army (560-15A)

Market Weston (near Bury) 1654 Mary Vincent mar John Tillot of Hasted. (p35)

Mary was servant to Thomas Page (20A) of Husted—maybe (Hawstead)

Martlesham—Suffolk—Robert/Barbara Page had Robert1717, John1719, John1722, Martha 1725—
Then Joseph/Mary Page had Mary1791, Sarah1793 (560-110)

Melton—Suffolk—Joan1569, Mary1716 and Anne1744 Page married (560-111)

Metfield—Co. Suffolk—Richard Page 2 fireplaces

Mickfield—Co.Suffolk William Page mar Ann Felgate 1Dec1605 near Winston(560-33D)

Middlesex, England—Col John Page arrived VA c. 1650

Millfield—Co. Suffolk—Ann Page mar Hawes (560-28)

Monk Soham—Suffolk (next to Ashfield) Elizabeth Page had Susan 1792 (560-112)

Monks Eliegh—Suffolk—1661 Jacob Page had Richard (560-113)

Moulton—Suffolk—Richard Moody (Knight) d.1574 and 20 acres to son George Moody.
        Wit: Thomas Page ((560-32A)

Mundford—Co. Norfolk—John Page (35) WILL 1650

Mutford—Suffolk—Robert/Alice Page & Thomas/Elizabeth Page had many children
        (560-114)

New Buckenham—Co. Norfolk—below Attleborough—

Nacton—Co. Suffolk—Robert/Martha Page family—1609 Robert/Dorothy Page
        Richard/Rebecca Page family—see 560-112

Naughton—Suffolk—1582 William Page had Elizabeth (next to Nedging) (560-113)

Nedging—Suffolk—John/Alice Page had Thomas, b.1602 (next to Naughton) (560-114)

Newmarket—Suffolk—mar: Elizabeth Page1649—Gresham Page1727—Robert Page 1731
        (560-115)

Norton—Suffolk—Robert/Grace Page had Elizabeth 25Oct1558—Robert is son of
        Thomas Page (6)
        23Sep1584 Andrew Page mar Margaret Gyllye—had Anna 1585.(560-60B & 119)
        Edmund had Anne Page b. 4Dec1698 (560-119)
        Mr. Page (9 fireplaces 1674) John Page (101) (560-60A)

North Cove (Suffolk) (formerly Sapiston)—1638 Thomas Page (15B/20A)(560-159)
        —next to Mutford—Thomas/Elizabeth Page (560-114)
        WILL—1627 of John Aldham, North Cove (formerly Sapiston) mentions
        Sir Edmund Bacon and John and Thomas Page, sons of Thomas Page—which might
        be from line of Robert Page (0-1) for years of 1341-1344 North Walsham—Co.

Norfolk—Thomas Page (13A) Thomas Page (23A)(p23-38-39)

Norwich Castle—The Knights of Bury St. Edmund did duty there. Had riot 1272. (p4)

Old Rappahanock County, Virginia—USA—Land ownership by William Garrett
        (Yarrett) is clear and "possible" birthplace of Thomas Page, b. around 1650's
        married to Alice Garrett—still poses a problem. (560-155) Both families Page/
        Yarrett
        (Garrett) lived in this area of Va and a marriage of this kind would be normal. These
        two families also had strong documented ties back to County Suffolk, England—so
        the marriage could have taken place in England or Virginia OR as it turns out on a
        ship in the mid-Atlantic as they were traveling to Virginia in 1659.

Old Buckenham—Co. Norfolk—Thomas Page line (560-75)

Ormesby, St. Margaret—(Co. Norfolk)—Robert Page, b.1604—arrived Mass 1635—
        (MASS 1—NH 1—VA 19-3—ENG 9-1)—**LINE L**

Otley—Co. Suffolk—Roberto Page—Burial 1327 (560-12C)(near Ashbocking and Grundisburg)

Pagefield—formerly named (Pakenfield)—but now called Lowestoft. (see p.16 & 47)

Port on channel—was a fishing village in 1300's and where a large naval battle was fought offshore in 1665.

Pakefield (Pagefield) 7 miles from Somerleyton. Ancient Viking settlement (560-14)

Pakenham—Co.Suffolk—St. Mary's church—home of school for Page's (560-9) (p6)

Phillip Page (96) had 4 fireplaces & Joseph Page—1 fireplace (560-12)

William Page (1558-1603)—**Thomas Page, bc.1641** (560-12D)

John Page WILL 22Oct1616 (560-17A)

Robert/Margery Page had Ales Page Sep1567, Agnes 1570, (560-17A)

Thomas/Elizabeth Page had William1667, Hester1669, John1670, (560-17A)

Robert/Elizabeth Page had Robert, 22Apr1733 (560-17A)

Pakenham or de Pirou—from Castle of Pirou, France (p.2)

Parham—Suffolk—Edmund/Catherine Page1598-John/Elizabeth Page had Francis 1648

John/Bridget Page children 1651—Benjamin/Susan Page children 1675—

Benjamin/Judith Page children 1681 (560-120)

Pettistree—Suffolk—Daniel/Anne Page children1702—

Edmund Page mar Katherina Turvye 1596 (560-?)

Polstead—Suffolk—1543 John/Grace Page children—1604 Thomas Page children

1494 John Page **WILL** (560-121)

Preston—Co. Suffolk—Thomas Page, b.1666, Preston (son of Thomas Page, b.1638) (560-12D)

Kersey—Suffolk—(near Alpheton)—Mary Page mar Thomas Locke & Susanna Page mar

Thomas Gleason & Rebecca Page was wit: to **WILL** of Thomas Page (30)

Thomas Page, b. 1666,(30A-1) attended school in Bury, for 2 years, then

Magdalene college, then Ipswich four years. (560-47)

1667 **WILL** of Thomas Locke, Yeoman—(560-47A)

Quierzy (Picardie), France—**LINE M**—Raymond Page, b. 1604

Rattlesden—Co. Suffolk—Robert Page (**LINE D AND L**)(p54) connected to Ormsby, Co.

Norfolk (see MASS 1 & 1-6) Lawrence Page, d.14Dec1632, Rattlesden.

LINE D Contact: June Page Saxton for LINE D info. (560-59) see 10-1A, p7

1707 Mary Page, Rattlesden mar Thomas Hawkin of Norton 1Jan1707.(560-33C)

Edmund/Ann Page had children—Thomas/Bridget Page had children—(560-59C)

LINE C-Thomas Page(30)had John1603,Mary1620,Susan1622,Robert1627-(10-1, p46)

Mary Page had Sara1642—Phillip/Ann Page had Phillip 2Jun1665
(see 97-1) (560-59C)

Redisham—Suffolk—Thomas/Sarah Page (560-124)

Rendham—Suffolk—Thomas/Margaret Page 1736—John/Elizabeth Page1755 (560-125)

Rickinghall (560-30A)—Thomas Page (15) 1 fireplace (see 560-p104)
Four Ashes House (p35)

Ringmer (Sussex)—Charles W. Paige line (LA, Cal) was William Henry Page, b.
19Feb1797, Ringmer (Co. Sussex) (560-67) but baptized at Swaffham, (Co.
Norfolk). maybe Parents: James/Mary Page. This appears to be just before
William, b. 1797 emigrated to America. A William Page married Martha Sanders
31Dec1817 at Ringmer (Co. Sussex) (being verified) see MICH 11

Risby (Co. Suffolk) (next to Bury St. Edmund) Walter Page (91)-then son James (91-1),
(White Lion) then son Roger (91-2), then son Thomas (91-3) &
John Page (91-4) moved to Westley.
1327 Waltero Page burial (560-12C)
1723 Henry Page (Walsham) mar Mary Prick (Risby) on 26Sep1723. (560-12)

Rishangles—Joshua Page, b. 1830—Dan/Moira Page

Rollo, born 846, Fakse, Denmark.(Baptized Robert I)(p.3)—d. Normandy, France
—looking for Y-DNA connection

Rotherhithe—London on Thames River—Joshua Page, b.1780, sailmaker, (560-46A) another
person in **LINE I**—appears to be from Edward Page, bc.1786, Maidstone, Co.
Kent, married to Catherine Stanford 1815, St.Margaret, Rochester, Co. Kent,
England.
This is port where the Mayflower—left for America. Contact robtpage@gmail.com
This port on the Thames river seems to be the port—that on 12Jun1783, John
Page and his son John Jr—debarked—that owns land in Lawnes Creek Parish,
Surry Co, Va.
Also Capt Robert Caufield transported Page Line C—Mary Newton Page (30F)
& husband Thomas Locke (30F-1) to Stafford Co, Va. in 1674 (See VA 8) (see
560-46)

Rougham—(Co. Suffolk) John Page (son of John Page) buried 2Jun1652 (560-68)
1639 John Page—Ship Money Returns (560-12E)

Sapiston—Suffolk—Robert Page (0-1) 1341-1344 (p.15/25)

Saxstead—Co. Suffolk—Rogero Page—Burial 1327—(560-12C) (near Worlingworth)

Saxthorpe—Co. Norfolk—George W. Page line G.

Scole—Co. Norfolk—William/Ann Page had son Miles Page 1567 (560-73) ENG 10-4

Semere—(Co. Suffolk)—Thomas Page (1) Priest at Dickle burgh church 1400-1402.

Shorne (Co. Kent)—George/Sarah Page ar Branford, Ct—1662. (George W. Page **LINE G**)

Shropham—Co. Suffolk—Henry de Pakenham (1367-d.1445) son of Agnes, wife of

Henry de Breton. Pakenham Hall, (1400)

Shotley—Suffolk—John/Susan Page had Phillip 1706 (560-123)

Somerleyton—Co. Suffolk—lies about 6 miles from Lowestoft. This place was seized just after 1066 by William the Conquerer and given to Roger Bigot and later was owned by the Jernengham (Jernigan) family that was close with the Page family. (560-14) (p.4)

Somerleyton, Castle Acre, connected to Sean Jarnigan/Jernigan. and Michelle Taunton. Knights had to pull guard duty there.

South Cove—Suffolk—Robert/Margaret Page children—Francis/Anne Page had Thomas 1646 (560-122)

Spexhall—Co. Suffolk—1691 John Page born—(see 560-54 & 127)

Stafford Co, Va—1674—Thomas Page (30A)) arrives. (16)

Stanton—James Page (20C) Wicken property from father John Page (15A-20)

Starston—Co.Norfolk—Richard Page—tanner—maybe **LINE D**

Stevenage (Co. Hertfordshire)—Line N—4th generation Londoner to Brisbane, Australia in 1980.

Stradbroke—Co. Suffolk—Ricardo Page—Burial 1327 (560-12C) (near Worlingworth)

Stratford St. Mary—Suffolk—Abakuk/bridget Page1588—Robert/Eleanor Page (560-129)

Stowmarket—Co. Suffolk—Isaak Page 1 fireplace—1674 Isaack Page buried (560-12)

Stoke by Nayland—Co. Suffolk—Widow Garrett, William Garrett, Richard Lee, William Page, William Baker—Many Page's see (560-128)

Sudbury—Co. Suffolk—Stephano Page—1327 Burial (560-12C) (near Action) Johanne Page—1327 Burial (560-12C) see (560-130) has too many names to list.

Sulgrave—Northamptonshire—Thomas Gleason and wife Susanna Page (**LINE C**) living in Sulgrave—when children Thomas, b.1637 & daug Susanna, b. 1639 were born.

Swaffham—Co. Norfork—William Page, b.19Feb1797, Co. Essex, Eng—(**LINE C**) had son Ebenezer, b. 8Apr1820, (Co. Sussex,) just before William, b.1797 emigrated to America. (See MICH 11)

Parents of William, b. 1797 were James/Mary Page—Line C—see MICH 11 & NY 56

Swefling—Suffolk—John/Ann Page (560-131)

Tacolneston—Co. Norfolk—Phillip Page land deal (560-49C)

Tannington—Suffolk—1574 John Page/Audrie Page had Henry— 1634 Benjamin/Ann Page had Richard (560-132)

Thorndon—Co.Suffolk—next to Rishangles—Thomas Page, d.1554- Elizabeth Page, d.1677

Thornham Magna—Co. Suffolk—Parish records. (1581-1616) (560-21) Abagail, b. 1601 (18) Henry Page (18B)

Thomas Page (12) owned one tenement or ancient cottage (p29)

In Great Thornham Magna. Thomas Page, b.1588, son of Thomas Page

Thornham Parva—Co. Suffolk-John Page (23B) (2 hearths) (560-21)

Thorpe Abbots—Co. Suffolk—Thomas Page mar Catherine Brewster on 23May1668
      (see 560-32A)

Thurston—Co. Suffolk—1655 Sarah Page mar Henry Fuller of Hesset. (560-33C)
      Sarah's mother was Elizabeth Page, a widow. Philip Page (560-49A)

Thurston is next to Pakenham—Blackborne family

Ten **WILLS** from 1524 thru 1695. (560-49A)
      1639 Buckell paid for Pages—Ship Money Returns (560-12E)

Thomas Page, b. 1676, Thurston (560-12D)

Tichfield Church—Co. Hampshire—Burial place of William de Pageham (p. 2)

Timworth—Suffolk—1544 Thomas Page born—

1548 Mrs. Thomas Page has female born

Timworth—Suffolk—Thomas Page had Susan1570 & Thomas1576 (560-133)
      1593 Thomas Page born

Timworth Green—Thomas Page (94) had Susan, bap22Nov1570 and Thomas, bp7Jul1576

Timworth is a few feet from Ingham. (560-12D)

Totton—Co. Hampshire—Next to Southhampton—Ernest Angus Totton is a close DNA
      67 match from this village of Totton—that is not far from Titchfield Church
      graveyard—where Rick Bentley Page—reveals he found a burial monument of
      William de Pageham
      IS TOTTEN A LONG LOST DESCENDANT OF THIS LINE?

Tuddenham St. Mary—Suffolk—1570 Thomas Page
      1743 William Page mar Elizabeth Veacher1743 (560-134)

Turin, Italy—1350 A.D.—Shroud discovered

Ubbeston—Co.Suffolk—1651 Joseph Page (30E) of Hawstead mar Mary Clayden (30E-1)

Ufford—Co. Suffolk—John Page's daug Anne mar John Cheeke. No date
      Robert/Margaret Page had William1575, Jacob1580, John1581 (560-137)

Walcot (Co Norfolk)—List of Page's born in Walcot—see (560-146)

Walsham le Willows—see (560-12 & 12A) for 1674 Burials & marriages-too many to list

Walsham le willows—1670 Thomas Page born (560-12D)

Walsham le Willows—John Page (2), Edmund Page (4C), Richard Page (21)

William Page (B) 1391—William, Thomas, John Page Hearth tax (560-12)

Walsham le Willows—Philip I. Page (ENG 10-2) assigned to Family **LINE K**—wrong
      (560-28)—There is a connection to LINE C

William Page (16), John Page (15A), Rand Page, Thomas Page (15B), Sam Page, (19)
      Joseph Vincent, Sr & Jr., John Vinsent, Henry Page (48), John Garrett (560-12)

Walsham le Willows—John, John Jr, Raynald, Thomas & Joseph Page Ship Money Returns (560-12E & 560-7D)

> 1638 Thomas Page (4 Ashes House) living next to William Page and near Joseph Page. (560-159)

Wareham, Co. Norfolk—Edmund Page (ENG 9-1) **LINE L**

Wells-next to the Sea—(Co. Norfolk) Thomas Page b.1650 (111) parents: James/Ann Page (560-70)

Wenham Magna—Co. Suffolk—Anne Page, widow of Chattisham (Abram Page) marries see 560-54

Wenham Parva (Little Wenham)—Co. Suffolk—1702 William Bacon mar Elizabeth Page (see 560-54)

Wenhaston—Suffolk—1541 John Page Yeoman (560-150)

Westerfield—Suffolk—Margaret Page mar Daniel Salter—(see 560-54)

Westhall—Suffolk—1654 Margaret Page mar Daniel Salter (560-139)

Westleton—Co. Suffolk—1327 Willmo Page—buried (560-12C) (near Aldringham)

Westley—Co. Suffolk,—(560-43) Lease dated 1535 to John Page (8) (91-4) from John Melford, Abbot for 40 years a manor called le Sexteyns in Westley.

> John Page, Gent (91-4), son of Roger Page-Risby was wit to many deeds in (1504-1513), (560-43) John Page gent, **WILL** 1547(91-4) (560-43) Thomas of Lackford (91-3) & John (91-4) Page move to Westley

Westthorpe—Co. Suffolk—1391 William Page (0-2) see 560-54 for more names

West Stow—Suffolk—Thomas Page b.1696 (560-138)

West Wickham, Co. Cambridgeshire—contact Helen Helen_griffiths58@yahoo.ca

Whatfield—Suffolk—1644 EdmundPage mar Alice Pegg and had Edmund1645, William1647 (560-140)

Wherstead—Co. Suffolk—William Page (88) & Mary had Mary1677, William1679 (560-141)

Whepstead (next to Hawstead) Co. Suffolk—1702 William Page/Mary (109) had daug Mary in 1677 and son William in 1679—(see 560-61 and 61A)

Whepstead—Co. Suffolk—Mary, William, & Elizabeth Page (560-61A)

Whepstead—Co. Suffolk—Joseph Page (93)

Wickhambrook—Co. Suffolk,—1585 to 1707—many Page's (560-62)

Wilby—Co. Norfolk—Henry Page (18A) (560-135)

Wingfield—Co. Suffolk—George Page, b. 1795—not LINE C but **LINE J.**

> Edward Page had John 1589, william1590, Edmund1592 (560-142)

Withersfield—Suffolk—Amy Page mar James Cornill 1686 (560-143)

Woodbridge—William Garrett, Samuel Page (3 fireplaces) James Crispe (2 fire)

> John Garrett 2 fireplaces Micah Page (96)
>
> Allen Page had Allen1548, & Samuel 1546,
>
> 1569 Robert mar Agnes (Bystome) and had Thomas1570—

John/Frances Page had Alis1602, Mary1604, John1600, Ellen1608,

Mary1612, Ann1619, Margaret1616—

Micah/Mary Page had Mary1651, Micah1654, John1660, Eliz1665, Joseph1657

(560-136)

Woolpit—Robert Page (13-34A-47) and Parish register (1628-1811) (560-23)

Woolwich—London—Thames River port—Capt Robert Caulfield ship left for Va (VA 8).

Woolverstone—Suffolk—Christopher Page b. 1549,

1620 Thomas Page mar Marie Paris (560-144)

Worlingham—Suffolk—**LINE D**—Thomas/Joan Page had John1614, Rose1617, Jane1622

John/Jane Page—Thomas/Elizabeth Page—John/Ann Page (560-145)

Aug 1664 Thomas Page born (560-12D)

Worlingworth—Co.Suffolk—Family **LINE** "C", "D" and "L" are in this area.

Henry Page (18A), son of Richard Page (21)—tanner, Edmund Page (33)

John Page (elder)(31) and his son John Page (31-1) (560-58)

1497 Richard Page, the Older—1601 Richard Page—1596, William Page,

Framlingham Castle, and Mary Page widow, 560-?

Wrentham—Suffolk—(by Covehithe) 1637 Francis/Frances Page had Thomas (560-147)

Writtle—Co. Essex—King Robert de Bruce of Scotland—born 1274 at village near

Chelmsford & Great Baddow where Abraham Page lived. (p.3)

Wymondham (Co. Norfolk) Not William Page line to Bedford Co, Va—BRACH SAYS NO

(see VA 58-1A & Miss 37) contact: John Brach jbrach@frontier.net

Wyverstone—Co. Suffolk—Stephano Page—burial 1327—(560-12C)

Robert Page/Alice—see ENG 10-1, p. 46. (next to Westhorpe, Bacton &

Finningham)

Yelvertoft, (Co. Northhamptonshire) WEJP line.

Yarmouth—Co. Norfolk—Phillip (31-2)

Prepared by Robert E. Page

CHAPTER FOUR

MEMBERS OF PAGE FAMILY "C".

SAXON #1 CHART—need help—to add any missing data or correct mistakes. 25 January 2013

The following is a list of those in Page Family Line "C" that have joined our SAXON group to compare our 37, 67 and 111 marker results. Everyone should get at least the Y-DNA 67 test. PLEASE VERIFY the below INFO Please send me your blood type and eye color for our list. I am missing a few Kit numbers—please furnish—BUT—also, everyone needs to ENTER THE SCORES in Ysearch, which gives others access to your scores and learn of a possible match (with a different surname). (see your personal page at FTDNA for instruction on this easy process.) Please furnish me your Ysearch I.D. number.

As more Y-DNA scores come in—**HAPLOGROUP** I—from the score M170—which is the grandfather of our M 253, which is the subgroup of I . . . which makes us **I1a3**. This makes us a small "unique" group which is the largest Haplogroup in Great Britian—which is good.

The below Y-DNA matches are compared to Robert E. Page Y-DNA.

I have recorded your oldest—**M**ost **R**ecent **K**nown **A**ncestor—and will see—**MRKA**—before that info. I did not request nor receive TMRCA—which is the = Time-To-Most-Recent-Common-Ancestor, but did provide that date, IF available. It would be interesting—if that information could be provided. Many of our Y-DNA results seem to indicate our "non-PAGE" name is around year 1000. The more results we get helps cement that data.

DNA LIST 3—Those that appear very close by paper trail and Y-DNA are probably the same line.

Needs more research—from youngest ancestor up paper trail to where the paper trail stops.

Anything past that is GUESSING.

BOBBY W. PAGE—bob_page@cox.net kit 4826 (Y-DNA 111) 108 of 111 match. MRKA is Thomas Page, b.7Feb1680, Isle of Wight, Va.—but "**CONFLICT**" supports that the oldest "documented" ancestor is really Thomas Page Sr, born about 1755 (location not known) (see NC 202), who died 1838/9, Marion Co, SC and then his son Thomas Page Jr, who appears, b. 1773, Sampson Co, NC—d. Miss married in 1794 to Mary Scott, b. 1774. The son of this Thomas/Mary was William Henry Page, b. 1801, SC. The father of this Thomas Page, bc. 1755 **is a son of ABRAHAM PAGE/Mary Lamb line, according to the PAGE Family Bible. (see charts AT1, AT1A-1, MISS** 36) Home: 7718 Park Ave, Broken Arrow, Ok, 74011 (918) 455-0630

Need some more research

JOHN BUFORD PAGE—sgmjohnny@aol.com kit 2752 (Retired SGM US Army) (Y-DNA 66 of 67) Blood type AB+ MRKA was Thomas Page, b. 7Feb1680, IOW, Va-d.1744, NC but now claims Thomas Page, b. 1633, Eng-d.1703, Va mar Alice Hearn, b. 1650, Va—d.1740, NC—Which is a serious conflict with Y-DNA results—which reflects his oldest known ancestor is **ABRAHAM PAGE** /Mary Lamb line. (see charts AT1, AT1a-1, MISS 36.—and others. Home: 4016 Oldstone Forest Dr, Waxhaw, NC, 28173 (828) 320-9475 Ysearch: KDTHC SNP M253+ and P19+—Has Hazel eyes. The family history chart of John Buford Page was put together in the 1980's with the help of author Jesse Page (Page Family in N.C.) and long before all the genealogical documents were available—as they are today. I have extensive documents of over 25 years of research and am missing some of the documented crucial connections of this line. In John's forward to his book EARLY PAGE FAMILIES—he indicates the connections are "possible". It appears that another close look should be conducted starting with himself and "slowly" going back up the line. Y-DNA results show him very close to many people on this list—which clearly point to ABRAHAM PAGE LINE. IF—he has an unbroken male line back to Thomas Page, Isle of Wight, Va—then he is the only one on this list.

Appears correct but Need verification.

KENNETH NEAL PAGE—kit N61443 blood 0+ hazel eyes (Y-DNA 63 of 67) is being handled by cousin Mary Ellen Wilkerson, maryellenwilkerson@carolina.rr.com 10808 Young Poplar Pl, Charlotte, NC 28277 (704) 541-5552. MRKA—ABRAHAM PAGE, bc.1704, England,—d.1778, N.C. Ysearch I.D. S73VF

Need re-action from Fred A. Page

FRED A. PAGE—maymoongal@yahoo.com—kit 97237 (YDNA 66 of 67) blood 0+ MRKA appears to be from **ABRAHAM PAGE**, b.1790-d. 1845—that had ten children in Barnwell Dist, S.C (see chart SC 1). Abraham, b.1790, SC had son Jacob, b. 1808 (see chart SC 1 & SC 1-1) with parents in Marion Co, SC and this appears to be the Fred A. Page line.

Home 1019 Kirkwood Ave, Murphysboro, Tenn, 37130. Ph: (615) 895-3712. Need Ysearch I.D. Daughter Tammy email is geroyfamily@united.net is assisting in this genealogy.

CLYDE EDWARD PAGE Kit #259932 (Y-DNA 111) (66 out of 67 Match) Blood type: 0+ eyes: brown MRKA—Abraham Page, b.1704-d/1778, NC—Solomon Page, b.1760 (chart AS 8) Home address: 1450 Plantation, Circle, Lincolnton, GA 30817. Match SNP M253 + Y-Search.org ID = RTQK2. Clyde is a descendant of McIver (MI) Page, born 1854, Dillon Co, S.C. died 1901, Ellisville, Miss. Info: Lake View S.C. Bear Swamp Baptist Church records. McIver Page left Dillon Co., SC Aug 1885 for Ellisville, Jones Co, Miss. Descendants of McIver Page moved to southern Louisiana and California.

OLIVER WINFRED PAGE kfrazier1190@gmail.com kit 247370 (YDNA 65 of 67 match) Blood type O eyes Hazel—MRKA—ABRAHAM PAGE, b.1704, England-d.1778, N.C—then his son SOLOMON PAGE, b.1760 (maybe N.C-d.19Mar1837) (AS1) (see AS 4-1) Home: Dillon, S.C. Ysearch RAZUW His daughter **Karen (Page) Frazier** kfrazier1190@gmail.com 6442 Red Pine Ct, Fruitport, Michigan, 49415 is assisting this genealogy.

ROBERT E. PAGE—flkeybob@terranova.net—kit 2932 (YDNA 111)(Z59 SNP) Blood type 0+ hazel eyes MRKA—ABRAHAM PAGE, b. 1704, England-d.1778, N.C.—then son David Page, b. 1744. (according to PAGE Family Bible) Home: 87465 Old Hwy, Apt 107, Islamorada, Fla, 33036 (305) 852-5337 Ysearch: 92R2U (See his chart AD1) Robert E. Page is matched 66 of 67 with Bobby W. Page, John Buford Page, James C. Page and Fred A. Page. SNP M 253+ Ysearch 92R2U—Y-DNA 111 results makes him a 108 match out of 111, with Stephen W and his father W. D. Page.

Need verification
GLENNDON EARL PAGE JR—bluechap42@gmail.com Kit 210031—(Y-DNA 66 of 67 blood 0+ green eyes. MRKA is Jehue Page, b. 1798, Washington Co, Ga—d.1849, Harris Co, Ga Oldest ancestor is Jehugh Page (unable to locate Jehue Page, b. 1798—but did find Jehugh, b. 15Feb1773 on chart AD1—as son of David Page, b. 1744/Sarah (see chart AD1) Which backs up to **ABRAHAM PAGE**, b. 1704-d.1778, N.C.—then David Page, b. 1744. Home: 249 Fawn Ridge, Cibolo, Tex 78108 (210) 501-0056 Y-search # ??? (see chart AD1) Glenn has a close match (66 of 67) with Robert E. Page, Harry L. Page and James C. Page— that are the ABRAHAM PAGE, b.1704, line in Marion Co, S.C. Glenn is active duty USAF. Need to add this info to Y-Search I.D. QW3RW

HARRY L. PAGE return1809@aol.com—kit 132081 (Y-DNA 66 of 67) Blood type 0+ (blue eyes) MRKA is **ABRAHAM PAGE,** bc.1704, England-D.1778, N.C.—then David Page, b. 1744—according to PAGE Family Bible. Home: Rt 2, Box 391, Dillon, SC. 29536. Phone: (843) 774-6879 (see chart AD1 and AD2C-1) Ysearch Q6RCP.

JAMES CLYDE PAGE—kit# 113627 golfdad84@roadrunner.com (Y-DNA 66 of 67) blood type 0+ (USMC retired COL) MRKA is **ABRAHAM PAGE, b.1704 England-d.1778, N.C./ Mary Lamb**—then David Page, b. 1744. Home: 611 Blue Street, Marion, SC, 29571 (843) 423-3654 Ysearch ZU7AD—eyes brown (see charts AD1, AD2C-1) Harry L. Page, James C. Page and Robert E. Page are 66/67 match SNP M253+

Need more info—linking him to WHO? Need to develop family history from him back to the oldest ancester ancestor without a break in the paper trail.

WILLIAM GORDON PAGE—pagebb@bellsouth.net—kit 6881 (DNA 65 of 67) Blood 0—MRKA Oldest ancestor Lemuel Page, bc.1750 Johnston Co, NC married to Elizabeth Powell and son of Jesse Page, b.1728 and Ann, b. 1730-d.1764. (SEE chart GA 6 & NC 102)—Home: 2016 N. Kirkwood Dr, Shreveport, La 71118 (318) 688-3318—Retired 1984 USAF Col. Ysearch: JQDC7 and AJMDZ. Helen J. Smith is assisting her cousin W.G. Page, who is on her mother's side of the family.

ALAN ALLS—kit ??? alanalls@hotmail.com (Y-DNA 64 of 67) Blood 0+ MRKA— Father appears to be Norman William Alls, b. Kingston Upon Hull, England-d. middle 1980's. Mother: Beryl Elizabeth Knox, b. Scarborough, England. Fathers line "seems" to back up to County Down, **North Ireland** and mother's line backs up to southwestern Scotland. Alan lives North England. Phone (England) 011 (44) 1482-856-365 Ysearch: 5DXQV Alan finally found his brother to participate in a sibling DNA test and it confirmed, they are brothers. So his confirmed family (Alan, brother and sister) currently living in Hull, East Yorkshire and his other brother and two sisters living in Barrow in Furness, in Cumbria, England. It appears this family was "maybe" connected with the (shipping) business. What is interesting, Alan Alls, is very close to our Thomas Page, bc. 1650's, PAGE line C, that "maybe" moved from Co. Suffork or Norfolk, England to Isle of Wight, Va between 1674-1679. A lot of Y-DNA matches are showing our line has a lot of matches in **SCOTLAND** and appears to be connected to the **KNIGHT TEMPLARS**—who fled France in 1307 and many fled to Scotland. See my document ENG 10-1 for more info on the Scottish connection.

NEW INFORMATION: (30Jul2012) Alan Alls reports he is involved in the FAMILY FINDER program and seems to have made a connection with Elizabeth Kaegi (and her cousin Warren Belt) and that she is the contact person. There seems to be a DNA blood connection with someone (maybe with the U.S. military—during WW II in Northern Wales)—that later served in the BURMA area in 1945. They feel he "might" be from the southern United States—born around 1920-1924. Can anyone in PAGE line "C" see any connection ? Slowly the pieces of the puzzle starts to fall in place. Please pass the word around—and not be afraid to reveal this search.

Need verification.

JIMMIE PAGE—kit 10751—bob.page@basic-ind.com (DNA 37) MRKA is ancestor Thomas Andrew Page, b. 1795/7, Duplin Co, NC. Who is a brother to Henry Page, b.1801-(AT1A-1) who is the ancestor of Bobby W. Page (see above) These brothers claim they are from Thomas Page/Alis Garrett, Isle of Wight, VA. But cannot produce a clear unbroken paper trail which produces a conflict on oldest ancestor. Records seem to indicate MRKA is **ABRAHAM PAGE, b.170, Eng-d.1778, N.C**/Mary Lamb, then Thomas Page Sr, b.1755/68, in N.C. (see chart AD1 & NC 202) Jimmie Page address is 904 Blount Street, Philadelphia, Miss, 39350 and Bobby W. Page is handing his interest.

Need verification

STEPHEN W. PAGE—kit 23173 coachpage@aol.com (Y-DNA 108 of 111) MRKA is Thomas Page, b.1769, Duplin Co, NC—d. early 1800, Covington Co, Miss. CONFLICT: Other documents indicate Stephen W. Page and father W.D. Page appear to be MRKA to the **ABRAHAM PAGE, b.1704, Eng-d.1778, N.C.**/Mary—then Thomas Page, b. 1755/68. (see AD1, AT1A-1, MISS 36) There does NOT appear to be an unbroken solid paper trail from W.D. Page back to his oldest ancestor. Home: 1911 65th Ave, W., Tacoma, WA, 98466 Tel: Home (253) 460-0651 work (253) 460-3000 (ok to call) Ysearch: Y542D and CKTZC. Steve Page's father, W. D. Page, also did his Y-DNA 67/111 and had same scores as Steve, but I do NOT show him on the master sheet,—ONLY because of space. Stephen W. and his father W.D. Page—both match Robert E. Page Y-DNA 108 out of 111 DYS results. I call that pretty solid. Steve Page has signed up (Dec2012) for the new Geno 2.0 test that National Geographic is offering.

Need verification

PERMAN HUDSON PAGE—kit 80242 p9jam@aol.com (BAD EMAIL ADDRESS) (DNA 25) NEED MORE INFO Perman's father was a brother of the father of John Buford Page.

MERLE SHEDRICK (PAGE) BAKER—kit 6012 (**BAD EMAIL**) mbaker9732@aol. com (DNA 37) MRKA is Thomas Page, b.1822, SC Home: 708 Elmwood Dr, Baytown, Tex 77520, Tel 281-422-6033. Ysearch: MB3ND green eyes

Need updated info—vague info

GARY ALFRED PAGE—kit 23254 lcpage@bellsouth.net (DNA 37) Blood type 0+— MRKA is John Page, b.1822, Staffordshire, England—d.1873, Staffordshire. And his son William Henry Page, b.8Aug1859, Handsworth, West Bromwich, Staffordshire, U.K. who emigrated to PA in USA in 1892. Home: 1955 Old Dominion Drive, Atlanta, Ga 30350 kit #23254 (Need Ysearch number).

Vague info—more exact info needed

THOMAS WAYNE PAGE—kit 5547 tgpage664@att.net (Y-DNA 63 of 67) MRKA is John Page, b. 1685, Va (see VA 52) Home: 998 E. Plaines Prt, Hudson Road, Zachary, La, 70791 (225) 654-6126. Ysearch AV647 Hazel eyes (need Ysearch #) GLENDA PAGE is contact. Thomas W. Page is descendant of Wiley Page, brother of Uriah Page.

Hoping for discovery of the missing link?

ROBERT B. NOLES—kit 2302 rbnoles@bellsouth.net (DNA 111) (61 of 67 match) MRKA is Benjamin Noles (Knowles), b.1765, Wake Co, NC HOME: 133 Acadian Lane, Mandeville, La, 70741 985-845-4688. Ysearch 4K6RN

Need some more research on this very close Y-DNA match.
There must be a NPE in the 1700's in the U. S. or maybe in England.

HAROLD BRUCE TANNER—research@wavecable.com Kit # ??? (Y-DNA 63 of 67) MRKA is John L. Tanner, bc.1810-d.1863 location unknown. He did later move from Georgia to Alabama, then Texas. Ysearch FZ7TB. There are THREE other Tanner's with almost same DNA and this grouping appears to show up in Duplin Co, N.C. around middle 1700's. They are not listed on the master chart but are: Donald Lee Tanner crittters@earthlink.net—John W. Tanner (62 of 67) johnwtanner@yahoo.com and Raymond Shields Tanner (62 of 67) btanner@wichitaeagle.com.

This line has the same problem of the Scottish link.—more research—
Might show where the—NPE or adoption—took place.

JAMES JEFFERSON TAYLOR taylorjj@hotmail.com Kit # 51153 (DNA 61 of 67) Blood 0+, Y-search ZZJR9 MRKA is Cornelius Alexander Taylor, b. 1794, Wythe Co, Va, then N.C, then TN and Ky.—served in War of 1812 and maybe goes back to John Taylor, bc.1478, Rothbury, Northumberland, England (next to **SCOTLAND**)—Home: 426 Pleasant Drive, Lucasville, Ohio 45648-8513 (740) 352-5541 Appears to be NPE probably in England or Normandy, France.

JAMES DEAN TAYLOR costfall@verizon.net—DID NOT DO DNA—MRKA is Isaiah "Jesse" Page, b. 1742 (see my chart AJE 1) married to Dicy Miller, bc. 1764 (Jesse was a son of ABRAHAM PAGE/Mary Lamb) See his chart **AJE2-3A** which appears to reflect William Taylor, b.1786, NC—d.aft 1860, Ga married Nancy Page, b. 1791, NC-d.aft 1860 in Ga. Looking above at James Jefferson Taylor, it also appears that this Taylor line has been carrying the PAGE gene for a long time. The PAGE line were "tailors" and it is strange that the Taylor line seems to be an occupational name—that fits the occupation of the PAGE family under consideration. Home address: 1124 Jeffery Trail, Irving, Tx, 75062—ph: 972-255-0159.

This Hunter family is probably the "most important MATCH"—we have (forgetting last names) because it backs us to around the year 1000. Other DNA research is ongoing to support this important Y-DNA genealogical discovery.

OLIVER GEORGE HUNTER oliver@thehunterfamily.co.uk (DNA 67) (match 23 of 25 then 61 of 67) Blood O—kit# H1101—No Ysearch number. MRKA is William Hunter, bc. 1560, BeneberrieYairds, County Ayr, **SCOTLAND** (same surname but different line) of Cunningham. His son, Patrick, b. 1591 married Jean Cunningham, b.1587—who was daughter of Rev. Robert Cunningham, bc. 1557, and wife Jean Hunter, b. 1575—daug of Robert Hunter, bc. 1544-d.9Aug1581. Line goes back to William Venator, bc.1090, Normandy, France-dc.1160, but is a broken line Y-DNA line. NEED HOME ADDRESS ? It appears—this makes the DNA connection (Halogroup I1) with the Normandy, France— maybe family of ROLLO (Robert I) and their descendant (William the Bastard) that were involved in the 1066 invasion of England.

ADDITIONAL CONTACTS with no Y-DNA results.
There are several that I correspond with that have a (solid) paper trail (NO y-dna) and I am going to add them to this mailing list—for information only and any comment they might wish to make.

Helen J. Smith—helenjs@aol.com—10208 N. Magna Carta Pl, Baton Rouge, La, 70815—phone: (225) 928-7121 is connected through her father to Thomas Page, b. 1755— son of ABRAHAM PAGE, b. 1704, England (chart AD1)—through a descendant Uriah Page, b. 1824/Sally Moore, b. 1819—son of Lemuel Page, b.bef 1760 married to Elizabeth Powell.—which is on GA 6, GA 18 and ALA 9-1 charts. She is assisting her cousin (on her mothers side) William Gordon Page, b. 1930, who is descendant of Uriah Page, son of Lemuel.

Delight Williams lacbeau@cox.net is also out of the Lemuel Page line through his son Uriah Page, b. 1814 line. NEED CURRENT CONTACT INFO.

Nichol L. Martin, msmartins@sbcglobal.net 128 N. Deerfoot Circle, Spring, Texas, 77380 is connected through her father to ABRAHAM PAGE, b. 1790-d. 1845, Barnwell Co, SC married in 1832 to wife #1 Sarah McLemore, b. 1795. SC-d.Miss. and their son ABRAHAM PAGE, b. 1833, White Pond, (Robeson Co), NC-d.1915, Miss married in 1856 to Mary Ann Kilcrease, b. 1840. (chart SC 1, SC 1B, GA 6, MISS 24-2 and NC 202).

Elizabeth Kaegi—ekaegi@qmail.com—for her cousin Warren Belt—and has a FAMILY FINDER connection with Alan Alls, who is a 64/67 Match with Robert E. Page. Seems to indicate a connection with a PAGE male from Southern U.S.—that served in the U.S. military during—WW II and maybe later served in Burma.

The following DNA list of matches are NOT that close—but are close enough—to keep an eye on them because they do fall into the pattern of our PAGE line "C" family—long before last names entered the scene—while for the most part was in the 1400's.

DNA List 4 Hopefully many on this list #4 will UPGRADE and see if they should remain or be removed from the list that is interested in seeing—if there is any blood relationship.

PHILLIP C. BRAY bpbray@mlecmn.net (**BAD EMAIL**) Kit # ???? (DNA 37) or Jacquie Hoggard jacquierk@cox.net MRKA is Henry Bray, d. 1794, Chatham Co, NC, 39081 Home: Hiway 18, Aitkin, Mn, 56431 or 40 Ridgewood Pkwy, Newport News, Va, 23608, Ph: 757-874-2297 There are a lot of Bray's in this Y-DNA line.

PETER J. ROBERTS peterebay@yahoo.com kit 08867 (DNA 67)(Z59 SNP) Home—1137 Eton Court, N.E., Atlanta, Ga, 30319-1904. MRKA is Thomas Barrett Roberts, bc.1816, Bahamas. SNP M253+ Peter J. Roberts ancestry begins at Marsh Harbour, Abaco, Bahamas but the family oral history says the Roberts ancestor was from Belfast, Ireland. Y-DNA suggest that prior to Belfast, the line comes from **SCOTLAND**. Closest Y-DNA with surnames appear to be associated with Scottish Clans (Murray, Douglas, etc.) which trace their descent from Freskin, who was a Flemish Knight (http//en.wikipedia.org/wiki/Freskin. Clan Murray in Atholl was a neighbor of Clan Donnachaidh (AKA Clan Roberson). It suggest that the "Robertsons" adopted the Roberts surname. The Flemish were located in what is now north Beligum and southern Netherlands which were areas often attacked by Vikings. Other near matches are also high in Denmark and Sweden, which is Viking country. This line is closely connected to below Richard Austin Roberts, kit 13630. Thomas Barrett Roberts immigrated to Key West with wife Elizabeth Russell, where both died in Key West. Thomas Roberts son, Thomas Jr, b.1856, lived on Matecumbe Key for awhile, before moving to Miami. Another son, Edward "Ned" Roberts, b.1845, remained in Key West, built an old historic "eyebrow" house on William Street, married and died in KW in 1905, of typhoid fever.

Peter J. Roberts recently received his positive results from FTDNA on his test for "Z59 SNP"—which defines I1a, (that all in PAGE Family "C" possess) and Z58—which defines I1a3, and Z9—which defines I1a3a. The ancestor for Z59 lived about 4,000 years ago—at the start of the Nordic Bronze Age. Charles W. Paige just ordered Z59 and Robert E. Page also just ordered his Z59 test for $29.00. I am encouraging those interested in "genealogy way back there" to also join our search for the PAGE family history back before last names became required. Contact Robert Page for details how to make the enrollment easy.

RICHARD AUSTIN ROBERTS—kit 153273 (DNA 37) is being handled by his cousin Donna Jean Robinson ConchGirrri@aol.com. This Roberts line is connected to Peter J.

Roberts line from Marsh Harbour, Abaco, Bahamas. They are a 25/25 match. The MRKA is ancestor is Benjamin Roberts, d.1839, Key Vaca, Florida and on 12Dec1820—in Abaco, Bahamas married Charlotte Russell, b. 20Jun1802, Harbour Island. They immigrated to Key Vaca, Florida around July 1836, but daughter Maria was born in the Bahamas.

WAYNE BRINLEE wbrin75@gmail.com Kit # 10237 (DNA 67) blood type AB+ MRKA is Mathias Brinley, bc.1720, dc.1785 York Co, Pa. Home: 4312 Athens St, San Diego, Ca, PH: (619) 287-7026

ROBERT OLIVER WILSON drrow0828@earthlink.net (BAD EMAIL) KIT # ??? (DNA 37) Blood type A+ MRKA is George William Grove, b. 1876, Pa but did use other last names. Home: 725 Sheppard Way, The Villages, Fl, 32162 (352) 751-6307

CHARLES ROBERT REEB maddmann@att.net KIT# ??—(DNA 37) MRKA is Johann Nicolaus Reeb, bc.1620, Keskastel, (Lorraine) France, which is just below Sarreguemines, France. Need his address and better contact info.—Mr. Reeb is blind and deaf. Peter J. Roberts assisted Mr. Reeb in this DNA. Ysearch 4376X and is listed as haplogroup R1B (this probaby eliminates him from our group)

GEORGE W. HESSER gwhesser@bigfoot.com Kit # ??? (DNA 37) MRKA is ???—need full info Ysearch XT38R

GLENN L. (Susan) BRAY plaidhearts@kc.rr.com Kit # ??? (DNA 67) Blood type AB+ MRCA is Henry Bray, d.1794, Chatham Co, NC. 4302 NE 56th Street, Kansas City, MO, 64119 (816) 454-8919 Ysearch XT38R

CHRISTOPHER PAGE (UK)—kit 65869 page.family@btinternet.com (DNA 67) MRKA is—Thomas Page, bc.1711, Ormesby, (St. Margaret), Co. Norfolk, England—but did NOT emigrate to America. Ormesby is where Robert Page, b.1604, England—d. 22Sep1679, Hampton, N.H.—that emigrated to America in 1637—and is Page Line L (see ENG 9-1 and NH 1 for detailed info). Chris lives in Dover, Kent, England. Need Ysearch ???

NOT SURE MY BELOW WORDING IS CLEAR!

RAYMOND R. PAGE—kit 188554—(DNA 25) who lives in Canada, and is—somehow related—but not by Y-DNA to members of Page Family "M". There is a "maybe" (adoption) connection to relatives—who are descended from Raymond Page (Ramoun Paget) who arrived in Quebec City, Quebec Province, Canada from Quercy, Guyenne, France in 1642. Nycole Page npage@bell.net (family "M") asked Robert G. Page to take the DNA test and Nycole considers him an "alien" (adopted) in family line "M". He is supposed to be of Raymond Page line from France, but something was wrong. He is a nephew of Raymond R.

Page from France. Contact: npage@bell.net OR yolandecat@mediom.qc.ca It has turned out there was an "unofficial" adoption.

ROBERT G. PAGE, kit # 213696—also Canada, and his proxie is the above "Nicole" npage@bell.net Both Raymond R. Page and Robert G. Page tested with Page Family line "M" but found closer to Line "C".

JERRY L. HAAG haagi@algorithms.com—(BAD EMAIL) KIT # ??? (DNA 37) blood type A+ MRKA is Johan Georg Haak, emigrated to Berks Co, Pa in 1733 from Europe. (must be Germany) Needs to upgrade to DNA 67.

JOHN FLAIG (JF) webmaster@johnflaig.com Kit# ??? (DNA 67) Ysearch TB2W5 He was born Brooklyn, NY and lives in Milwaukee, Wisconsin. He was shown on DNA List 3, as very close to our Page surname connection, but as other scores came in, he was moved to List 4 because of the score results, and then, the rest of his 67 scores, are on list 6. To see This is interesting, because John Flaig is fairly close to begin with, but as the numbers came in, he still remains close, but the particular DYS numbers do NOT match, to most everybody on the list.

John Flaig's MRKA documented ancestor Georg Flaig, b. 1808, Gruenchbach, Southern Prussia and oldest likely ancestor is Hans Flaig, b. 1642, Moenchweiler (near Villingen), Wurttemberg, Germany. What little is known, is his line "on paper", backs up to early 1600's in area, south of Stuttgart, Germany, in the Swabia (Necker River Valley) around the town of Rottweil, on the eastern side of the Black Forest (very near the Rhein River), and also the source of Danube (Donau) River. This is area that the Vikings often attacked, and when the French King in 1307 arrested many of the Knights Templars—a small group of **KNIGHT TEMPLARS** escaped and settled in the Swiss Alps, not far from this location.

MAGNUS SCHILLER magnus@lawyer.com Kit # ??? is a very close Y-DNA 67 to John Flaig, both coming from Schwaben (Black Forest) area of Germany. Magnus traces his line MRKA to Johan Schiller, on commercial island of Marstand, north of Gothenburg in the 1540s. At that time, this part of Sweden, belonged to Denmark and name was spelled Sekilder. The family moved to Sweden from southern Germany, being invited by Swedish King Gustaff II Adolf, who in 1630 was in Germany fighting in the 30 years war (1618-1648). In the middle of 1500s, there was a big immigration, to this Island, from Germany, Denmark and England and the family name originated from some Anglo Saxon name like "Seekilder".

This area is also the source of the Danube (Donau) River, just over the mountains from the Rhein River. This is interesting because, he does show the **VIKING** gene DYS 392 (11) is present, but . . . did that gene "gets maybe dropped off", in that Germany area, as the gene line moved north, out of Africa into Turkey, then traveled into Europe (probably by sea) to southern France and then northward on up, to the Scandinavian area, (probably by sea) ending around the North Germany/Denmark area, where it seemed to settle, developed, and then in later years, sent out raiding parties, all over Europe, Iceland and Greenland, and maybe even . . . . what later became North America. "Or" did the German Y-DNA gene later, get transplanted, as the Vikings, moved south, in the years around beginning around 800 A.D, as many Viking attacks, occured in England and inside France and Germany, by going up the Rhein River, and that group of Vikings, "maybe" settling, around the Necker River (the source of the Danube River) to later invade more eastern parts of Europe. Somebody jump in on this speculation!

CHARLES WILLIAM PAIGE—kit 80186 charlespaige@netscape.net (DNA 67)(Z59 SNP) Home: Los Angeles, Calif. MRKA is—William Henry Page, b.19Feb1797, Co. Essex, England, (NY 56)—WHO may have been born William Page, who was baptized at St. Peter and St. Pauls Church in Swaffham, County Norfolk, England on 5Jul1797. If this is so, then his parents are James and Mary Page, and a daughter Mary was also baptized at the same locale 1Nov1795. It is not known for sure where the family was living during those years. William married Martha Sanders (formerly thought to be Martha Hudson) By whom he had four known (maybe five) one was Ebenezer, b.4Apr1820, Co. Sussex, according to American Civil War military records. It is possible that Charles ancestor was William Page who married a Martha Sanders at Ringmer, Co. Sussex, England 31Dec1817. (Charles's ancestor William's 1st child—Ester, was b.Oct1818).

After all children of William/Martha Page were born they immigrated to America in 1829, settling in Wayne Co, NY where Martha soon died. (See chart NY 56) (Ysearch NYWPF). The Y-DNA is very close so, this Co. Essex info indicates some of Page Family Line "C" later moved south of Co. Suffolk to Co. Essex, which puts this family back to early 1300's around Bury St. Edmund in our research. Charles is generally believed to e descended from William through William's American-born second wife, the widow Mrs. Chloe (Thaver) Robinson, through their son Rilev Preston Page. However, there is some chance that Charles is descended from William's son Ebenezer Page and thus descended from William and Martha. The case being provided by the following document: http://freepages.genealogy.rootsweb.ancestry. com/~pagebarnes/Who_were_Rilevs/parents.pdf. OR http://freepages.genealogy.rootsweb. ancestry.com/~SOP_TOC_Page-castner-html.

CLARENCE PAGE—kit 109770 pmaceacher@msn.com (DNA 25) Pat MacEachern is handling his account. MRKA is Abial Page, b.1794, New York (see chart NY 32) This line might be connected to Charles William Paige line (chart NY 56) Waiting for Y-DNA 67 scores.

BERRIS REID bspreid@aol.com kit # ??? (DNA 37) MRKA is James Reid, b. 1863, Jamaica. His father was **SCOTTISH**—101-12 Donora Drive, Toronto, Ontario, M4B Ph: 416 752-5852

DAVID LOGAN HANKS JR hanks88@yahoo.com (BAD EMAIL) Kit # ??? (DNA 37) Blood type A+ MRKA is John Wesley Hanks, b.20Jul1872, Ala. He believes his real father was a Thompson. Home: 1787 Highway 82 West, Prattville, Ala, 36067 (334) 358-4470

PAUL HENRY BARRETT mcjar@mindspring.com (BAD EMAIL) kit # ??? (DNA 37) MRKA is George A. Barrett, b.1776, Va married Ruth Rutherford, b. 1775, Cowpens, S.C.—had son Thomas R. Barrett, b. 1802, SC and family moved to Indiana in 1809. Home: 4568 Via Clarice, Santa Barbara, CA, 93111 (805) 967-0298.

ERNEST ANGUS TOTTON (Totten) Rosemary Totton krisstott@gmail.com Kit # ??? (DNA 67) His daughter Rosmary Totton (New Zealand) is handling his account. The patronymic Totton seems to have its roots in the south of England, and seems to have been derived from an Anglo Saxon hamlet/farm/village on the edge of the New Forest, now known as the town of Totton, next to Port of Southampton. This area was invaded by Jutes (Danish-German) in the 5th century, then again in 1066 by the Norman Invasion of England by William the Conquerer. (See ENG 10-1) In a nearby town of Titchfield—Genealogist Rick Bentley Page found a burial monument of **William de Pageham**, at Titchfield Church, in County Hampshire, England. Recently in the 1870s the Totton's came from **Northern Ireland** (Belfast) to settle in the Newcastle-upon-Tyne area, UK. Ernest A. Totton emigrated from there to New Zealand after WW II. The MRKA is John Totton (Totten), farmer, b.circa 1815, in or near Belfast, possibly Glenavy area. His son was James Totton, bc.1844, same place. James married Agnes Morrow in Belfast in 1873. Could this family name "Totton" (Tutten) be a descendant of William de Pageham ? More information has been developed by daughter Rosemary Totton that has indicated a connection with this family in the Lanarkshire or Ayshire in Scotland. Then another connection is the Tottenham Manor and a connection with Robert de Bruce at http://british-history.ac.uk/report.aspx?compid=26987 and then the Bruce Castle Park in London.

ROBERT DALE NICHOLSON—Kit # ???—(DNA 37) being handled by daughter, Lois Haile haileab@q.com this line backs up finally to MCRA—William Nicholson, d. 1826, Montgomery Co., Ind. Was living in Madison Co, Ky and Ross Co, Ohio and was married to Dorcas. His son, was Henry Nicholson, bc.1785, Montgomery Co, Ind.

SEAN JACOB PAGE—kit 143201 (DNA 67) (brown eyes & type AB blood) is being handled by cousins Bob & Marge Crews Telerski. Marjorie.Telerski@gmail.com Marge

Telerski's mother was a Page. The MCRA is Jacob O. Page, b. 1823, Quebec, Canada, that later moved to Vermilion Co, Ill. See ILL 60 chart.

Page Family Line "K". NOT PAGE LINE "C".

This is not our PAGE line "C", but the earliest known Page ancestors from this different Y-DNA line, came from the SAME town, Walsham le Willows, County Suffolk, England where our particular PAGE line "C" appears to have lived at the same time, in the same place. I have added them to this list to "maybe" discover any blood or marriage connections, that might have occurred in error. I suspect an NPE occurred later on just the Philip Ian Page line because the genealogy before that—does appear—to be connected to the PAGE line "C" in Walsham le Willows, England.

Researcher Philip Ian Page, b.1924, currently living in Henley-on-Thames, (just west of London) has traced this line back to Walsham le Willows, Co. Suffolk, England. His very limited OXFORD ANCESTORS Y-DNA results reflect, that he is NOT in Page Family "C" FTDNA line, but I am putting this group on our mailing list, because of this strange occurrence. His oldest known ancestor is Richard Page, d. 31May1639, Walsham le Willows, Co. Suffolk, England, which puts him, according to George W. Page, Administrator of the Page Family, into line "K". Philip I. Page, one of the lead researchers, is a retired British Officer and served in South Asia, in the Royal Norfolk Regiment (founded 1685) and in 1950 that Regiment was amalgamated with the Suffolk Regiment, which was renamed the Royal Anglian Regiment, which recently returned from Afghanistan. His many years of employment history reflects, he has worked in many locations, such as in Chicago, for several years with International Harvester Co., of Chicago as Human Resources Director, then later as Director of their British manufacturing plants, in many parts of England. He is still active in management and I hope he can find time to assist in this genealogy research.

Also connected to this PAGE "Family "K" line is Christine (Page) Barnes, living at 230 N. Luzerne Ave, Baltimore, Md, 21224 tel: 410-276-2232, for about half the year and then at 7586 Sunny Ridge Loop, Highland, Cal, 92346 Tel: 909-862-6977 in the winters. Cell 443-862-6977. Her Oldest Page ancestor is Richard Page, d. 31May1639, Walsham le Willows, Co. Suffolk, England. This is Page Family Line "K". She has a "paper trail", but no Y-DNA results to support the paper trail.

It is interesting to "guess" at how these two PAGE families seem to originate, from this "very small village", in County Suffolk, England. What is known is, that just a few miles down the road, there was a school for young men to learn how to become a "Page" in the court system of England and some went on to become schooled and trained to be "Knights". Many young men, that might be a son of a famous or rich person, or just a favorite of an important person, could be sent this "special school". (560-2, p. 37 & 99) There were only two such schools in all of England, at that time. When the young man finished his schooling, he adopted the name PAGE and of course his offspring, continued with that adopted "occupational" name. (SEE MY ENG 10-1 DOCUMENT for details)

What has just been discovered is most of the Page Line "K" is really line "C". It now appears that the paper trail of Philip I. Page is flawed and only his particular line—appears to have either an adoption or NPE in his line. Since he only did the "Oxford Y-DNA 10"—test, Philip needs to "upgrade" and get more results to figure out who he really is.

67 marker results so far
    Bobby W. Page—James Jefferson Taylor Magnus Schiller W.D. Page
    John Buford Page Gerald J. Benton John Flaig Glenndon Earl Page Jr
    Fred Arley Page Robert B. Noles Thomas Wayne Page Steve W. Page
    Robert E. Page Ernest Angus Totton Alan Alls William Gordon Page
    Harry L. Page Charles William Paige Sean Jacob Page Christopher (UK) Page
    James C. Page Raymond S. Tanner Harold Bruce Tanner Kenneth Neal Page
    Peter J. Roberts Donald Lee Tanner John W. Tanner

Y—DNA 111 marker results so far—need more to sign up
    Robert E. Page Stephen W. Page Robert B. Noles
    Bobby W. Page W. D. Page Clyde Edward Page

DEFINITIONS
    Admittance—means by which tenants took up a holding of a house or land.
    Hayward—a manorial official elected annually by means of rotation of villein.
    Messauage—a plot of land with a dwelling house or houses or the house itself.
    Surrender—by which villein property was sold through the court, the Lord being paid a fee.
    Tenement—a landholding or the house itself.
    Villein—an unfree tenant
    Yeoman—a mark of status of a landholder below that of a gentleman, and the beginning of the middle class.
    1 rood = 40 perches 4 roods = 1 acre
    12 pennies = 1 shilling 20 shillings = 1 English pound

To learn more about Walsham le willows in County Suffolk, England go to:
www.walsham-le-willows.org/maps/walking/historictrail

For information on Scottish DNA go to: scotlandsdna.com
For free information on Great Britian genealogical information to www.freereg.com.

To see a map of Scandinavian settlements in England, go to:
www.viking.no/e/england/danelaw/ekart-danelaw.htm Thanks to David Weston.

UK National Archives www.nationalarchives.gov.uk OR
UK National Archives www.nationalarchives.gov.uk/a2

For those that might have a Scottish connection try: www.scotandspeople.gov.uk
Wills, testaments, coats of arms, some censuses (1513-1911) Not Free
And Scotlandsdna.com—Free

Since we have an interest in Virginia go to: www.virginiamemory.com/collections free and
North Carolina go to: www.archives.ncdcr.gov (1799-1893) free

Research information and credit for finding most of this valuable information was provided
by: Christopher Page (Ark), Bobby W. Page (Okla), Harry L. Page (SC), George W. Page,
(Md), Philip Ian Page (England), Christine (Page) Barnes, (Md), Jo Church Dickerson (SC)
and others.

Anyone wanting to receive updates on this genealogy research should contact the below to be
added to the email address list.

Prepared by Robert Page, 87465 Old Hwy, Apt 107, Islamorada, Fl, 33036 (305) 852-5337
Email—flkeybob@terranova.net